PASSING JUDGMENT: THE POLITICS AND
POETICS OF SOVEREIGNTY IN FRENCH
TRAGEDY FROM HARDY TO RACINE

HÉLÈNE E. BILIS

Passing Judgment:
The Politics and Poetics
of Sovereignty in French
Tragedy from Hardy
to Racine

UNIVERSITY OF TORONTO PRESS
Toronto Buffalo London

© University of Toronto Press 2016
Toronto Buffalo London
www.utppublishing.com
Printed in the U.S.A.

ISBN 978-1-4875-0026-9 (cloth)

Printed on acid-free, 100% post-consumer recycled
paper with vegetable-based inks.

Library and Archives Canada Cataloguing in Publication

Bilis, Hélène, author
Passing judgment : the politics and poetics of sovereignty
in French tragedy from Hardy to Racine / Hélène E. Bilis.

Includes bibliographical references and index.
ISBN 978-1-4875-0026-9 (cloth)

1. French drama – 17th century – History and criticism.
2. French drama (Tragedy) – History and criticism.   3. Sovereignty
in literature.   4. Judgment in literature.   5. Politics in literature.
I. Title.

PQ528.B54 2016   842'.409   C2016-901969-1

University of Toronto Press acknowledges the financial assistance
to its publishing program of the Canada Council for the Arts and the
Ontario Arts Council, an agency of the Government of Ontario.

Canada Council   Conseil des Arts
for the Arts   du Canada

ONTARIO ARTS COUNCIL
CONSEIL DES ARTS DE L'ONTARIO
an Ontario government agency
un organisme du gouvernement de l'Ontario

Funded by the   Financé par le
Government   gouvernement
of Canada   du Canada

Canadä

To my mother, who taught me how to read,
Katharine Bilis-Bastos (1946–2016)

Contents

Preface

Seventeenth-century France witnessed the concurrent rise of absolutist politics and tragedy's establishment as the preeminent literary genre. Scholars of this complex period have not reached a consensus as to how these two developments may be tied, especially since as the tragic genre gained in prestige, French playwrights steered clear of presenting characters from French history, most often choosing their subjects from Roman culture or Greek mythology. What was, then, the relationship between the fictions of tragedy created by playwrights and the theories of power advanced by absolutist thinkers of the same period? Did French tragedians give artistic form to absolutist ideas, or were political themes and portrayals in tragedy largely ornamental, divorced from the contemporary realities of monarchical power?[1]

In *Passing Judgment*, I seek to answer these questions from a new perspective: I suggest that invoking abstract notions of sovereignty in determining where politics and theatre intersect fails to capture the specificity of tragedy's engagement with royal power and political thought. Turning the focus instead towards the royal judge – a persistent but controversial tragic "type" – exposes the distinct challenges playwrights faced in seeking to consolidate the demands of poetic practices and political rhetoric. In short, I argue that the royal judge, perhaps more than any other tragic character because he is meant to embody sovereignty, can serve as a sharp measure of the intertwinement of political theory and theatrical practice in the seventeenth century.

Scholarship on seventeenth-century French literature tends to divide the century in two. *Le premier dix-septième* is everything leading up to, roughly, 1660, the date around which Louis XIV decides to rule without a prime minister and Pierre Corneille publishes his poetic manifesto,

the *Trois discours sur le poème dramatique*. Pre-1660 studies on theatre focus
on what is known as "irregular theatre" (theatre not subject to Aristotelian poetics) and the rise of neoclassicism, as the growing importance of
the Académie Française founded in 1635 by Cardinal Richelieu began
to encourage adherence to the "rules" of tragedy. *Le second dix-septième*
siècle, i.e., the post-1660 era, is seen as the heyday of both French monarchical power and neoclassical tragedy, which the great works of Jean
Racine are said to exemplify. Yet, as this study will show, the royal judge is
present across these chronological divisions and the debates around his
portrayal constitute a thread that ties together tragic works at both ends
of the century, including canonical and lesser-studied plays. Taking the
long view of this tragic type allows us to grasp how, suddenly, as Cardinal Richelieu becomes invested in promoting tragedy over other genres,
judgment scenes of tragedy became an urgent aesthetic and political
problem. The royal judge appears onstage in the early tragedy of Alexandre Hardy, in the baroque world of Jean Rotrou, and in the canonical
plays of Corneille and Racine, tragic works long considered in isolation
from the earlier drama. In following the winding path of the king as
judge, we come to see how playwrights reconfigure and recast earlier
tragic models of royal judgment as they attempt to anchor their fictions
in the politics of the day. This lens allows us to understand the role theatre played in legitimizing political power in a period intensely preoccupied with royal portraits, but also how difficult it was to consolidate such
demands with the necessary goal of entertaining spectators.

The royal judge constitutes an overlooked portrait, one that brings
to light the distinct challenges inherent in the theatrical presentation of kings, or what we might describe as the double bind of tragic
royal representation: how to navigate between the increasing emphasis
on safeguarding the dignity of the royal function while also placing a
monarchical character at the heart of the tragic drama. As critics close
to the Crown emphasized the need for admirable royal characters, playwrights were faced with two options. In the first, the king may be represented as completely detached from the action of the play, uninvolved in
the merely human dramas of the narrative. This detachment preserves
the king's dignity and specialness, his splendid isolation from ordinary
human concerns, but this threatens to reduce him, ultimately, to a mere
function (the function of rendering judgment). This reduction leaves
him looking like little more than a bureaucrat (a *magistrat*, not a *souverain*) who lacks the dignity crucial to the respect of the monarchical
function. Such a strategy generates a dramatic problem as well: though

his judgment seals the play, the king is not at the centre of the drama. He lurks in the sidelines while the main action goes on without him.

The second possibility is to present the king as fully immersed in the theatrical action, a human being with agency and desires – a dramatic character, in other words. This strategy maintains the centrality of the monarch, but again threatens to reduce him, though this time not to a function, but to being a mere man. He is a powerful man, to be sure, but still a man marked by the instability of passions, ignoble feelings, and human frailties. Such a diminished portrayal inevitably leads characters within the play and spectators watching it to question the legitimacy and validity of the king's judgments. While the development of absolutist politics and rhetoric intensified the problem of royal representation and shaped the solutions the playwrights and critics proposed, this fundamental contradiction persists throughout the drama of the period, precisely because the dilemma it encapsulates has no solution. *Passing Judgment* tells the story of seventeenth-century playwrights' successive attempts to resolve this problem. Each author offers answers that address the issue in new and creative ways, but each one ultimately falls short of resolving the contradiction inherent in the conflicting aesthetic and political imperatives the plays try to embody.

Playwrights, as I understand them, tried to escape the double bind and hit a poetico-political bull's eye in which absolutist discourses and entertaining tragedy might converge. Ultimately, however, these efforts resulted in the subtle destabilization of the political doctrine they were intended to promote. The margins afforded to the playwrights for pleasing a theatre-going public with notoriously unstable tastes, while also adhering to a poetic theory of monarchical admiration, were simply too tight. *Passing Judgment* is invested in reflecting on these moments of breakdown in the project of tragedy, the instances where the theatrical-political feat playwrights were asked to accomplish proves impossible. The approach consists of deliberately not regarding the plays of Corneille and Racine as masterpieces of neoclassical tragedy, nor as the products of pure geniuses who exhibited an impeccable grasp of theatrical composition and alexandrine verse. Instead, these plays constitute pieces of the larger puzzle of ancien régime theatrical production. This perspective enables us to see how the canonical playwrights and their fellow tragedians tried out new models as they went along. Far from possessing a homogenous and consistent poetic viewpoint, they constantly grappled with conflicting demands as they shaped their tragedies in response to specific critiques, to the context of the moment, to one another, and to their own desire to innovate within the tragic genre. If there is any homogeneity to be identified, it stems from the fact that seventeenth-century theatre is, at its core, about the performance of sovereignty. As we will see, different performances were expected according to different genres, but even as the margins for acceptable royal characters narrowed, in staging the king as judge, playwrights blended this tragic type with dramatic types taken from other theatrical forms, especially comedy and tragicomedy, thus blurring the barriers erected between genres.

Hippolyte-Jules Pilet de La Mesnardière, the influential theatre critic and author of *La Poétique* (1639), describes the king onstage as necessarily conforming to, and confirming, the social-historical ideal of the royal judge put forward in monarchical treatises of the period:

> un Roy qui paraît au théâtre doit être si courageux qu'il n'appréhende aucun danger [...] Il doit être si prudent, qu'il n'ait jamais aucun sujet de rétracter ses jugements [...] Enfin, il doit être si bon qu'il vive avec ses sujets comme [...] s'il eût été homme privé.[2]

> [a King who appears in theatre must be so brave that he will fear no danger ... He must be so prudent, that he will never have reason to retract his judgments ... Finally, he must be so good that he can live with his subjects ... as if he were a private man.]

One can imagine a playwright reading such prescriptions and tearing out his hair in frustration at the narrowness of La Mesnardière's formula. If a theatrical king must always be brave, prudent, clever, and clear-sighted in his judgments, on what will the tragic conflict rest? Can a genre thrive if it aims to illustrate "une sorte de distribution de prix ou plutôt un jugement dernier" [a distribution of prizes or rather a last judgment], as the critic René Bray has described the ideal ending in the poetician's view?[3] La Mesnardière writes that tragedy should "établir sur le théâtre le trône de la justice" [establish on the theatre a throne of justice] and that it should be "semblable aux bons législateurs [en] donnant aux vertus & aux vices la récompense qui leur est dûe" [similar to good legislators in giving just reward to virtues and vices].[4] Though La Mesnardière's stark terms of reward and punishment may seem overly rigid, his was the prevailing view among commentators of tragedy.

Writing a decade after the publication of *La Poétique*, in his influential treatise *La Pratique du théâtre* (1657), l'Abbé d'Aubignac calls for a similar constriction of monarchical roles:

Quand un Roi parle sur la Scène, il faut qu'il parle en Roi, et c'est la circonstance de la dignité contre laquelle il ne peut rien faire qui soit vraisemblable, s'il n'y avait quelque autre raison qui dispensât de cette première
circonstance, comme s'il était déguisé.[5]

[When a King speaks on Stage, he must speak as a King, and it is the circumstance of that dignity against which he cannot do anything that would not
be plausible, if there was not any other reason that dispensed him from this
first circumstance, as for example if he were in disguise.]

Thus, although the catalogue of theatrical kings on the seventeenth-
century stage is vast, with a panoply of roles attributed to monarchical
characters who may be by turns heroic, Machiavellian, aging, *galant*, and
so on, d'Aubignac wishes to make royalty the king's defining characteristic, a consistent quality evident in the theatrical monarch's every action.
Playwrights realized that in devising a king for the stage who would act
and speak "as a king," the "as" constituted the key problem. Theatre, and
the tragic judgment scene in particular, underscores the performance
that sovereignty constitutes. The moment of royal decision pointedly
asks spectators to evaluate the behaviour of a sovereign character and
the moral nature of his judgment. Paying attention to the royal judge
onstage allows us, therefore, to perceive the antinomy between theatrical performance and idealized kingly portraits. At best, the depiction of
tragic passions, the dialogism of the stage, and its materiality create ambivalent images of sovereignty in which the royal character appears weak
and all too human. At its worst, the tragic judge can seem comical, even
farcical – an outright failure in the portrayal of royal grandeur.

In Corneille's 1659 *Œdipe*, the playwright seeks to outdo d'Aubignac's
precept of royal distinctiveness by having the heroic Thésée state
unequivocally: "Mais jamais sans forfait on ne se prend aux rois, / Et
fussent-ils cachés sous un habit champêtre, / Leur propre majesté les
doit faire connaître"[6] [But never without crime does one attack kings /
Even if they are hidden beneath rustic garb, / Their own majesty must
make them recognizable]. Poetic practices and the maxims proclaimed
within the tragic genre seek to extend the contemporary emphasis on
the historical monarch's unique status and person to fictional kings.
Such examples, however, also illustrate the divide between poetics and
practice, as the most basic plot elements of *Œdipe* undermine the idea of
a unique royal majesty since the tragedy stems precisely from the hero's
inability to recognize Laius as king.

Passing Judgment seeks, therefore, to examine the contradictions of what "speaking as a king" entails. What, precisely, is the determining identifier of kingship? The recent scholarly focus on "decisionist politics," and in particular on the theories of Carl Schmitt, has emphasized the "sovereign decision," as the ultimate identifier of personal authority. Schmitt's much-quoted phrase, an echo of the French jurist, Jean Bodin, states that, "he who decides the exception is sovereign."[7] Such a statement implies a conviction of the effectiveness of decision-making and a belief that the sovereign will successfully give his decision the necessary weight and consequence. This study demonstrates, however, that the performance of decision-making onstage was far less certain to designate monarchical grandeur. Playwrights and critics became painfully aware that the act of decision-making itself was insufficient to ensure an unassailable sovereignty, and that the royal character appears particularly fragile and subject to criticism at the moment when he articulates a judgment.

By situating the political and poetic discourses on sovereignty alongside the theatrical works themselves – the theory against the practice – we perceive how playwrights had to confront the impossible task of royal representation: making the monarch a tragic character while maintaining spectator admiration for a royal function increasingly presented as infallible by political authorities. Nonetheless, my argument is not that the sovereign who comes to occupy the tragic stage towards the end of the century is the result of an inevitable and linear march towards monarchical ascendency, nor that the rise of absolutism correlates with the tragic king as a mouthpiece for the Crown. On the contrary, careful attention to the sovereign's transformations on stage reveals a multiplicity of portrayals and perspectives at work in staging a royal figure in the act of judgment. Playwrights, most notably Corneille and Racine who both authored successful comedic works, were acutely aware of the fragility of monarchical dignity, and of its proximity to ridicule, and they keenly understood the potential for their tragic sovereigns to lapse into comedic figures. This led them to justify and explain their representations retrospectively, sometimes denouncing their characters entirely, in the prefaces and commentaries they wrote in the wake of the theatrical representations.

Despite the strict principles of *bienséance* theorists assigned to the royal image conveyed in French tragedy, monarchical portrayals proved to be elusive and unruly. Though playwrights struggled to embody absolutist thinking in their works, they were continually defeated because absolutism generated a set of demands that could not be satisfied in theatrical terms. *Passing Judgment* seeks to offer a revised understanding of French tragedy and monarchical representations, which have similarly been lauded for their prestige, unity of purpose, and effective articulation of royal narratives. The guiding claim I advance is that keeping our eyes on the king as judge reveals a tragic genre in flux and an eclectic range of royal personations. Playwrights persistently searched for acceptable models of royal judgment, experimenting with new structures, drawing inspiration from comedy and tragicomedy, and revisiting old types; critics imposed formal constraints and established new "rules" for presenting a glorious king. The combination of these theatrical practices and political strategies, however, could never entirely erase the disturbing potential for the king's dignity to fail and for him to lapse into ridicule. That is the story *Passing Judgment* seeks to tell.

Chapter 1, "The Critique of *Le Cid*: Richelieu, Royal Judgment, and the Rules," seeks to reshape the way we understand the relationship between seventeenth-century historical and cultural models of royal judgment and the rise of tragedy's "rules." At a time when legal frameworks within France were shifting and monarchical theorists sought to replace the old paradigm of the monarch as guardian of the law with a new ideology of the king as law incarnate, judicial fictions under Louis XIII increasingly stressed the king's independence in the legal domain. Simultaneously, Richelieu placed ever more emphasis on highly visible public trials, thereby actively changing the ways those close to the king and throughout the French kingdom perceived monarchical justice. In understanding the portrayal of royal judgment that emanates from these political-historical developments, we are able to grasp their connection to the rise of tragic imperatives, such as *bienséance* and *vraisemblance*, especially as the institution of these rules aimed to eliminate negative portrayals of royal justice in the theatre. The chapter brings to light how the quarrel around Pierre Corneille's *Le Cid*, a polemic in which Richelieu played a decisive role, was a turning point for dramatic figurations of monarchical justice. In reading the "quarrel of *Le Cid*" through the lens of critical efforts to articulate new standards for tragic portraits of sovereignty, we come to see how the major texts of this debate constituted an official rebuke of Corneille's adherence to an antiquated model of kingship.

Chapter 2, "Failed Judgments, Thwarted Justice: Alexandre Hardy's *Scédase ou l'hospitalité violée*," takes a step backwards historically from the 1630s to the drama of the first quarter of the century, before the

codification and narrowing of the tragic genre, in order to illustrate what
it was the critics close to Richelieu were reacting against. Specifically, I
offer a reading of Alexandre Hardy's tragedy, *Scédase ou l'hospitalitée violée* (1615) that allows us to contemplate the image of the sovereign the
doctes will reject. Hardy stands as an early model of tragic royal judgment,
one in which the king is presented as an explicit judge: he mounts a
trial, calls upon witnesses, imprisons suspects, and decrees a verdict that
seals the plot. By emphasizing the implications of the king's recourse to
a formal legal procedure, the chapter demonstrates why Hardy's model
of royal judgment – in fact a convention of early French tragedy – is condemned and abandoned by later playwrights.

Chapter 3, "The Ceremony Unravels: Tragedy's Comedic Turn,"
returns to the elaboration of rules in the 1630s–40s surrounding what
should and should not be staged, specifically with respect to the exercise
of royal justice in tragedy. As critics close to Richelieu increasingly theorize the "noble genre" as needing to persuade audiences of the dignity
and grandeur of royal figures, playwrights must become more attuned to
elements that would disrupt the audience's admiration for monarchical
characters. In juxtaposing such theories alongside the practice of tragedy, the chapter challenges critical efforts, of the seventeenth century,
and of the twentieth and twenty-first centuries, to define tragedy as a
"ceremony." Far from a perfectly stable, strict, and carefully orchestrated
ritual with set-pieces, predictable outcomes, and an exact performance
of conventional gestures, the chapter examines how the tragic genre is
always at risk of devolving into comedy. In examining specific examples
of such moments, and the critical interdictions that result from them, we
become aware of the fluidity and constant dialogue between the comedic and tragic genres. Finally, a reading of Racine's comedy, *Les Plaideurs* (1668) alongside his tragedy, *Britannicus* (1669), written only a year
apart, demonstrates the shared preoccupation of both genres with the
dangers of imperfect royal performances of justice.

Chapter 4, "Learning from Experience: On Corneille and Coherence," focuses on the plays of one of France's foremost tragedians whose
works span most of the seventeenth century. Although Pierre Corneille
is best known for a unity of vision within his corpus (expressed through
the Cornelian hero and his embrace of generosity), this analysis draws
out his struggle and ongoing search for just the right royal role. In tracing the fluctuating presence of royal judges from *Clitandre ou l'innocence
délivrée* (1631) to *Le Cid* (1637) and *Horace* (1641), we see Corneille hesi-
tating between the allure of tragicomedy and the nascent demands of

modern tragedy. Reading his great works against the grain, the chapter shows that instead of perfectly integrated models of Cornelian tragic and heroic values, the characters within these plays, and in particular the royal judges present in all three, result from a challenging and fluctuating process of creative trial and error. The chapter goes on to consider how the lessons learned from these early models shaped Corneille's later theatre, including the portrayal of sovereign judgment in *Rodogune* (1645), *Sertorius* (1662), and *Suréna* (1674). The question of timing – when in the intrigue to stage the royal verdict, and how quickly the judgment should be articulated – becomes a central preoccupation of tragic productions, always guarding against the disintegration of royal grandeur.

Chapter 5, "Corneille's *Cinna* and Rotrou's *Crisante*: A Search for the Emperor's Judgment," disrupts the longstanding parallel between Corneille and Racine to insert the model of another influential tragic playwright who, as part of Richelieu's dramaturgical circles, similarly grappled with theatrical portrayals of royal judgment. In bringing to bear the examples of Jean Rotrou's *Venceslas* (1647) and *Crisante* (1637) alongside Corneille's *Cinna ou la clémence d'Auguste* (1642), we can compare the authors' similar shift away from the early model of the king as explicit judge and royal judgment as a theatrical device. The dénouement by royal decision, once only an element of theatrical surprise motivated by dramatic necessity – a *rex ex machina* of sorts – takes on a distinct political flavour as the closing element of surprise is recast in tragedy. Beginning with a focus on the playwrights' staging of clemency, we observe how, as Corneille and Rotrou embrace the "monarchical genre," they invest their sovereigns with a new understanding of the relationship between law and the legal process, similarly emphasizing the sovereign's ability to move past simple dichotomies of guilt and innocence. The model of the "clement prince" seems to coincide well with the demands of absolutist narratives: the sovereign sides with virtue and refuses brutality. Looking more closely, however, these portrayals of clemency, in which the royal judge simply erases a crime through his verdict, paint a disturbing picture of the sovereign's dominance over the aristocrat whom he judges.

The second half of the chapter offers a close reading of *Crisante*, a tragedy often deemed to be emblematic of the chaos of Jean Rotrou's baroque aesthetic. Questioning facile labels, I show how *Crisante* stages a world of competing reigns: one of violence, disorder and excess, and another of limits, law, and authority. Caught between the end of the monarchy and the advent of Roman authority in the wake of the empire's invasion of Corinth, the eponymous queen who is raped by a

Roman embodies tragedy's search for order in the mid-seventeenth century. The play's quest for a sovereign to install Roman authority reveals Rotrou's investment in the new tragic aesthetic and demonstrates his shared focus with France's more "classical" tragedians on protecting the sovereign character onstage.

Finally, chapter 6, "Racine and Royal Fathers of Injustice – *Mithridate* and *Phèdre*" turns to the portrayal of royal judges who are also dominant fathers. Although the father/son tragic struggle has garnered extensive critical attention, no one to my knowledge has situated this hallmark of Racinian tragedy in the context of French tragedy's long-standing engagement with the royal judge. The chapter offers new insight into Racine's corpus, focusing most closely on two of his last three tragedies *Mithridate* (1673) and *Phèdre* (1677), written before he left the stage to become Louis XIV's official royal historiographer. We are now able to recognize how the structural changes the playwright introduces to the established model of tragic royal judgment constitute a decidedly political gesture. For Racine, the royal verdict no longer forms the basis for the play's dénouement; it becomes instead the foundation for the tragic intrigue. Misjudgment moves to the centre of Racine's plot as his sovereigns misread accusations, are unable to decipher the clues brought before them, misinterpret evidence, and fail to ascertain guilt from innocence. Beyond an Oedipal presence or an avatar of absolutism, Racine's father-judges are fresh models of an old character-type. Ultimately, however, the dénouements seek to absolve the sovereign and the chaos he provoked by demonstrating how his ill-advised judgments become unexpected benefits for the larger community.

Passing Judgment concludes with a consideration of how the royal judge and his weighty decisions gradually dissipate in the eighteenth century, loosening this character's hold on the tragic imagination. As the power of royal judgment no longer captivates audiences, the tired conventions of the tragic genre lose their relevance; tragedy ossifies and flounders. The old tragic character-type whose dignity was always fragile and on the verge of ridicule, morphs into an explicitly comical figure (as in Beaumarchais's Comte d'Alma Viva in *Le Mariage de Figaro*), or simply develops into a father, devoid of royal trappings.

Acknowledgments

On the path towards getting this book finished, I encountered many generous and encouraging people who have enriched my journey. They have taught me the many meanings contained in the word "helpful," and showed me its multiple nuances and facets, and the depths of it possibilities. I am grateful for their support and pleased to acknowledge them in published form.

I wish to thank Suzanne Rancourt, generous and supportive editor, the anonymous readers of the University of Toronto Press who shrewdly guided this book towards completion, and Miriam Skey, a most assiduous copy editor. I am grateful to Wellesley College for the Faculty Awards Grants I received and for the junior leave which allowed me to make crucial progress on this project. At Wellesley, I warmly thank the members of the French department who welcomed and mentored me, including Venita Datta, Scott Gunther, Andrea Levitt, Barry Lydgate, Catherine Masson, Jim Petterson, Anjali Prabhu, Michèle Respaut, and Vicki Mistacco. For providing last-minute comments and good models, I am grateful to Francesca Southerden, James Noggle, and Helena de Bres. Bill Cain was an encouraging and patient reader with keen insights. Laura O'Brien, Sarah Allahverdi, and Codruta Morari were always ready to provide answers. Elizabeth Yazgi, Melody Pao, and Elizabeth Loxtercamp were diligent students and research assistants.

The world of *dix-septiémistes* is populated by supportive souls and sharp thinkers, among whom I wish to recognize especially Déborah Blocker, Steven Bold, Mathilde Bombart, Juliette Cherbuliez, Timothy Hampton, Katherine Ibbett, John D. Lyons, Ellen McClure, Larry Norman, Harriet Stone, Hélène Visentin, and Rainer Zaiser. Jennifer Tamas and Sylvaine Guyot belong in a category all their own, true allies beside me on the long path towards the finish line. Guillaume Peureux, a model of generosity, provided me with the extra push, the helpful suggestion, and the vote of confidence I needed.

From Berkeley days to the present, I have benefitted from the lasting friendships and insightful observations of Orlaith Galli, Margo Meyer, Ayelet Ben-Yishai, and Silvia Valisa. Over the course of many years now, Liz M. Young, Sarah Wall-Randell, and Sally Theran have been friends *hors pair*, providing the intellectual engagement one needs to keep progressing and the laughter one needs to exist. Vernon Shetley, friend and critic extraordinaire, shaped my thinking, provided conclusions, and made me aspire to write like him. To Nicholas Paige, eternal mentor, whose guidance drives me, pushing me to plug away and stay "full speed ahead": thank you.

Papy Boubou, Mamichèle, and ma Léounette, on one side of the Atlantic, Ellen and Dave Van Arsdale, on the other, never allowed me to contemplate anything but forward movement. Katharine Bilis-Bastos, who so loves French literature, grew sick over the course of this writing, but lived to see its dedication to her. Flora, Anthony, and Vincent joyfully and turbulently took me away from writing and back into their worlds: I love you and thank you for supporting your *maman*, each in your own special way. Finally, to the biological anthropologist most attuned to seventeenth-century theatre, the person who, quite simply, makes everything possible, every day, words cannot convey what Adam Van Arsdale has given me, but it would not be an exaggeration to say that he has fuelled my mind and soul.

I thank the *Modern Language Review* for permission to use my article, "Corneille's *Cinna*, Clemency, and the Implausible Decision" which was published in volume 108 of that journal (January 2013) and now forms part of chapter 5, as well as *Littératures classiques* for use of "Voir la Sorcière de Colchis d'un nouvel œil ou comment rendre visible la dignité," which appeared in volume 83 (2013) and which I draw upon in chapter 4. I wish to recognize the Wellesley College French Department for its generous Book Subsidy Award.

PASSING JUDGMENT

Introduction

Un Roi sera grave, jaloux de son autorité, mêlera la rigueur de Maître avec la douceur de Père, et punira généreusement les manquements de respect que l'on commettra devant lui.

La Mesnardière[1]

1 Tragedy as the Monarchical Genre

French tragedy underwent a transformation in status beginning in the 1630s. Georges Forestier has convincingly shown the "complete reversal" from the genre's unpopularity in 1628, a year when not one of the eight new plays offered to Parisian audiences fell under the label of tragedy, to its unquestionable renaissance six years later when Corneille, Rotrou, Mairet, and Scudéry, the up-and-coming playwrights of the day, inaugurated its revival.[2] By the end of the first quarter of the century, humanist tragedy's pedantry and heavy moralizing had grown stale, especially in comparison to the light-heartedness of tragicomedy's entertaining intrigues. Though both genres displayed characters of noble rank, the boundless plots of adventure and surprise offered by tragicomedy had displaced the staid models of the classical genre.[3]

Almost in the blink of an eye, at the start of the 1630s, discussions surrounding the form and proper design of tragedy began to occupy Parisian literary circles, prompting a flowering of theoretical texts and prefaces debating the value of respecting the genre's rules and imperatives.[4] In response to tragicomedy's appeal, tragedy's defenders erected classical tragedy as the only truly reasonable, instructive, and noble theatrical form. Within the span of a decade, tragedy was beset by a poetic baggage – an intricate series of rules, conventions, and interdictions – whose weight paradoxically served to elevate it above the competing dramatic genres. Suddenly, no playwright could ignore the "rules" with impunity.[5]

The political impetus driving the codification of tragedy has begun to garner much-needed critical attention, bringing to light the intertwinement of developments in neoclassical aesthetics and French monarchical politics.[6] It is in the decisive decade of the 1630s that Richelieu's Académie Française notoriously condemned *Le Cid,* and that the tenets of *vraisemblance* and *bienséance* became the defining principles of the tragic genre.[7] Neoclassical tragedy became intensely preoccupied by what Gérard Genette has dubbed the "*devant être*" – the "what should be" – of the tragic world.[8] This preoccupation endows tragedy with a framework inherently exterior to the play: what is plausible equates with what is morally acceptable. Tragic portrayals must pass the test of French cultural standards and clichés, opening the way to the influence of ethical debates and political ideology in determining tragic composition. Absolutist rhetoric fostered more stringent attitudes towards royal portrayals and increasingly demanded that playwrights diverge from their classical sources. Staging the royal judge represents a struggle to determine, long before the quarrel of the Ancients and Moderns in the last quarter of the seventeenth century, what is appropriate for French tastes.

2 Fictions of Royal Judgment

This study draws on recent scholarship that has examined the blurry demarcation between ancien régime legal culture and the development of literary plots. Christian Biet holds that for the majority of seventeenth-century authors, law and legal vocabulary were part of their "*culture générale,*" what he describes as, "un mode de raisonnement presque banal tant il est partagé, une des manières de voir et d'écrire (sur) le monde"[9] [a mode of reasoning almost banal in its commonality, a way of seeing and writing (about) the world]. Educated Frenchmen received similar training to their English counterparts in the arts of rhetoric based on Cicero's *De Inventione* and Quintillian's *Institutio Oratoria,* works concerned with judicial oratory and the ability to organize arguments in such a way as to be most convincing. The average Frenchman did not, however, actively participate in the justice system. In the British context, Lorna Hutson has argued that the participatory structures of English criminal justice, which called on ordinary people to be involved in the judicial process (as litigants, as witnesses, as members of the jury), increasingly taught Englishmen to weigh evidence and think in terms of evidential concepts.[10] According to Hutson, this juridically based mode of thinking shaped how playwrights and spectators perceived plot structures and the *inventio* of dramatic fictions, leading to the development of more plausible theatrical plots.

To consider the French model in light of Hutson's argument brings us full circle since the author of *The Invention of Suspicion* writes that she owes her focus on changes in British law and the concurrent development of English tragedy to Andrea Frisch's study of French legislation of amnesty and French tragedy. Frisch examines a variety of laws conceived in the wake of the Wars of Religion, and argues that they fostered a culture of amnesia, which influenced the development of the French tragic imperatives of distance in the seventeenth century.[11] According to Frisch, the trauma of sixteenth-century violence led to neoclassical tragedy's embrace of ahistoricity and an "aesthetics of distance": "Tragedy played and would continue to play a privileged role in the flowering of this myth [of timeless universality] since one function of an aesthetics of distance in neoclassical theater was to buttress the fiction of a timeless French culture."[12] Though Frisch is right to point to the marked transformations the tragic genre undergoes from the sixteenth to the seventeenth centuries, especially how tragedy moves away from depicting violence in the theatre and events taken from French history, I disagree with the notion that the stage turns to subjects meant to be taken as "timeless" representations. A close study of the poetics and plays developed in such proximity to monarchical power and alongside absolutist discourses reveals a constant engagement with the precise contemporary French historical-political context, including much commentary on the necessity of presenting admirable and dignified theatrical sovereigns to monarchial subjects. Rather than stemming from a will for collective amnesia towards events of the preceding century, I see the seventeenth-century's ever-rising influence of the imperatives of *bienséance* and *vraisemblance* as a direct result of increased attention to absolutist models of royal behaviour, and in particular as a sign of the growing awareness (not always successfully translated into practice, albeit) of the need to protect the portrayal of the king's relationship to the law.

Michel Foucault has memorably described how the French judicial process under the ancien régime remained almost entirely hidden from public view until crowds were called upon to witness the spectacular and carefully organized rituals of punishment on the scaffolds of city squares.

The aim of such displays was not to involve French subjects in the carrying out of justice, but rather to demonstrate the king's all-powerful authority to punish:

> Over and above the crime that has placed the sovereign in contempt, [the public execution] deploys before all eyes an invincible force. Its aim is not so much to re-establish a balance as to bring into play, as its extreme point, the dissymmetry between the subject who has dared to violate the law and the all-powerful sovereign who displays his strength [...] The punishment is carried out in such a way as to give a spectacle not of measure, but of imbalance and excess in this liturgy of punishment, there must be an emphatic affirmation of power and its intrinsic superiority.[13]

Foucault's language of "dissymmetry," "imbalance," and "excess" captures how the violent execution of the criminal was a necessary declaration of the monarch's unsurpassed power against those who would break his laws. In contrast to the British model, then, the French judicial process fostered a culture of witnessing and spectatorship, not of active involvement. The French public's role, in the monarchy's view, was to convene in contemplation of the brilliant and bloody dénouement brought about by the royal decision.

If the historical monarch could rely on spectacles heavy with such shock-value to emphasize his supremacy, and if this narrative of unsurpassed legal power could be reaffirmed in royal panegyrics and iconography, the theatrical stage was a unique space in the ancien régime where the image of royalty conveyed did not uniformly celebrate the institution of monarchy.[14] As Biet has argued, because of their "plurivocité interpretative" [plurivocal interpretation], literary texts could displace topics at the core of ancien régime legal discussions into territory where law could only venture with difficulty.[15] In theatre, in particular, where there is no narrator to guide the reader/spectator, and no monological perspective, the development of a variety of characters and points of view jeopardizes the promotion of one uncontested normative behaviour.

This attention to the multiplicity of voices particular to dramatic works is at the core of Sylvaine Guyot's readings of the royal body in neoclassical tragedy. In contrast to critics who have focused on the unique charisma, *éclat,* and dignity of the royal person,[16] Guyot has shown how the "sidération" [paralysis] associated with glimpsing the royal body is limited in tragedy by the dialogical and temporal constraints of the theatrical stage.[17] Whereas in royal panegyrics and other encomiastic texts and performances, including royal ballets, the sovereign can appear as the "Soleil de la France," and impose silence and admiration through a simple self-display, it is quite the contrary in a tragic fiction. Playwrights verify the king's grandeur by resorting to a variety of practices: the creation of a character witness who identifies and verbalizes the king's magnificence, or they resort to a discourse of *galanterie* to emphasize the king's sexual appeal.[18] Although the stage may promote fictions whose themes and lessons are meant to converge with contemporary narratives of sovereignty, theatre resists a direct application of monarchical discourse and must find other means of conveying similar messages.[19] The difficult task of rendering visible onstage what is a given in the political arena (i.e., the king's unequalled greatness) is a central concern of *Passing Judgment*. Yet in charting the transformations in poetic discussions and theatrical practices regarding how a theatrical king should look, sound, and act, we see that the problem of making the king "*parler en roi*" was not always, in fact, a problem. The aim is to study the rise of this concern, and how it affected theatrical production and critical responses to dramatic works.

3 Centring the King – The "Examen de *Clitandre*"

As the tragic genre garners prestige, the issue of the royal character's proximity to the central dramatic action and to those he must judge becomes a dominant preoccupation. By 1660, when Corneille reviews the entirety of his dramatic production for a new edition of his complete works, the playwright's unease towards the status of the royal character culminates in the "Examen de *Clitandre*."[20] In the "Examen," Corneille articulates an outright prohibition against a sovereign character whose only role is to judge. The playwright rules out the possibility of staging a king who would have no personal involvement in what he judges:

> Je dis qu'un Roi, un héritier de la Couronne, un Gouverneur de Province, et généralement un homme d'autorité, peut paraître sur le Théâtre en trois façons: comme Roi, comme homme, et comme Juge, quelquefois avec deux de ces qualités, quelquefois toutes les trois ensemble. Il paraît comme Roi seulement quand il n'a intérêt qu'à la conservation de son Trône, ou de sa vie, qu'on attaque pour changer l'Etat, sans avoir l'esprit agité d'aucune passion particulière [...] Il paraît comme homme seulement, quand il n'a que l'intérêt d'une passion à suivre ou à vaincre, sans aucun péril pour son Etat [...] Il ne paraît enfin que comme juge quand il est introduit sans aucun intérêt pour son Etat, ni pour sa personne, ni pour ses affections,

mais seulement pour régler celui des autres, comme dans [*Clitandre*] et dans *Le Cid*; et l'on ne peut pas désavouer qu'en cette dernière posture, il remplit assez mal la Dignité d'un si grand Titre, n'ayant aucune part en l'action que celle qu'il y veut prendre pour d'autres, et demeurant bien éloigné de l'éclat des deux autres manières.[21]

[I say that a king, an heir to the throne, a governor of a province, and generally a man of authority, can appear on the stage in three ways: as a king, as a man, and as a judge, and sometimes with two of these qualities, sometimes with all three at once. He appears as only a King when he has interest solely in the conservation of his Throne, or of his life which is attacked to change the state, without his spirit being agitated by any private (*particulière*) passion. He appears solely as a man when he has an interest only in a passion he must follow or vanquish, without any peril for his state … He appears, finally, solely as a judge when he is introduced without any interest for his state, nor for his person, nor for his affections, but only to settle those of others, as in [*Clitandre*] and *Le Cid*, and we must admit that in this last posture, he fulfils quite poorly the Dignity of such a grand Title, taking no part in the action, other than what he can do for others, and remaining very far from the *éclat* of the two other postures.]

In this passage we follow Corneille as he ponders the political and theatrical dimensions of portraying a sovereign onstage, deciding, ultimately, to turn away from a long-standing trope of French theatre. The conclusion he reaches – the rejection of an earlier model – stands as a clear example of how royal narratives and theatrical fictions converge in asserting that the king should be omnipresent onstage and always play a leading role. As the seventeenth century advanced, the Crown aggressively tried to assert the king's relevance and unequalled authority in the domain of justice by concocting fictions of his ubiquitous and all-knowing presence. Although in the political sphere the sovereign might call on a plurality of ministers and councillors to enact his will, the king's presence should always be felt in expressions of authority. Even if he is physically absent, the king should always maintain an "interest in his state" (to echo Corneille) and all decisions should be viewed as an enactment of his will.[22] In the "Examen" passage, Corneille shows new sensitivity to the intertwinement between contemporary monarchical rhetoric and the stage, as he expresses an awareness of the need to protect the "Dignity of such a grand Title" and guarantee a royal "*éclat*" for his character.

However, despite Corneille's recognition of the inadequacies of the royal judge onstage, this passage also enables us to discern fundamental differences between the logic of theatre and the monarchical narratives of the day. The last sentence of the "Examen de *Clitandre*" passage quoted above, where Corneille rejects the "solely as judge" option, underscores the development of the principle that a good sovereign (in the theatrical sense, if not in the moral sense) should have a personal *and* political stake in the action. In other words, the "Dignity of such a grand Title," depends precisely on what the contemporary political ideal of the virtuous monarch sought to avoid – the intermingling of personal passions and political action.[23] A commonplace of royal encomia was to praise the king for instituting a clear separation between his personal or private concerns and those of his subjects. In contrast, the theatrical ideal Corneille advances delineates a strange intermediary position for the king as neither only a public persona preoccupied by matters of state, nor only a "man" defined by his private passions. To provoke the audience's emotional attachment to him, the tragic king must be fully invested and entangled in what he judges, not defined by a reactive posture to what others have precipitated. When the king is simply a judge, personally removed from the matters over which he must rule, as in the example of *Clitandre* or *Le Cid*, his dignity suffers too hard a blow.[24]

Antoine Furetière's *Dictionnaire universel* (1690) suggests "dignité" is a characteristic that manifests itself through laudable language and behaviour:

Dignité. f., Qualité de ce qui est digne. Ce Prédicateur a bien soutenu la dignité de son sujet par ses belles expressions.

On dit d'un Président, d'un Grand Seigneur, qu'il parle avec dignité, qu'il agit avec dignité, qu'il marche avec dignité, pour dire qu'il soutient bien son rang, qu'il ne dément point son caractère, qu'il parle, qu'il agit bien, qu'il a grand train. Cet homme constitué en dignité.[25]

[Dignity. fem., Quality of that which is dignified. That Preacher upheld the dignity of his subject by his beautiful expressions.

We say of a President, of a Great Lord, that he speaks with dignity, that he acts with dignity, that he walks with dignity, to say that he upholds his rank, that he does not refute his character, that he speaks, acts well, and has great resources. This man is constituted by his dignity.]

For both Corneille and Furetière, acting with dignity means satisfying public expectations regarding a predefined behaviour, remaining faithful to the qualities associated with a social condition. The notion of social rank that Furetière invokes, as well as the examples he includes – the Preacher, the President, the Great Lord – reveal that *dignité* cannot be separated from a strict social hierarchy. *Dignité* is based on a demonstration, i.e., displaying the trappings or giving an expected performance of a prestigious social condition rather than behaving in a morally virtuous way.

Having become convinced that royal characters need to flaunt their royalty, Corneille outdoes even his most stringent critics by going so far as to articulate a "new rule" stipulating that royal characters cannot play "solely judges" nor supporting characters:

> Le roi et le prince son fils paraissent [dans *Clitandre*] dans un emploi fort en-dessous de leur Dignité: l'un n'y est *que comme juge*, et l'autre comme confident de son favori. Ce défaut n'a pas accoutumé de passer pour défaut: aussi n'est-ce qu'un sentiment particulier dont je me fais une Règle, qui peut-être ne semblera pas déraisonnable, bien que nouvelle.[26]

> [The king and the prince his son appear [in *Clitandre*] in a function far beneath their Dignity: one is there *only as a judge*, and the other as the confidant of his favourite. This defect has not usually been recognized as a defect: therefore it is only a personal feeling from which I make a Rule for myself, that perhaps will not seem unreasonable despite its newness.]

We see how by 1660 the scope of *bienséance* extends to practical considerations when deliberating how to stage the royal character with sufficient respect. Furthermore, Corneille demonstrates a practical understanding of the matter. If a king is given the "*emploi*" [role] of a supporting character, a secondary actor will play the royal role, further deteriorating the royal person's *éclat*: "Aussi l'on ne donne [le rôle du roi-juge] jamais à représenter aux meilleurs Acteurs; mais il faut qu'il se contente de passer par la bouche de ceux du second, ou du troisième ordre"[27] [Indeed we never give [the role of the royal judge] to the best Actors; we must be content to see it spoken by second, or third rate ones]. Monarchical parts can no longer be given out indiscriminately. The new rule Corneille announces decrees that the most recognizable members of the troupe should play the characters with the most prestigious and the highest social rank.

4 The Performance of Royalty

A central tenet of my argument is that because of the particular performative qualities attributed to royal decisions in the seventeenth century, the king's declaration of judgment onstage necessarily differs from the judgments of all other characters. Only the king's will makes law; only his judgment is a binding verdict. The decisions of others can certainly influence the dramatic intrigue, but they simply do not have the same legally binding force. This view counters Hélène Merlin-Kajman's contention that the royal judge disappears entirely from the stage when he is supplanted by an absolutist model of kingship.[28] Writing in response to Louis Marin and Jean-Marie Apostolidès's exclusive focus on the king, Merlin-Kajman argues for a broader application of the "two bodies" metaphor in which literary texts theorize a sphere separate from the king's authority.[29] Drawing on the "Examen de *Clitandre*" passage, she argues that the role of the royal judge as arbiter and guarantor of order ceases to be played by royal characters alone and that others, be they noblemen or bourgeois, or even servants, come to replace the royal judge onstage. She suggests, for instance, that the maid, Toinette, in Molière's *Le Malade imaginaire* is a character who takes on the mediating function of the royal judge, thereby constituting a prime example of a playwright turning the judge into a "figure plurielle" [plural figure], one in which many different characters can adopt a role previously reserved for the sovereign alone.[30]

It is certainly true that within a tragic plot we find numerous scenes involving a variety of characters exerting judgments over others. However, sustained attention to the representation of a legal authority reveals how playwrights and critics saw the sovereign character in a unique light and distinguished his role as exceptional. It is important to recognize that the "royal judge" is not only, or not necessarily, "royal." Depending on the particular source upon which a playwright bases his tragic plot, the "royal judge" may be a general, a prince, an emperor, etc., for all these terms designate the person in command who possesses the highest authority within the character hierarchy of the play. The "royal judge" is the authority towards whom the characters turn for a decision in the realm of justice. In grouping together different titles under one category, I follow Corneille for whom "king" is shorthand for the person in charge – the sovereign of the plot: "Je dis qu'un Roi, un héritier de la Couronne, un Gouverneur de la Province, et généralement un homme d'autorité peut paraître sur le Théâtre en trois façons: comme Roi, comme homme, et comme Juge; quelquefois avec deux de ces qualités, quelques fois toutes les trois ensemble"[31] [I say that a king, an heir to the Crown, a Governor of a Province, and generally a man of authority can appear onstage in three ways: as a King, as a man, and as a Judge; sometimes with two of these qualities, sometimes with all three]. Corneille amalgamates power and authority, a blend in which the governor of a province can coalesce into the heir to a throne. Not every play stages a monarch, but every tragedy presents an "homme d'autorité" (and sometimes as in *Rodogune* [1645], "une *femme* d'autorité") who possesses an objective sovereignty over the state and its subjects; that character stands alone in his or her ability to articulate immediate verdicts of life and death, and to determine the turn of (dramatic) events.

If in a twenty-first century television series the character chosen to play the commander-in-chief is cast according to his ability to "look the part" and to seem "presidential," the royal judge on the ancien régime stage also needed to convey a unique dignity through his physical presence. Moreover, the symbolic power of his person as an embodiment of judgment needed to be made immediately recognizable for audiences. The extensive narratives of power that accompanied the royal person and the mythology it evoked posed a serious challenge to playwrights attempting to make a fictional character behave in a manner that resembled a culturally resonant but ever fluctuating ideal of kingship. The king onstage was not *the* sovereign of course; no French playwrights by the seventeenth century sought to represent the *actual* king, nor, for the most part, did they stage kings from their national history, as did Elizabethan and Spanish playwrights.[32] But the theatrical king needed to speak, look, and behave in ways that did not cast a shadow on the contemporary monarch nor damage the dignity of the monarchy as an institution. As Corneille's great rival Scudéry quipped regarding the Spanish monarch in *Le Cid*, "[Corneille] devait traiter avec plus de respect, la personne des Rois que l'on nous apprend être sacrée; et considérer celui-ci dans le Trône de Castille, et non pas comme sur le Théâtre de Mondory"[33] [Corneille should treat with more respect the person of Kings that we are taught to regard as sacred; and consider this one to be on the throne of Castille, not on Mondory's stage]. If the mot d'ordre was to forget that the king onstage was a king onstage and to view him instead as an extension of the historical king, deserving of all the respect due to royalty, playwrights were left to rethink theatre's peculiar role in relaying political fictions while also supplying their plots with engaging characters.

Understanding the extraordinary achievement of French neoclassical drama also entails understanding its failure to accomplish what it was theorized to do. In following the tragic genre's emergence from a context of fierce aesthetic and ideological debate, we see the ongoing struggle for authority between playwrights, critics, and political theorists in the representation of monarchical power. Even as playwrights sought to confirm and celebrate royal authority, they were haunted by the politically explosive possibility of an undignified king, one who was in some form inadequate to his position.

Chapter One

The Critique of *Le Cid*: Richelieu, Royal Judgment, and the Rules

L'ambition, l'orgueil, l'audace, l'avarice,
Saisis de son pouvoir, nous donnèrent des lois,
Et bien qu'il fût en soi le plus juste des rois,
Son règne fut pourtant celui de l'injustice.

Corneille, *Sur la mort du Roi Louis XIII*[1]

1 The Politics of Royal Judgment

When Louis XIII was born on 27 September 1601, under the zodiacal sign of Libra, royal astrologers emphasized the newborn king's natural association with the balance scales of justice characteristic of that sign. They hailed the timing of his birth as a divine portent of what would become the king's defining royal virtue. Eventually, more as an incentive than as a reflection of his character, Louis received the sobriquet, "le juste" [the just].[2]

The timing of Louis's birth did prove premonitory of socio-political transformations in the French monarchy's relationship to the law, though astrologers would have been hard-pressed to predict the consequences of such sweeping changes, much less to identify them as decidedly "just." Political theorists close to the Crown responded to the chaos of the French Civil Wars and to the consecutive regicides of Henri III and Henri IV by affirming the king's position as the supreme legal entity of the kingdom.[3] There begins to be a shift in rhetoric from assertions of the king's duty to promote an immutable and universal justice towards a new focus on the king's divinely invested will. This latter perspective accentuates the independence of royal authority from positive law, stressing its contingent and efficient nature; the king's will should institute order rather than simply uphold law.[4]

Pro-monarchical theorists (most of them trained as jurists) insisted on the indisputable primacy of the sovereign in the field of justice: all law was said to be made in the king's name, and even in cases when his absence required him to delegate his judicial duty, his presence was implicit. Jean Bodin's widely read *Les Six Livres de la République* (1576) famously articulates a lasting definition of the king's sovereignty according to his unique power to make law:

> Il faut que ceux-là qui sont souverains ne soient aucunement sujets aux commandements d'autrui et qu'ils puissent donner loi aux sujets et casser ou anéantir les lois inutiles pour en faire d'autres [...] La puissance de donner loi emporte aussi le commandement. En ce sens, 'le prince est absous de la puissance des lois.' Les lois dépendent de sa pure et franche volonté, ce qu'exprime la formule, "Car tel est notre plaisir."[5]

> [Those who are sovereigns must not be in any measure subject to the commands of others and must be able to give laws to their subjects and break or repudiate useless laws in order to make others ... The power to give law includes the enforcement of them. In this sense, "the prince is absolved of the power of laws." Laws depend on his pure and frank will, which the expression, "for such is our desire" expresses.]

Bodin's wording accentuates the sovereign's isolation from the needs and influences of others. The prince's relationship to law is characterized by a remoteness and a violence – the power to "break or repudiate" at will. The sovereign Bodin describes possesses an unflappable resolve and is free to enforce his decisions as he sees fit.

Starting from the premise that God has chosen the king to rule as his living image, his judgment was celebrated as infallible, as the *main de justice* – the golden regalia which the king received at his coronation and which accompanied him in official portraits – illustrated. For pro-absolutist theorists, the contestation of a royal decision amounted to a sacrilegious act. As the historian Fanny Cosandey describes it, justice was defining of the monarchical identity and function:

> Désignés par Dieu, les souverains ont pour mission première de faire régner la justice, laquelle est, par définition, d'émanation divine puisque relevant

de la perfection. Seule la justice, en effet, justifie à la fois leur dignité et leur autorité, l'une permettant de la représenter, l'autre de l'appliquer.[6]

[Designated by God, sovereigns have as their first mission to make justice reign, which is, by definition, of divine origin since it stems from perfection. Only justice, in fact, justifies both their dignity and authority, the first enabling its representation, the second its application.]

The *lit de justice* held one day after Henri IV's assassination is emblematic of the early seventeenth-century monarchical eagerness to actively assert the Crown's legal prominence. Against the *parlementaires'* emphasis on the juridical basis for the transmission of the royal *dignitas*, Queen Marie of Medici and the child-king, Louis XIII sought to underscore the legitimacy of the dynastic line in designating Henri IV's successor themselves. Rather than speak of an office that would be passed from king to king, they stressed a sameness between Louis and his father, putting forward a biological oneness uniting their two bodies.[7] Furthermore, the prevalence of royal mottoes such as "Ce que veut le roi est loi" [The king's will is law] or "Un roi, une loi, une foi" [One king, one law, one faith] attests to the monarchy's will to found the French kingdom on the basis of the king's legal supremacy, not on a constitutional basis. Pro-monarchical theorists insisted on the king's singular ability to make law through his pronouncements and to force submission through his simple command.[8]

In order to grasp the distance separating this emerging seventeenth-century conception of royal judgment from the feudal ideal that preceded it, we have only to turn to the royal iconography of another French king named Louis – Saint Louis – after whom Louis XIII was christened. The folklore of the fatherly monarch, Louis IX, depicted him as an arbitrator-king who would patiently ponder his subjects' needs, resolve their quarrels, and guide them along a virtuous path. Saint Louis's biographer, Jean de Joinville, famously described the revered king's personal approach to justice: "Il advint maintes fois qu'en été, il allait s'asseoir au bois de Vincennes après sa messe, s'adossait à un chêne et nous faisait asseoir autour de lui. Et tous ceux qui avaient un problème venaient lui parler sans en être empêchés par un huissier ou quelqu'un d'autre"[9] [It happened often in the summer that he would go sit in the Bois de Vincennes after Mass, reclining against an oak tree and have us sit around him. And all those who had a problem came to speak to him without being prevented to do so by a royal officer or other]. Available and approachable, Saint Louis was physically and spiritually close to his subjects' concerns. He exercised a local, public justice with conciliatory aims, under a protective tree.

In contrast, over the course of the first half of the seventeenth century, the French monarch is increasingly depicted as the head of a vast administration of justice. The proximity of the feudal arbitrator-king's body is replaced by a corpus of officers who enforce legal decisions in the name of a physically absent king.[10] As Roland Mousnier describes it, the monarch's role as supreme lawgiver was forged by the broad concerns of efficiently administrating a state; the image of kingship that results is one of efficiency and order, not an intimate caring for the everyday travails of subjects seated around the royal person:

> Le roi est le premier justicier du royaume et sa justice découle de toutes ses autres fonctions, la "police" ou l'administration, la défense et la sécurité du royaume. Le roi, n'ayant pas, avant la résurrection des corps, le don d'ubiquité, ne peut pas exercer lui-même, partout, toutes ses fonctions. En vertu de la plénitude et de l'universalité de son pouvoir, le roi fait exercer par ses officiers une portion de l'autorité qui lui appartient. Cette autorité est celle du roi et non la leur.[11]

> [The king is the first guarantor of law within the kingdom and his justice results from all his other functions, the "police" or administration, the defence and security of the kingdom. The king, not having, before the resurrection of bodies, the gift of ubiquity, cannot exert, everywhere, all his functions. By virtue of the plenitude and universality of his power, the king has his officers exert a portion of the authority that belongs to him. This authority is his, not theirs.]

Changes in the royal exercise of justice were extensive and perceptible for subjects across France. For many, they were seen as a dangerous application of Machiavellian politics stemming from cynical uses of royal judicial power.[12] The divisions and massacres of the French Civil Wars had damaged the image of the monarch as a figure of justice. In the *Histoire universelle*, the historian and president of the Parlement of Paris, Jacques-Auguste de Thou, portrays a royal perversion of justice facilitated by Henri III's recourse to royal officers enacting justice in his name. In what reads as a full-fledged caricature of the idealized image of Saint Louis, de Thou's scene insists on the king's morbid fascination for torture:

Lorsqu'il fut mis à la question, le Roi y assista caché derrière un Rideau: il alla même à l'Hôtel de Ville pour le voir écarteler. Il y eut bien des gens qui trouvèrent qu'un pareil spectacle ne convenait guère à la dignité royale.[13]

[When he was put to torture, the King attended, hidden behind a Curtain: he even went to the Hôtel de Ville to see him drawn and quartered. There were many people who found that such a spectacle was unbecoming to the royal dignity.]

If de Thou undeniably assigns the part of the victim to the nameless punished man, from behind the curtain the king occupies the role of sadistic voyeur, demonstrating a strange blend of feebleness mixed with cruelty. Crucially, the monarch stands at the sidelines of the main event as he watches the pain inflicted on the condemned man by unnamed henchmen. De Thou switches to the passive voice, "when he was put to torture," emphasizing a lack of clarity regarding who exactly is responsible for inflicting the suffering. Then, he reverts to an active voice, "many people found," to assert the popular consensus that the king has sullied himself by viewing this episode. This description of Henri III, one that the seventeenth-century nobility angry at the execution of their peers will readily apply to Louis XIII, highlights the blend of brutality and undignified behaviour that comes to characterize the century's theatrical portrayals of tyranny.

The changing depictions of royal justice were, of course, not only the result of changing theories, but changing practices as well. Under Louis XIII, legal reforms were conspicuous and widespread enough to be observed by French subjects of all social conditions. On scaffolds mounted in city squares for all to see, noblemen were put to a bloody and tortuous death at the behest of the king's prime minister – Cardinal Richelieu. Not only were men from prominent noble families executed publicly, but the wide geographical range in which their death sentences were enacted made it even more likely that a large swathe of French subjects would have witnessed them first-hand or would at least have been familiar with the various accounts that circulated in their wake. A list of only a small sampling of those put to death in Richelieu-directed political trials illustrates their geographical breadth: the Count of Chalais was decapitated in Nantes in 1626; the Duke of Montmorency was executed in Toulouse in 1632; the magistrate de Thou and the Marquis de Cinq Mars died on the scaffolds of Lyon in 1642.[14]

Cardinal Richelieu was deemed personally responsible for overseeing the violent deaths of these men, having played a decisive hand in their trials and aggressively promoting the guilty verdicts they received. The judicial process was quickly becoming a weapon in Richelieu's arsenal against challenges to the Crown.[15] These demonstrations of judicial violence were accompanied by other legal measures designed to promote the monarchy's strength, independence, and authority. Practices such as the exile of influential nobles, the confiscation of their land, the revocation of their titles of nobility, and the humiliating parade of noblemen through the city on their way to prison became increasingly common punishments for those found guilty of *lèse-majesté*. For the monarchy, the goal was to silence the power of the Parlements and quell the influence of leading members of the nobility who sought to weigh in on matters of import to the Crown.[16] The aristocracy saw these legal reprisals as cruel means of satisfying private grudges and considered them to be flagrant examples of judicial abuse.

Aristocrats targeted by Richelieu responded to his judicial attacks with a blend of consternation, alarm, and anger, but, as correspondence and pamphlets penned in anti-Richelieu circles attest, the dominant tone of their reaction was contempt. The nobility ridiculed his efforts as those of a lowly comedic figure – undignified, vulgar, inefficient, and disrespectful of noble *privilèges*. Faced with Richelieu's edicts forbidding duels, aristocratic commentators continued to propagate the view that these prohibitions were a disgrace and that true noblemen would settle their differences by the sword not by trials.[17] As the following letter written by an aristocratic hand attests, to many, Richelieu's legal meddling resembled the crude habits of the crafty and specious *chicaneurs* of comedy:

La première fois que l'on dit chez la Reine, que le Cardinal de Richelieu travaillait à faire mon procès, cela fut trouvé si étrange et si éloigné de tout ce qui s'est jamais pratiqué en Justice, qu'au lieu de s'en ébahir, on le prit pour une raillerie, et une chose qui ne pouvait tomber sous le sens commun. Il semblait premièrement que ce serait contrevenir aux maximes qu'il a, d'abaisser le moins qu'il peut sa toute puissance prétendue, et de ne pas se commettre ouvertement à une action, qui ne se pratique point entre la Noblesse; sentant plutôt son petit Chicaneur et solliciteur de procès, que son homme de conséquence.[18]

[The first time it was announced in the Queen's quarters that the Cardinal of Richelieu was working on my trial, it was considered so strange and so foreign to anything that has ever been practised in Justice, so much so that instead of being shocked by this, we thought it was a joke, something that

made no sense. It seemed, first of all, that it would go against the maxims
he has set for himself, to denigrate as little as possible his supposed all-
powerfulness, and commit an action that is not practised among the Nobility; smelling more of a pithy lawyer or solicitor of trials, than of a man of
consequence.]

Despite the potentially ruinous consequences of the cardinal's legal pursuits, they are belittled and mocked; critics make his dignity their first
point of attack, casting him in the role of the well-known comedic type
of the lawyer obsessed with judicial proceedings. This character will continue to be a source of scorn, as in the second half of the century in the
comedy *Les Plaideurs* (1668) where Racine engages with the ludicrous
figure of the *chicaneur* and draws laughter from the presentation of a
father so taken with criminal pursuits that he puts a dog on trial. To cast
Richelieu in that role is to turn his reliance on judicial practices into a
ridiculous penchant for legal meddling, and thus, to deny the legitimacy
of his claims and position.

In parallel to the derision of the king's minister, widespread anecdotes
criticized Louis XIII's complacency regarding the cardinal's behaviour:
how could the king knowingly support these disgraceful practices? He
was deemed to be either too passive or else too cruel. Rather than link
the king to his father, Henri IV, who was known for his clemency, anecdotes tied Louis's troubling ways to the turbulent Henri III, the monarch
de Thou depicted hiding behind the curtain, watching as others torture
in his name. Whether Louis's inaction alongside Richelieu stemmed
from indifference and passivity, or from a ruthless cruelty, his behaviour
was deemed by many of his opponents as undignified and a disgrace to
the royal function.

It is within this turbulent context of monarchical-aristocratic legal
battles and reforms, so characteristic of Louis XIII's reign, that I situate the stinging critiques directed at Pierre Corneille's royal judge, Don
Fernand, in his immensely successful play, *Le Cid* (1637). As we have
seen, precisely in this period the issue of royal decision-making, its
portrayal, its basis, and its consequences, were an active source of concern for the French Crown and for many of its subjects. In the wake
of the palpable legal-political changes of this era, theatrical portrayals
of royal judgment suddenly elicited pointed discussion in poetic works
and fuelled passionate commentary among critics and playwrights. As
we will see, critics found Corneille guilty of presenting a king who was
at once worthy of ridicule and capable of terrible cruelty – flaws that so

distinctly echo the criticism directed at Richelieu and Louis XIII. Moreover, Don Fernand was deemed too marginal to the main intrigue of the play, and his judgment was found to be implausibly immoral. Situated at the height of Richelieu's influence over the Crown's political and cultural policies, the question of Don Fernand's improper judgment set in motion a debate over theatrical representations of royalty that drove playwrights to rethink the role of the sovereign within their plots. It also transformed the terms of discussion of kings onstage and inaugurated a period of intense concern for the safeguarding of royal dignity in theatrical performances.

Much scholarly attention has been paid to the quarrel over *Le Cid*, especially with regards to its decisive influence in shaping a critical public and a politically active literary sphere. Its role in emerging debates surrounding authorship, institutional censorship, and questions of literary translation and adaption has been well explored.[19] *Le Cid*'s quarrel serves to legitimize tragedy as a superior "art" with rules, norms, practitioners, and experts. More than any other literary genre in this period, tragedy's forms and themes result from a politically invested codification whose principles are laid out in response to Corneille's play.[20] Furthermore, the quarrel's place in defining the notions of *bienséance* and *vraisemblance* has been well examined, and my aim is not to rehearse these debates here.[21] I wish to shift the focus away from the play's heroine, Chimène. Critical discussion has dwelled on the controversy surrounding the unseemliness of her enduring love for Rodrigue, the man who killed her father in a duel. Instead the analysis will turn towards the discussion of the sovereign's improprieties. Little scholarship has been devoted to the critical reception of Don Fernand, though it is his decision that places Chimène in the position to marry her father's assassin at the close of the play.[22]

My readings of these critiques will centre around two of the most influential critical texts of the quarrel: the one that launched the polemic – Georges de Scudéry's *Observations sur* Le Cid (1637) – and the one that officially put an end to it – Jean Chapelain's *Les Sentiments de l'Académie française sur la tragi-comédie du* Cid (1637), a response penned in the name of the newly founded institution. These texts highlight the negative appraisals of Don Fernand and they decisively shape future portrayals of royal decision-making on the French stage, culminating in the theorization of a *bienséance* specific to royal characters and actions. The remainder of this chapter examines the period's critical articulation of what is deemed to be an entirely misguided royal portrayal within Corneille's play.

What follows, then, is not a reading of *Le Cid*, but a survey of how influential critics close to royal power read Corneille's most popular play. For the most part, I will hold off on providing Corneille's response and his own meditations on these matters until chapter 3, when I will ally a study of his practice with his theoretical discussions of royal portrayals. Starting with the critical reception of *Le Cid* and allowing the voice of Corneille's critics to resonate will make clear what playwrights writing after the polemic had to take into account as they set about devising royal characters for the stage. Perhaps more so than the play itself, *Le Cid*'s criticism coloured royal portraits to come.

2 Judging Judgment

Judgment, and more precisely, the notion of a judgment rendered before a watchful public, lies at the heart of *Les Sentiments de l'Académie Française touchant les observations faites sur la question de la tragi-comédie du* Cid. The opening lines of Jean Chapelain's long-awaited official intervention into the quarrel begin by immediately asserting, in the language of jurisprudence, the Académie Française's legitimacy in pronouncing a verdict over a published work:

> Ceux qui par quelque désir de gloire donnent leurs Ouvrages au public ne doivent pas trouver étrange que le Public s'en fasse le Juge [...] Ils ne peuvent avec justice désirer de lui qu'il fasse même estime des fausses beautés que des vraies, ni qu'il paie de louange ce qui sera digne de blâme.[23]

> [Those who out of a certain desire for glory give their Works to the public must not find it strange that the public becomes judge of them ... They cannot with justice desire that [the public] judge in the same way false beauties against true ones, nor that the public give praise to what is worthy of blame.]

With this emphasis on the public's right to judge, Chapelain, at the behest of his powerful patron, stakes out the Académie's jurisdiction over the domain of letters and extends the Crown's supremacy of judgment over poetic works.[24] The "public" Chapelain first alludes to in broad terms, but soon reveals to be the Académie, has not only the right to judge, but also a moral-social obligation to do so, just as the king must judge the behaviour of his subjects. Throughout *Les Sentiments*, Chapelain has recourse to the language of justice, calling the *Querelle* a "trial" and developing the position that the Académie is a recognized "tribunal" based on the model of the Roman Censor, working to encourage "glorious progress" in the realm of letters.[25] In parallel to French courts of law where, after careful deliberation, an informed tribunal of judges renders a verdict in the king's name, the literary court consists of knowledgeable arbiters of good taste who will articulate opinions that instruct and benefit society.

Thus, in contrast to the messy reality of the quarrel over *Le Cid*, which spawned pamphlets rife with ad-hominem attacks and charges of artistic ineptitude, Chapelain paints the Académie's response as a model of judgment. This exemplary text, in the author's view, demonstrates how the verdict of a legitimate authority will uncover the truth – "la vérité est le prix que l'on court dans cette lice" [the truth is the price that one is after in this pursuit] after each side has entered its *plaidoyers*, "civilement et sans animosité" [civilly and without animosity].[26]

Diminishing the opinions of the theatre-going public, the spectators who had received *Le Cid* with such enthusiasm, Chapelain's text relegates the broad audience of the play to the position of witness to the Académie-judge's decision.[27] Chapelain intentionally sheds the bellicose language of Scudéry's *Observations*, and stresses the impartial, reasonable, and measured critique of *Les Sentiments*. In situating itself above the disagreement of individuals, the text models an articulation of judgment based on fact, equity, and careful consideration, thereby conforming to and accentuating the contemporary ideals of proper sovereign judgment. It is important to keep in mind Chapelain's pointed demonstration of the decorum and virtue of the Académie's judgment, especially as it contrasts with what he deems to be the deplorable and improper judgment of Don Fernand in *Le Cid*.

The Académie Française paints itself as a careful judge who has listened to the prosecution – Scudéry – and has attentively considered the evidence – *Le Cid* – so that an unassailable verdict can be determined. We will begin our analysis, therefore, with the charges Scudéry lays forth. In contrast to Corneille, among the great many faults the nobleman playwright Georges de Scudéry found with Don Fernand, he does not explicitly address the matter of the king's supporting role. This contrast encapsulates Corneille's and Scudéry's differing critiques of royal judgment – the first is less interested in the king's virtue and focuses on his structural position within the plot, while the second dwells on representational matters such as Fernand's lack of authority and feeble demeanour. Scudéry deplores, for example, that Fernand's orders were not followed and that the royal subjects' submissiveness to their king in the play is insufficient:

> il faut que je dise que jamais Roy ne fut si mal obéit que Don Fernand, puisqu'il se trouve que malgré l'ordre qu'il avait donné dès le second Acte de munir le port [...] il se trouve que Séville était prise, son Trône renversé, et sa personne et celles de ses enfants perdues si le hasard n'eût assemblé ces bien-heureux Amis de Don Diègue.[28]

> [I have to say that never was a King so ill-obeyed as Don Fernand, since despite giving the order as early as the second Act to reinforce the port ... Seville would have been taken, his Throne toppled, and his person and that of his children would have been lost if chance had not assembled these lucky Friends of Don Diègue.]

Above all, Scudéry focuses on the moral implications of the Spanish king's decision. He states: "Ainsi le quatrième acte s'achève après que Fernand a fait la plus injuste ordonnance que prince imagina jamais"[29] [Thus the fourth Act ends after Fernand has made the most unjust command that a prince ever imagined]. Scudéry's comment should not be abstracted from the debates of the Richelieu era surrounding the historical king's controversial judicial role and image. The king's behaviour, which he describes as "vulgar," as lacking in seriousness, and as childish, evokes the attacks against Richelieu and explains the heightened sensitivity to Fernand's character flaws by the critics close to Louis XIII's prime minister.[30]

The strongest claims Scudéry makes against the king's portrayal stem from this "unjust command," that the critic believes places Fernand in an unacceptable light. Scudéry is referring to the close of Act IV, when Don Fernand calls for a duel between Chimène's two suitors – Don Sanche and Don Rodrigue – and promises that whoever wins will receive her hand in marriage. Earlier in the play, Fernand had promised to reflect earnestly on his verdict when Chimène had insisted, "Je demande justice" (II.7. v. 653) [I demand justice]. Despite her love for Rodrigue, she had turned to the king to punish the nobleman for killing her father in a duel. Fernand, at that point, seemed to take his role of judge seriously: "L'affaire est d'importance et, bien considérée, / Mérite en plein conseil d'être délibérée [...]/ Qu'on me cherche [le fils de Don Diègue]. Je vous ferai justice" (II.7. vv. 743–7) [The matter is of importance and well considered, it deserves to be deliberated over in full council ... Go get him. I will give you justice]. By Act IV, however, when Fernand orders a second duel it is not as an explicit punishment of Rodrigue. Instead, he offers Chimène up as a prize to the last man standing. In other words, his decision does not ensure retribution for the murdered nobleman-father. Though Scudéry and the critics on his side will vociferously protest against Chimène's "unnatural" behaviour ("cette fille dénaturée"), they see the king's judgment as the indisputable cause of the disturbing alliance between a daughter and her father's assassin that marks the play's ending.

According to Scudéry, such a portrayal of royal judgment was unbearably shocking to French audiences who could not stomach such immoral reasoning from a king. Scudéry's polemical text frames its principle grievance regarding Don Fernand as an issue of *bienséance*. He turns to Aristotle as an incontrovertible authority for his argument. In the fifteenth chapter of *The Poetics*, the ancient author notes that fictional characters must adhere to larger conceptions of propriety. Aristotle gives only one example: it is not in the habit of women to be virile or unscrupulously clever. He adds that a character cannot be uneven in his behaviour unless his defining trait is unevenness.[31] In Scudéry's transposition of this rule, consistency becomes a matter of social condition. No noblewoman and no king should act in such an undignified manner. Tragic fictions should promote respect and admiration for characters of elevated social status, and for that reason they should be presented as consistently virtuous. The Aristotelian consistency of character is converted in seventeenth-century French poetics into a consistent display of morality for royalty and nobility. Since the Spanish monarch of *Le Cid* had not been introduced from the start of the play as tyrannical or utterly irrational, a king of sound mind could not plausibly make such a suddenly unjust decision.

This conviction leads Scudéry to underscore the importance of *vraisemblance* as a cultural necessity on the French stage. According to him, tragedy traffics not in the reproduction of reality, but in the production of an ideal world:

Cet événement [the mariage between Chimène and Rodrigue] était bon pour l'Historien, mais il ne valait rien pour le Poète; et je ne crois pas qu'il suffise de donner des répugnances à Chimène; de faire combattre le Devoir contre l'Amour; de lui mettre en la bouche mille antithèses sur ce sujet; ni de faire intervenir l'autorité d'un Roi; car enfin tout cela n'empêche pas qu'elle se rende parricide, en se résolvant d'épouser le meurtrier de son Père.[32]

[This event was good for the Historian, but it was worthless for the poet; and I do not think it sufficient to have Chimène express her disgust; to make Duty fight against Love; to put in her mouth a thousand arguments on this subject; nor to make the authority of a King intervene; since all this does not prevent her from being a parricide, by agreeing to marry her Father's assassin.]

Scudéry distinguishes between history and tragedy, insisting on tragedy's necessary departure from historical fact, but in his critique it becomes apparent that neither Chimène nor Fernand are isolated from the seventeenth-century historical reality. The behaviour of these characters is condemned because it reflects poorly on all noblewomen and on all kings; it is faulty above all because it taints in the eyes of the public the position of superiority the characters of high rank must occupy.

In the *Sentiments de l'Académie*'s response, Chapelain's definition of *vraisemblance* adheres to this discussion of Fernand. The Académie's text expresses a critical eagerness to replace the morally disturbing dénouement of royal judgment with what we might call a "monarchical aesthetic" – a poetics that despite its claim to prefer "universal" under-standings of behaviour, in fact, dictates a very narrow, culturally and historically specific view of how noble characters should behave. The repeated injunctions not to depict the historical but to prefer the uni-versal result in drawing attention to what sort of behaviour this atem-poral monarchical code of conduct for theatrical sovereigns advances. *Vraisemblance* becomes shorthand for censoring history in favour of pro-moting idealized representations. The alarm raised by Fernand's royal decision-making in *Le Cid*, and the passion with which the critics seek to erase it from the stage is revealing of the danger they see in such portrayals:

C'est alors que [le poète] la doit plutôt changer [la vérité] toute entière que de lui laisser une seule tache incompatible avec les règles de son art; lequel cherche l'universel des choses et les épure des défauts et des irrégu-larités particulières que l'histoire, par la sévérité de ses lois, est contrainte d'y souffrir.[33]

[It is then that the poet must change [the truth] entirely rather than leave a single stain incompatible with the rules of his art; which seeks the universal in things and cleanses the defects and the particular irregularities that his-tory, because of the severity of its laws, must suffer.]

The newly established "rules of [tragic] art" are synonymous with an elimination, or "cleansing" of those "marks" which thwart the monarchical ideal of the Richelieu era. Faulty kings such as Fernand stand as historical aberrations that no longer have a place on the tragic stage.

François-Hédelin abbé d'Aubignac, a critic and playwright in favour with Cardinal Richelieu, authored the influential treatise on theatre, *La Pratique du théâtre* (1657). In the passages dedicated to *vraisemblance*, d'Aubignac echoes and expands on Chapelain's discussion, emphasizing further the dangers of not showing proper respect towards the royal person. He describes *vraisemblance* as "le fondement de toutes les Pièces du Théâtre" [the foundation of all Dramatic Plays] and insists on the need for drama to conform to "l'opinion et le sentiment ordinaire des hommes"[34] [the opinion and regular feeling of men]. By this, he means that the common opinion of men (French men) should be that kings are just and make enlightened judgments. D'Aubignac distinctly foregrounds the question of sovereign portrayals by choosing to focus his first example of *vraisemblance* on the emperor Nero's unacceptable actions. The critic references the Roman sovereign's infamous brutality towards his mother – he first strangled her and then opened her abdomen. D'Aubignac's definitive statement in reaction is, simply, that "cela ne devait point arriver"[35] [that shouldn't have happened]. The French critic insists that while these events may be historically grounded, no French audience could, or should, believe a sovereign capable of such monstrosities. In other words, according to this rigorist approach, even Nero cannot be shown in all his evil because of the limits of what royal subjects are willing to believe about sovereigns. There is little room for *a contrario* examples, the *éloge paradoxal* that stems from painting a frightening portrait of tyranny in order to cast a favourable light on the magnanimity of the sitting monarch. In d'Aubignac's mindset it is best to simply offer a pleasing royal portrait.

The discussion of *vraisemblance* leads d'Aubignac to return to the definition of theatrical action, which he sees as aiming to display a "perfect" image in its entirety:

> Il n'y a point d'action humaine tellement simple, qu'elle ne soit accompagnée de plusieurs circonstances qui la composent, comme sont le temps, le lieu, la personne, la dignité, les desseins, les moyens, et la raison d'agir. Et puisque le théâtre doit en être une image parfaite, il faut qu'il la représente toute entière, et que la Vraisemblance y soit observée en toutes ses parties.[36]

[There is no human action so simple that it is not accompanied by a number of circumstances that compose it, such as the time, location, person, dignity, design, means, and reason for acting. And since the stage must be a perfect image of the action, it must represent it entirely, and *Vraisemblance* must be observed in all of its parts.]

Though he does not expressly state that by "perfect image of the action," he means "flawless," d'Aubignac's emphasis on an awareness of a character's "circumstances," especially his "dignity" and "means," in defining him entails painting a respectful and admiring portrayal of royalty.

Writing a few years later in a critique of Corneille's *Œdipe* (1659), d'Aubignac's concerns regarding unfavourable representations of royalty have grown even more pronounced.[37] Although Aristotle himself hailed Sophocles's *Oedipus Rex* as a tragic exemplar, d'Aubignac reproves the dangerous lessons such a portrait of royal misery offers to a society structured around royal distinction:

Il faut entretenir [les spectateurs] dans cette pieuse croyance, que les Rois sont toujours accompagnés d'une faveur particulière du ciel, qu'ils sont partout innocents, et que personne n'a droit de les estimer coupables.[38]

[It is necessary to maintain [spectators] in this pious belief that Kings are always particularly favoured by the heavens, and that they are always innocent, and that no one is entitled to judge them guilty.]

D'Aubignac invests French playwrights with the duty to protect and promote theatrical kings in general. "Les rois," no matter their mythology or chronology, deserve particular safeguarding when it comes to the public's opinion of them. No latitude exists between the esteem owed to the French monarch and the reverence owed to all crowned heads onstage. On the spectrum of royal theatrical portrayals, d'Aubignac's poetics fall on the most conservative end, but this perspective proves to be very influential. D'Aubignac and his fellow critics reject the notion of a superseding literary tradition or historical context that would divorce theatrical portrayals from the immediate cultural standards of respect due to the historical king on the French throne.

Reasoning according to seventeenth-century pro-monarchical standards, Corneille's critics found Don Fernand unacceptably lacking in authority. *A la Richelieu*, they wanted to see a sovereign's forceful judicial response to the events described by the plot. A ruler, according to the critics' understanding of kingship, must be shown to actively police his state to ensure that peace and order are maintained. In this view, if the kingdom's noblemen threaten each other, or if the state is shown to suffer from some imminent threat, the king must intervene decisively and demand submission to his authority.

Corneille, in response to *Le Cid*'s detractors, adopts a relativistic approach, giving examples from his Spanish source, and insisting that he aimed to depict a different type of kingship, one that evokes a time before the king's legal force was so dominant:

> il reste néanmoins quelque chose à examiner sur la manière dont agit [le roi], qui ne paraît pas assez vigoureuse, en ce qu'il ne fait pas arrêter le Comte après le soufflet donné, et n'envoie pas des Gardes à Don Diègue et à son fils. Sur quoi on peut considérer que Don Fernand étant le premier Roi de Castille, et ceux qui en avaient été maître auparavant lui n'avant eu titre que de Comtes, il n'était peut-être pas assez absolu sur les grands Seigneurs de son royaume pour le pouvoir faire.[39]

> [there remains, however, something to examine regarding the manner in which [the king] acts, which does not appear vigorous enough, since he does not have the Count arrested after the slap is given. We may consider that since Don Fernand was the first King of Castile, and that those that were sovereign before him had only possessed the title of Count, his power was perhaps not so absolute over the great Lords of his kingdom as to be able to do so.]

In this passage, Corneille frames royal behaviour explicitly as a matter of context by explaining that Fernand's feebleness is grounded in a historical dynamic different from the one that prevails in seventeenth-century France. The playwright justifies the behaviour critics oppose by pointing to his Spanish source-text, *Las Mocedades del Cid*, as proof that, at one time, noblemen acted with disregard for royal commands:

> Chez Don Guilhem de Castro, qui a traité ce Sujet avant moi, et qui devait mieux connaître que moi quelle était l'autorité de ce premier Monarque de son pays, le soufflet [de Dom Gomes à Don Diègue] se donne en sa présence et en celle de deux Ministres d'Etat.[40]

> [In Don Guilhem de Castro, who treated this Subject before I, and who must have known better than I do what was the authority of this first Monarch of his country, the slap is given (in the king's) presence and in the presence of two Ministers of State.]

Corneille emphasizes Don Fernand's temporal and royal Otherness, insisting that the king's *mollesse* [limpness] is the product of another era, a time and place when the monarch did not intercede in aristocratic affairs: "C'est sur cet exemple que je me suis cru bien fondé à le faire agir plus mollement qu'on ne ferait en ce temps-ci où l'autorité royale est plus absolue"[41] [It is on the basis of this example that I thought it well-founded to make him act more limply than we would do in these times when royal authority is more absolute]. Corneille underlines the profound shift between the contemporary French context that governs relations between the monarch, the "Ministers of State," and the noblemen, and contrasts this with the Spanish context when aristocrats responded directly to each other. In alluding to the foreign nature of his representation in answer to his critics' attacks, Corneille astutely transforms the critique of weakness directed towards his theatrical king into an opportunity to flatter the contemporary monarch whose power over the "great Lords," he suggests, is nowadays so formidable.

Against this vein of justification, however, d'Aubignac argues that monarchical subjects can only be satisfied by fictions that coincide with their cultural expectations. In other words, the French can only relish tragedies that glorify the monarchy. Depictions that run counter to these expectations would inevitably fail to please them. In this respect, then, the Ancients are no example to follow:

> La plainte de celui qui aurait entrepris de tuer un Tyran, et qui serait surpris sans exécuter son dessein, ne nous plairait pas comme aux Athéniens, et nous l'aurions en abomination, au lieu d'avoir quelque compassion de son Malheur: parce que vivant dans un Etat Monarchique, nous tenons comme sacrée la personne des Rois, quand même ils seraient injustes; au lieu que les Athéniens nourris dans un Gouvernement populaire, condamnaient tous les Souverains, et ne les pouvaient souffrir.[42]

> [The complaint of one who sets out to kill a Tyrant and is surprised before he executes his plan, would not please us as it would the Athenians, and we would hold him in abomination, instead of having some sort of compassion for his Misfortune: because living in a Monarchical State, we hold the person of Kings to be sacred, even if they are unjust; while Athenians nourished by a popular Government condemned all Sovereigns, and could not stand them.]

Once again the line between poetic precept and monarchical flattery blurs. "Nourished" in a culture of respect for the sacred royal body,

French spectators could not stomach an attack on the sovereign, even onstage. Such a rule is clearly contradicted by the success of tragedies like Corneille's *Cinna ou la clémence d'Auguste* (1642) or Tristan l'Hermite's *La Mort de Sénèque* (1644), but points to the period's growing concern for protecting the royal image and the desire to isolate it from criticism. Specifically, d'Aubignac erects a taboo against attacking the sanctity of the "person of Kings," echoing an earlier criticism by Scudéry of Don Fernand: "[L'auteur] devrait traiter avec plus de respect la personne des Rois, que l'on nous apprend être sacrée, et considérer celui-ci dans le Trône de Castille et non pas comme sur le Théâtre de Mondory"[43] [The author should treat with more respect the person of Kings, that we are taught is sacred, and consider this one on the Throne of Castile and not on Mondory's Stage]. I take this reference to the royal "person" as a willingness to underscore that it is not the concept of monarchy alone that should be protected, but also the individual onstage who embodies that institution, no matter which throne – Roman, Castilian, French, etc. – he occupies. This vision leads to the development by these critics close to the Crown of a *vraisemblance* that should be particular to France and to the love of the French for their monarchs. The character on the throne, they insist, must be made to reflect the flattering cultural assumptions that govern king-subject relations in monarchical discourses of the first half of the seventeenth century.

3 Demonstrating Good Judgment

Le Cid's success with Parisian audiences coincided with Richelieu's new-found focus on the moral lessons the tragic genre could deliver to French audiences. Louis XIII's prime minister had founded the Académie Française in 1635, only two years prior to *Le Cid*'s début, with the aim of legitimizing theatrical practices and influencing the content of theatrical fictions.[44] For playwrights and critics who hoped to ingratiate themselves with the cardinal, including Scudéry, La Mesnardière, and especially Chapelain, respect for decorum (*bienséance*) became a central concern.[45] *Bienséance* is described in their works as what is reasonable and expected, with the implicit understanding that the evaluation of that is determined by "polite" society, i.e., noble Parisian circles. When Chapelain articulates the Académie's judgment of *Le Cid*, he agrees with Scudéry in condemning the illogical nature of Don Fernand's justice: "le Dénouement de l'intrigue n'est fondé que sur l'injustice inopinée de Fernand qui vient ordonner un mariage, que par raison il ne devait pas seulement proposer"[46] [the intrigue's Dénouement is founded only on the unexpected injustice of Fernand who orders a wedding, that by reason he should not even countenance]. Chapelain's critique of Don Fernand's verdict is twofold: first, he laments the "unexpectedness" of the decision; nothing in Fernand's character prepared spectators to expect such a bizarre judgment. Second, Chapelain disapproves of the unreasonableness of a dénouement that rests on a verdict that seems to be no more than a contrivance, an artificial and nonsensical means of resolving the plot. By this judgment, the French critic takes an Aristotelian rule and gives it a monarchical flavour. In *The Poetics*, Aristotle specifies that tragic endings should not be arbitrary and should stem from "earlier facts" alluded to within the plot:

> It is therefore evident that the unraveling of the plot, no less than the complication, must arise out of the plot itself, it must not be brought about by the *Deus ex Machina* [...] The *Deus ex Machina* should be employed only for events external to the drama – for antecedent or subsequent events, which lie beyond the range of human knowledge, and which require to be reported or foretold [...] Within the action there should be nothing irrational.[47]

Aristotle's precept takes on a political dimension with Chapelain's insistence that the king's judgment not appear haphazard or arbitrary. To end the play with such an unpredictable verdict reflects badly on royal decisions in general and conveys a negative impression of the consequences of royal judgment.

The concern Chapelain voices is a distinct product of the Richelieu-influenced-1630s understanding of tragic fictions; it stands in contrast to earlier models prevalent in the first quarter of the seventeenth century when it was commonplace for the king to be, in fact, not much more than an effective means to bring the play to an end – the *deus ex machina*-like figure Chapelain now denounces.[48]

Chapelain goes on to insist that a disturbing decision such as Fernand's would need to be presented as aberrant, or else simply not presented at all:

> Mais nous maintenons que toutes les vérités ne sont pas bonnes pour le théâtre, et qu'il en est de quelques-unes comme de ces crimes énormes, dont les Juges font brûler les procès avec les criminels. Il y a des vérités monstrueuses, ou qu'il faut supprimer pour le bien de la société, ou que si

l'on ne peut les tenir cachées, il faut se contenter de remarquer comme des choses étranges.[49]

[But we insist that not all truths are appropriate for the theatre, and that some are like those enormous crimes where Judges choose to burn the evidence with the criminal. There are monstrous truths that one must either hide for society's wellbeing or, if they cannot remain hidden, must be described as abnormal.]

Chapelain insists on the tragic genre's promotion of the public good, a function which entails eliminating "monstrous truths" from the stage, including the notion that a noblewoman and her king could be capable of such undignified behaviour. For "society's wellbeing," a passion such as Chimène's and a royal judgment such as Don Fernand's should remain a dark secret. For this reason, Chapelain maintains that Corneille should have entirely disregarded the historical nature of his story and changed the ending, "with no concern for fact."[50]

In the passage quoted above, Chapelain turns the playwright from a poet into a judge; when writing a tragedy, an author must evaluate the moral and social consequences his fictions will have on spectators, and protect them from harmful truths. In articulating this precept, Chapelain alludes to seventeenth-century judicial practice, including the secrecy inherent to it. If burning a criminal may seem cruel and excessive to onlookers, Chapelain props up the virtue of the French legal system – and the virtue of tragedy – by insisting that a judge and a playwright take the appropriate measures to spare the public from painful discoveries. With this parallel between the judicial realm and theatre's protective social role, Chapelain highlights the commonalities between two spheres that work together and compliment each other to ensure the moral improvement of French subjects.

Chapelain's parallels between crimes onstage and societal crimes do not end there. Echoing the principles of necessary punishment of the wicked laid out by La Mesnardière, *Les Sentiments de l'Académie* insists on theatre's role in chastising bad behaviour. Public virtue depends on the display of criminals condemned onstage:

Les mauvais exemples sont contagieux, même sur les théâtres; les feintes représentations ne causent que trop de véritables crimes, et il y a grand péril à divertir le Peuple par des plaisirs qui peuvent produire un jour des douleurs publiques. Il nous faut bien garder d'accoutumer ni ses yeux ni

ses oreilles à des actions qu'il doit ignorer [...] si nous ne lui apprenons en
même temps la punition, et si au retour de ces spectacles il ne remporte du
moins un peu de crainte parmi beaucoup de contentement.[51]

[Bad examples are contagious even on the stage; imaginary representations
cause only too many real crimes; there is great peril in entertaining the
people through pleasures that can lead to public suffering. We must not
accustom either the public's eyes or ears to actions it must remain ignorant
of, if we do not also teach the punishment for these, and if upon returning
from these spectacles the public does not carry home at least a little fear
among much contentment.]

If theatrical representations can contaminate society, leading to "real
crimes," the solution according to Chapelain is not to eliminate them
outright, but instead to require scenes of retribution where spectators
witness evil characters suffering "punishment" intended above all as a
deterrent for the onlookers. He repeats this point when addressing the
"scandalous" and "depraved" behaviour of Chimène specifically:

Ces pernicieux exemples rendent l'Ouvrage notablement défectueux, et
s'écartent du but de la Poésie, qui veut être utile; ce n'est pas que cette
utilité ne se puisse produire par des mœurs qui soient mauvaises; mais pour
la produire par de mauvaises mœurs il faut qu'à la fin elles soient punies, et
non récompensées comme elles le sont en cet Ouvrage.[52]

[These pernicious examples render this Work particularly defective, and
stray from the aim of Poetry, which is to be useful; it is not that this usefulness cannot be attained through bad behaviour; but for it to be achieved
by bad behaviour it is necessary that at the end it be punished, and not
rewarded as it is in this work.]

Royal judgment becomes a means of suppressing and escaping the perilous behaviour depicted within a plot. In this view, the ethics of royal
decision-making and the king's demonstration of sound reasoning constitute not just good theatrical practice but also an effective method for
encouraging lawfulness within the French kingdom. Thus, in step with
Richelieu's contemporary legal reforms, Chapelain delineates a crucial
new role for the royal character or the "man of authority" within tragedy:
he is charged with maintaining order, rewarding the good, and castigat-
ing the criminal.

This new conception of the king's necessary portrayal as a solemn law-giver and teacher of moral lessons leads to the condemnation of another disturbing facet of Don Fernand's character: his lack of seriousness and authority. In the *Observations sur* Le Cid, Scudéry had lamented the king's antics:

> Là dans une action de telle importance, où sa justice devait être balancée avec la victoire de Rodrigue, il s'amuse à lui [Chimène] faire pièce; il veut éprouver si elle aime son amant; et en un mot, le Poète lui ôte sa Couronne de dessus la tête pour le coiffer d'une Marotte.[53]

> [There in an action of such importance, when his justice should be balanced with Rodrigue's victory, he enjoys giving her a hard time; he wants to test if she loves her lover; and in short, the Poet takes the Crown off his head and replaces it with a Bauble.]

The king resembles a court jester, not a sovereign. The crown – the greatest symbol of his divinely invested authority – is replaced and denigrated by a mere plaything, a mock ornament of power that underscores Don Fernand's failure to adopt the demeanour required of his function. The denigration of royal authority Scudéry detects in Don Fernand echoes Richelieu's denigration as a comedic character by aristocratic circles. Given this context, the motivation to decry the Spanish king's behaviour as a threat to ensuring widespread respect for royal legal legitimacy constitutes a political stance flattering to the French Crown.

Furthermore, Scudéry insists on the lack of balance between the exploits of the great noble hero, Rodrigue, and the king's ignoble tricks. While the aristocrat saves the kingdom, the king clowns around. Corneille's critics rail against the unacceptable depiction of sovereign-aristocratic relations in *Le Cid*, with even the nobleman Scudéry going so far as to reprove how the aristocrat in the plot responds to the king's orders. He complains: "il faut que je dise, que jamais Roi ne fut si mal obéit que Don Fernand"[54] [I have to say, no King was ever so little obeyed as Don Fernand]. Chapelain in *Les Sentiments* will pick up on this irreverence as well, complaining that once the nobleman Don Sanche is told by the king to be silent (*Le Cid*, vv. 579–82) he should not be permitted to utter another word: "Après avoir dit j'obéis et me tais, il ne devait point continuer de parler. Car ce n'est pas se vouloir taire, que de demander à dire deux mots en sa défense"[55] [Once he has said I obey and will be silent, he should not continue to speak. Because that is not to be silent to ask to say two more words in his defence]. Thus, both Scudéry and Chapelain denounce the king's farcical behaviour and emphasize the need for respect and admiration regarding the portrayal of royal decisions.

Lamenting this vein of weak judgment, Chapelain deems that Corneille failed to present Don Fernand as making proper decisions to preserve his throne when he hears of a potential Moorish invasion of Castile: "Il est vrai que l'excuse est pire que la faute, ou ce qu'il y aurait moins d'inconvénient qu'un Roi fut mal obéi ayant donné de bons ordres, que non pas qu'il périt faute d'en avoir donné aucun"[56] [It is true that the excuse is worse than the mistake, or that it would have been less inconvenient if the King were badly obeyed, having given good orders, rather than he die because he failed to give any]. The royal figure cannot be seen to make poor decisions or to act without authority, for these displays of feebleness are appallingly lacking in the respect owed to kings in general, and they upset the notion of royal *bienséance*.

Criticizing Don Fernand became an occasion for critics close to Richelieu to define what constituted acceptable (political and theatrical) royal portrayals. The Castilian king's political weakness, aloof character, marginality to the plot, and lack of dignity were framed as precisely what a tragic king should not be. Corneille will eventually agree for the most part with this view when he returns to the discussion nearly twenty years after the quarrel over *Le Cid* and invents a proscription for kings such as Don Fernand in the "Examen de *Clitandre*," as we have seen. Such an intense reaction to the Spanish monarch, however, and his eventual dismissal by the playwright as a royal type, begs the question of why Corneille presented such a king in the first place. How could he have so completely failed to anticipate such a negative reaction to his royal figure when he wrote *Le Cid* in 1637? The answer lies, I suggest, in understanding Don Fernand in the context of Corneille's previous works. Rather than view *Le Cid* as the apogee of the great playwright's career, the play should be viewed as an early attempt at getting the sovereign figure right.

4 Changing Models, Changing Standards

Corneille was caught off guard by the dismay his Spanish monarch generated. Before Don Fernand, he had only staged kings in two previous plays. In his first tragedy, *Médée* (1635), the playwright freely admits that he gave paltry roles to the two kings present in that plot: the first, Egée, spends time behind bars in an onstage prison until the heroine frees him;

the second king, Créon, is cruel and whiny, leading Corneille to conclude that his spectators should only shrug in indifference at his violent
death.[57] Beyond these two, the playwright's only other king before Don
Fernand was a nameless monarch, featured in the tragicomedy *Clitandre
ou l'innocence délivrée* (1631). This king will be the basis for Corneille's
1660 prohibition against royal judges when he pairs him with the Spanish monarch Don Fernand under the category of a "royal judge" who has
no "intérêt pour son Etat, ni pour sa personne"[58] [no interest in his State
nor his person]. These earlier examples of Corneille's royal portrayals
attest to his lack of familiarity with, or at the very least, his reluctance to
embrace, the new poetic precepts established in the period leading up
to *Le Cid*.[59] Writing from the vantage point of experience, in 1660 in the
"Examen de *Mélite*," Corneille describes a sort of poetic coming of age
and plainly admits to his initial ignorance. He explains straightforwardly
that he did not obey poetic rules, "puisque je ne savais pas alors qu'il y
en eût" [I did not know then that there were any], and he stresses that
he was following an earlier model set by Alexandre Hardy: "Je n'avais
alors pour guide qu'un peu de sens commun, avec les exemples du feu
Hardy, dont la veine était plus féconde que polie"[60] [I had at that time as
a guide only a little common sense, and the examples of the late Hardy
who was more fertile than polished in his creations]. I will return in
chapter 2 to the importance of Hardy's model of sovereignty up until the
1630s, but for now it should alert us to Corneille's designation of him as
an early source of inspiration, one where igniting respect for the royal
character was of little concern.

In the tragicomedy, *Clitandre*, Corneille's follow-up to *Mélite*, the playwright continues to underscore his scepticism vis-à-vis the rules when
he states that if he did not follow them in this play it is not because he
was not familiar with them, but simply because he chose not to do so:
"Aujourd'hui, quelques-uns adorent cette règle [des vingt-quatre heu-
res], beaucoup la méprisent, pour moi j'ai voulu seulement montrer
que si je m'en éloigne ce n'est pas faute de la connaître"[61] [Today some
adore this rule (of the unity of time), many have contempt for it; I only
wanted to show that if I stray from it, it is not for the lack of knowing it].
Hence, in the lead up to *Le Cid*, Corneille did not embrace the new focus
on the rules, and he was even more reluctant to recognize an authority
beyond his own.[62] Not only does he seem oblivious to the political stakes
at work in his royal portrayal, but he also seems to operate in a different
mindset from Chapelain and Richelieu's entourage – he was thinking in
terms of the norms of tragicomedy.

In Hélène Baby's meticulous inventory of 122 tragicomedies published over the course of the seventeenth century, she establishes that rarely in this genre is the main character a king; when he is, the plot dwells on the political vacancy of his reign, staging, for example, the regency of a woman ruling in his place, or the necessity for the king to wear a disguise.[63] In other typical portrayals of monarchs in tragicomedy, the king is taken prisoner or suffers from temporary madness. Most often, however, kings in this irregular genre are secondary characters, rivals to the main characters who are usually noblemen. The kings' authority over the noblemen and the women they love has no political consequences; their power serves only as an obstacle to the lovers' happiness. Along similar lines, John D. Lyons sums up the difference between the questions pursued between tragedy and tragicomedy in the following way:

> Generally speaking the dominant issue in tragedy is, what is to be done? Which ethical or social value should be supreme? In tragicomedy, on the other hand, there are often two intertwined questions (or the same question asked of the outer and inner worlds): what is real? And whom do the hero and heroine truly love?[64]

Within the worlds presented by these contrasting genres with contrasting aims, the king necessarily plays very different roles. Take, as a point of contrast, La Mesnardière's definition of tragedy: "un poème qui a pour sujet ordinaire la révolution des Etats, la récompense des bons Princes & la punition des méchants"[65] [a poem whose subject is ordinarily the revolution of States, the reward of good Princes and the punishment of the wicked]. The king's stature and centrality to the plot simply cannot be equal between a genre concerned with ethical-political dilemmas and another whose focus is on the illusions of love, disguise, and theatre.

According to Baby's census, the royal figure in tragicomedy falls into three categories – the royal rival, the royal father, and the royal judge.[66] In the first of these types, the king sheds his *dignité royale* and acts out of personal motivation to satisfy his amorous desires. In the second type, his authority allows him to impede a marriage he deems unacceptable on the grounds of familial alliances. In both of these circumstances, the king's relationship to the state disappears behind the romantic or paternal interaction at the plot's centre. Even in the cases where the king of tragicomedy decides to wage war, negotiate with an enemy, or resist a military offensive, all of his actions are carried out for the sake of his amorous interests. In the third type of tragicomedic situation, where the king is a judge, his role is to put an end to debate through a last-minute discovery of evidence or the announcement of a decision. This portrayal contravenes openly with Aristotle's (and eventually Chapelain's) directives since the royal judge ends the intrigue through a verdict that has no earlier preparation, no anticipation within the plot. That is the case in Corneille's *Clitandre* where a man and a woman with no prior attachment or even interest in each other are told by the royal judge that they will wed as the play comes to a close. This type of contrived ending, leading to a dénouement depicted as happy and peaceful was perfectly acceptable in tragicomedy where political and moral debates are blithely skipped over.

The king in that irregular genre, when he is not a judge, is above all an oppositional authority-figure that stands in the way of the hero's happiness:

> Dans la tragicomédie, les rois sont "homme(s) seulement" et la parenthèse tyrannique est bien un caprice d'homme, simplement amplifié par la fonction de celui qui y succombe.[67]

> [In tragicomedy, kings are "men solely" and the tyrannical parenthesis is indeed a man's fancy, only amplified by the function of the person who falls prey to it.]

In this context we come to see how Corneille's depiction of Don Fernand was unusual for tragicomedy because of the extent to which *Le Cid* dwells on matters of state – the education of the *dauphin*, the rivalry between nobles, the plight of the *Infante*, the issue of justice (although vengeance, especially through duelling, is a commonplace of tragicomedy), and the Moorish invasion. Yet, these more political elements were taken from Corneille's source, Guillen de Castro's *Las Mocedades del Cid*, which could explain the tragicomedy's atypical accent on political matters.

When Corneille wrote *Le Cid*, he had not yet shown any inkling of the great political tragedies that would lead to his renown. Despite Jean Mairet's *Sophonisbe* (1634) and *Marc-Antoine* (1635), the vogue of historical tragedies had not yet overtaken Parisian theatres, and Corneille had not yet turned to history, especially Roman history, to explore questions of legitimacy and sovereignty. Hence, Don Fernand was not conceived to be a model of regal virtue and authority: he was a king of tragicomedy.[68]

In keeping with the dénouements common to that genre, Corneille had assumed that the royal decision offered him an effective means to disentangle the dramatic intrigue. Don Fernand's command would enable Chimène to marry the man she loved, albeit her father's assassin, and love would conquer all, as it is prone to do in tragicomedies. Without the king's judgment, the divisions between the main characters would have lingered, and the lovers' future would have remained unacceptably unresolved. Fernand's royal decision, just like the royal decision six years earlier in *Clitandre*, heralds a wedding – the expected end to such tales. Furthermore, having drawn his plot from a pre-existing source, Corneille failed to anticipate the moral-political taboos Don Fernand's judgment infringed. He did not gauge the extent to which his royal character's judgment would be perceived as a negative reflection on, and an insult to, contemporary monarchical justice.

For the Richelieu-inspired critics, *Le Cid*'s dénouement by royal decision was not just another instance of a tragicomedic device. Instead, it encapsulated the shocking lack of *bienséance* towards royal characters they sought to entirely eliminate from the French stage. In assessing Corneille's reasons for the flawed dénouement, Chapelain blames him for thinking in terms of the conventions of genre, rather than grasping the dangerous political-moral implications of his ending:

> Le Poète voulant que ce Poème finît heureusement, pour suivre les règles de la Tragicomédie, fait encore en cet endroit [le dénouement] que Chimène foule aux pieds celles que la Nature a établies, et dont le mépris et la transgression doivent donner de l'horreur aux ignorants et aux habiles.[69]

> [The Poet wanting the Poem to end happily, in order to follow the rules of Tragicomedy, makes it so that in this part (the dénouement) Chimène tramples those that Nature established, and whose contempt and transgression must provoke horror in the ignorant and the wise.]

Corneille should have recognized the supremacy of the new theatrical precepts of morality over both conventions of genre and the authority of source texts. The author of *Les Sentiments* oddly attributes Corneille's mistake to following the rules of the wrong genre, whereas Corneille was, in fact, working within the framework of tragicomedy, a theatrical genre notorious for its lack of rules. Chapelain insists that Corneille's desire to resolve the plot backfired. Rather than create a sense of reconciliation that would settle the spectators' spirits, the playwright offered a horror-inducing ending, a sensation no longer acceptable on a stage that demands positive royal closure. Though Chapelain stresses here the necessary allegiance to the laws of nature, earlier in *Les Sentiments* he has clearly articulated the need for an artificial (in the sense that it may go against historical fact) demonstration of punishment for immoral behaviour.

Corneille's mistake lay in thinking that he could tie up *Le Cid*'s loose ends quickly, if awkwardly, as he had done in *Clitandre ou l'innocence délivrée*. He failed to fully recognize the political-aesthetic shift that had occurred since that play and to what extent matters regarding royal judgment onstage and off had become of prime critical concern. Don Fernand's "unreasonable command" becomes a symbol of the type of monarchical portrayal the Richelieu-inspired critics deemed necessary to condemn and suppress, all the more so if it constitutes the closing image of royalty spectators will take away with them as they leave the theatre:

> Or cette ordonnance déraisonnable et précipitée, et par conséquent peu vraisemblable, est d'autant plus digne de blâme qu'elle fait le Dénouement de la Pièce, et qu'elle le fait mauvais, et contre l'art. En tous les autres lieux du Poème cette bizarrerie eût fait un fâcheux effet, mais en celui-ci elle en gâte l'édifice, et le rend défectueux en sa partie la plus essentielle.[70]

> [However this unreasonable and precipitated command, and as a result implausible, is all the more worthy of blame because it constitutes the Dénouement of the Play, and makes it bad, and against the art. In all the other parts of the Poem this bizarreness would have made a negative impression, but in this part it ruins the edifice, and makes it defective in its most essential section.]

Le Cid's ending is particularly troubling to Chapelain's poetic mindset according to which a rigidly constructed tragic plot should culminate in a didactic lesson, a closing scene of restitution where the just are rewarded and the guilty are punished. The called-for demonstration of justice is replaced in *Le Cid* by a portrayal of a royal judgment that perpetuates the disorder it needed to resolve:

> Que si le Roy voulait le récompenser [Rodrigue] du grand service qu'il venait d'en recevoir, il fallait que ce fut du sien, et non pas d'une chose qui n'était point à lui, et que les lois de la Nature avaient mis hors de sa puissance.[71]

> [That if the King wanted to reward [Rodrigue] of the great service he had just received from him, he needed to give him what has his to give, and not

something that was not his, and that the laws of Nature had placed beyond
his power.]

The intertwined moral and structural considerations of *Le Cid*'s unexpected dénouement make Fernand's actions particularly improper and
illegitimate since the play ends with an act of moral "*bizarrerie,*" height-
ening the sense of disarray and *invraisemblance* that should be markedly
absent from a fifth Act.

5 How to Untie Tragic Knots

In his 1635 "Discours de la poésie representative," Chapelain describes
a precise, Act-by-Act formulaic arrangement of action, a rational build-
up of the intrigue meant to eliminate the randomness of tragicomedy's
dénouements:

> Dans le premier [Acte], les fondements de l'Aventure se jettent; dans le sec-
> ond, les difficultés naissent; dans le troisième, le trouble se renforce; dans
> le quatrième, les choses penchent vers le désespoir; dans le cinquième, le
> nœud se démêle avec vraisemblance par des voies imprévues, d'où résulte
> la merveille.[72]

> [In the first (Act), the basis for the Adventure is laid down; in the second,
> difficulties are born; in the third, the trouble increases; in the fourth, mat-
> ters lean towards despair; in the fifth, the knot is untied with *vraisemblance*
> by unexpected means, from which the marvel stems.]

Chapelain makes an optimistic assessment of playwrights' abilities to
put into practice the coherence and organization of such a formulaic tragic plot. The fifth Act "marvel" Chapelain alludes to imagines
an ideal culmination of action that should be surprising and awe-
inspiring, but also, crucially, *vraisemblable.* Furthermore, the "marvel"
should produce consensus and satisfaction in the audience while also
convincingly silencing the antagonistic views onstage. In short, the
new French conception of tragic dénouements, in contrast to the dénouements of the Ancients, demands setting things right in surprising
ways, not reinforcing the ambient chaos and "trouble" that formed the
heart of the intrigue.

The critical frenzy surrounding Don Fernand's Act V injustice and
the negative implications of his closing decision highlights the newly

political-moral role attributed to the dénouement. For Chapelain and his allies, the dénouement becomes the locus for a careful demonstration of the sovereign's command over the disturbing impressions and actions generated throughout the first four acts of the theatrical plot. This painstaking construction of what Chapelain terms an "edifice," also the play's "most essential part," cannot be undone by a non-linear action, a judgment without a clear cause-and-effect underpinning.[73] Beyond all moral considerations, Chapelain targets what he deems to be Corneille's clumsy and unlearned attempt to create an overall positive effect by relying on an inappropriate form – the *deus ex machina*.

Tragic dénouements, especially Pierre Corneille's, have been a matter of prime focus and controversy in the wake of Georges Forestier's seminal studies of the "genetic approach," which consists of reading a play backwards from its endpoint – its destination, i.e., its dénouement – to uncover the coherence of its *agencement* or organizational order.[74] In an echo of Chapelain's act-by-act formula for tragedy, Forestier pinpoints the dramatic dénouement as the determining factor of a plot, arguing that the various parts of a tragic structure are but stepping stones that add up to a logical and fixed resolution. As Forestier describes:

[Le travail créateur de Corneille] consiste à dégager de l'histoire non pas un ensemble, mais un seul élément fondamental – le dénouement, qui est en même temps le sujet de l'œuvre – à partir duquel est reconstruit à rebours un enchaînement de causes et d'effets qui donne l'illusion de conduire l'histoire à sa fin selon les modalités de la logique et du probable (qui peuvent être transgressés pour produire un effet de surprise).[75]

[(Corneille's creative work) consists in finding in the story not a whole, but one single fundamental element – the dénouement, which is at the same time the subject of the work – from which a concatenation of causes and effects is constructed backwards, which gives the illusion of driving the story to its end according to the modalities of the logical and probable (which can be transgressed to produce an effect of surprise).]

In this line of thinking, the dénouement constitutes both the subject of the play, its ultimate action, and its moral lesson. Forestier, fully adopting Chapelain's precepts, stresses the dénouement's status as the focal point of the plot, its "end," as in extremity, but also as in "purpose." Dénouement as "end" of the play gives way to the metaphor of a string or chain, making it the result of a precise *enchaînement* [concatenation] of events that build upon each other, creating the dramatic *nœud* [knot], until the intrigue's impasse can finally be resolved and untied.

If Forestier's genetic readings have been so insightful, it is because, at least in theory, the French tragic genre's five-Act configuration depends so much on a meticulous structural framework. In practice, however, as we have seen over the course of our examination of *Le Cid*'s reception, the dénouement of Corneille's canonical play was a far cry from the consensus-making, logical structural outcome Chapelain and his fellow critics prescribed. Corneille's Act V belonged to a different, earlier, tragicomedic conception of theatrical endings. As the playwright learns from the polemic his play spawned, he will wrestle with the new norms of royal *bienséance*. He will modify his presentation of royal judgment and alter the king's role in bringing the plot to an end. In short, he will search for portrayals that will not generate such scandalized reactions. While Corneille remains faithful to the framework of the dénouement by royal judgment in *Horace* (1641), *Cinna ou la clémence d'Auguste* (1642), and *La Mort de Pompée* (1644), each one of these plays represents a continued experimentation with, and modification of, the role of the royal judge within the tragic intrigue.

In this chapter, we have focused on a model of royal judgment that is suddenly considered unacceptable by critics insistent on encomiastic royal portrayals onstage. The impetus to refine tragic dénouements to reflect royal grandeur emerges from this critical pressure, shaping the form and content of the tragic genre and making the plot's outcome the focal point of the play's message. A first impression suggests that after *Le Cid*'s theatrical-political storm, Corneille switches gears and begins to depict his sovereigns as both central to the dramatic action and in step with the monarchical ideals of the era: *Horace* and *Cinna* present all-powerful monarchs who come onstage to *decide*, to give a verdict which, at the core of the dénouement, enables order to reign and the play to end. These fictions seem to simultaneously illustrate the prince's ability to squelch debate, give a moral lesson, and literally end the dramatic action, a seemingly drastic improvement from the awkward judgment scenes in *Clitandre* and *Le Cid*. And yet, when we peer more closely at these scenes of judgment, it becomes apparent that, in fact; the royal verdicts in *Horace* and *Cinna* generate intense debate regarding the structural and moral basis for the sovereign's decision at the close of these plots, and that these dénouements by royal decision prompt as many questions as they provide answers to regarding the legitimacy of the sovereign decision onstage.

Before pursuing the analysis of Corneille's experimentations in royal judgment, I wish to halt the chronological progression of this study so as to underscore the multiplicity of models that shaped the century-long discussion of the king as judge. In privileging an anti-teleological view and taking a step backwards in time from the defining moment of *Le Cid*'s polemic to an earlier portrayal of judgment, we will better understand the stakes underpinning the critical turn towards "regular tragedy" and the call for stricter parameters surrounding royal portrayals. As we saw in this first chapter, *Le Cid*'s dénouement provides a telling account of the degree to which playwrights operated according to recognizable models, in this case inspired by the genre of tragicomedy. But other examples of royal judgment propelled playwrights as well. Although *Le Cid*'s quarrel did not dwell on Alexandre Hardy and the "Tragedy of the Scaffolds" royal judge, that vein of theatre stood as a distinct marker against which to evaluate later, more flattering, portraits of the king onstage. Despite the literary canon's faint record of Hardy's dramatic model of judgment, it represents a reference point in the changing norms of royal portrayals. An exploration of Hardy will therefore expand our understanding of the gallery of royal judges in French tragedy and enables us to gauge the lasting influence of a disregarded model.

Failed Judgments, Thwarted Justice: Alexandre Hardy's
Scédase ou l'hospitalité violée

Hardy fut celui qui fournit le plus abondamment à nos Comédiens de quoi divertir le peuple: ce fut lui sans doute qui tout d'un coup arrêta le progrès du Théâtre, donnant le mauvais exemple des désordres que nous y avons vu régner en notre temps.

D'Aubignac, *La Pratique du théâtre*[1]

1 Tragedy of the Scaffolds

Alongside the exuberant emotion and moralizing verses of sixteenth-century humanist tragedy, there flourished another vein of serious drama, which privileged onstage spectacle and violent action. The differences between these two veins were especially remarkable in regard to their presentation of death. In the works of Etienne Jodelle and Robert Garnier, two renowned playwrights of humanist tragedy, death silently, invisibly, and unfailingly overtakes the plot, and the lamenting hero meets a woeful end; in the competing vein, death is a decidedly more gruesome matter.[2] The latter form of serious drama has been placed under the broad category of "Theatre of Cruelty" and, more specifically, "Theatre of the Scaffolds," two labels that define it as part of a French baroque aesthetic.[3] This theatre stands in contrast to humanist tragedy and the neoclassical theatre to come, especially for the prominence it gives to onstage portrayals of pain inflicted on the human body: "le corps, livré à ses pulsions désirantes et meurtries, détient sur scène un facteur emblématique de désordre et participe à un mouvement de dérèglement de l'écriture tragique qui permet l'explosion de ses limites"[4] [The body, left to its desiring and ravaging impulses, possesses onstage a factor of disorder and participates in a chaotic movement of disturbance of tragic composition that enables the explosion of its boundaries]. The rhetorical elements of the play recede while the graphic display of suffering bodies becomes the dominant characteristic of the tragic genre which emerges in the last quarter of the sixteenth century.

The "macabre tragedy" as Jean Rousset calls it, in which "une trainée de sang inonde le théâtre français" [a trail of blood floods the French stage] possesses a conspicuous proximity to the historically contemporary judicial domain, reproducing and expanding upon early modern displays of punishment and death.[5] Although the boundaries between the judicial and theatrical scaffolds never entirely blur, the correspondences between the two are undeniable. The tragic stage explicitly reenacts a legal-political procedural with which spectators are familiar, thereby asking them to evaluate its accuracy and enjoy its imitation.[6] In a manner distinct from the way tragedies of the later century will make only veiled allusions to contemporary judicial practices, this vein insists on the specificity of the sovereign's role as guardian of society, vividly displaying how his articulation of verdicts inflicts violent punishment and leads to brutal death.

Compare, for instance, Jodelle's *Cléopâtre captive* (1553) to Jean Bretog's *Tragédie française à huit personnages* (1571).[7] In the first, the heroine intones a forty-four verse soliloquy bemoaning her fate; then she commits suicide. In the second play, the audience watches as an accused servant is tried for sleeping with his master's wife; he is found guilty by a magistrate who judges him in the king's name. Bretog's *Tragédie française* ends with the guilty man's body swinging from a rope on the gallows as the onlooking villagers comment on his crime and evaluate for themselves and for the theatre audience the culprit's punishment. Death arrives as the result of a judicial sentence, the product of a societal condemnation, not as the inescapable destiny of a great character. Rather than an occasion for shedding tears in response to the lyrical beauty of the verses and the fatality with which the tragic hero accepts death, the violence onstage is meant to provoke a jolting visceral response from the spectators.

Paradoxically, if the graphic violence of such theatre is a sensationalistic means of entertaining the audience, the dénouement of the "Theatre of the Scaffolds" genre is tied to a supremely rational mode of legal thinking. The excruciating pain carried out on the body of the condemned man is triggered by a judicial decision, which becomes both a determining plot device and an occasion for socio-political reflection. In Bretog's play, as in others of its kind published in the late sixteenth and early seventeenth centuries, a royal sentence brings about the tragedy's dénouement through the enactment of a specifically judicial violence staged in response to a criminal act of violence.[8] By "judicial violence," I am referring to the brutal punishment brought before the eyes of the spectators that comes as a result of a decision in the legal realm – a trial scene in the most basic sense – where the royal judge sentences the guilty party to death. This decision does not belong to the tradition of the dilemma monologue – the stylized rhetorical set-piece where a tragic character reviews the pros and cons of an action.[9] It is, rather, the staging of an authoritative decision to punish. Royal judgment occupies such a decisive position in these plots, both structurally and thematically, that Biet has described the "Theatre of the Scaffolds" genre as staging a "hyperbolization of the sovereign."[10] By this, he means that within plots notable for their depictions of violent civil upheaval, including onstage portrayals of rapes, murders, suicides, and executions, these so-called "pre-classical" tragedies present the monarch as more powerful, more exacting, and more brutal than all other members of society.[11] Biet describes the sovereign's hyper-violent response as a dramatic means to buttress royal power:

> Et s'il y a, à tous les niveaux de la représentation du pouvoir, la nécessité de le représenter par l'hyperbole, ne serait-ce que pour le conforter comme pouvoir actif et effectif, la conséquence qui en dérive sera que la représentation frappante de ses crises sera hyperbolique et fondée sur l'excès.[12]

> [And if there is at every level of the representation of power, the need to represent it through hyperbole, even if only to buttress it as an active and effective power, the consequence that comes of it will be that the striking representation of its crises will be hyperbolic and founded on excess.]

Although Biet does not dwell on the notion of "hyperbolization," expressed by the sovereign's evident dominance and his unambiguous portrayal as the incarnation of social control, this model of authority represents a determining stage in early modern French theatre's representation of royal judgment. Biet's line of reading adheres closely to Foucauldian descriptions of justice in the early modern era as a means for the king to visibly reassert his authority through the physical punishment and death of the criminal, who in disobeying the law disobeyed the sovereign:

> The public execution [...] is a ceremonial by which a momentarily injured sovereignty is reconstituted. It restores that sovereignty by manifesting it at its most spectacular.[13]

In this first quarter of the seventeenth century, before the Académie Française turned its attention to royal portrayals, the theatrical and the judicial stages were aligned in similarly emphasizing the sovereign's unique ability to exact punishment and demonstrate his superior force in a spectacular retaliation against those who have transgressed his laws. This model of graphic retribution, which Richelieu will expand upon in the judicial sphere, will be cast off in the theatrical domain. Neoclassical poetics will reject such ostentatious and unsettling exhibits of the torture the sovereign can commit, forcing playwrights to express the monarch's unequalled power through less strikingly visual means.

If the critical reception of these plays has emphasized how "Tragedies of the Scaffolds" fundamentally celebrate the sovereign's ability to reinstitute order through his punishment, I want to expand the exploration of this model by focusing on a playwright whose works, while often categorized as belonging to this genre, markedly diverge from the usual narrative of social disorder pacified by the royal decision. In this chapter, I will examine *Scédase ou l'hospitalité violée* (written circa 1610, published in 1624), a tragedy by Alexandre Hardy where the outcome determined by the king's verdict is not a victory of royal judgment, but, instead, a failure.[14] Moreover, the judgment scene in this tragedy constitutes the moment when the royal character reveals himself to be most flawed: the judicial verdict tarnishes the monarch instead of elevating him. Though Hardy is generally considered to have lost the battle between "regular" and "irregular" tragedy, and his works have often been relegated to the footnotes of literary history, I argue that the model of king as judge he advances stands as an important chapter in the development of scenes of royal decision-making in the "regular" tragic genre that follows.

No single author is more associated with the rise of spectacular early French tragedy than Hardy. Introductory volumes to early modern French theatre commonly refer to his works, and in particular to *Scédase ou l'hospitalité violée* with its onstage rapes and murders as a prime example of the seventeenth-century's "Theatre of Cruelty," divergent from the static humanist form, but not yet representative of the codified form embraced by Corneille and Racine.[15] Hardy's prolific output (thought to exceed 500 plays) and his position as the principal author of the Hôtel de Bourgogne's troupe, afford him the status of an icon of this "pre-classical" dramaturgy – the irregular, violent, and baroque vein of tragedy – which stands as the foil to the aesthetic restraint of "classical" tragedy which will come to define the century's dramatic canon.[16] We know that Corneille read and admired Hardy's *Scédase*, and, despite its marked aesthetic distance from the conservative 1660 standards, the author of *Le Cid* considered it to be worthy of tragedy, the theatrical genre deemed noblest by the second half of the century:

> Scédase n'était qu'un paysan de Leuctres, et je ne tiendrais pas la sienne [son histoire] indigne d'y paraître [sur le théâtre] si la pureté de nôtre scène pouvait souffrir qu'on y parlât du violement effectif de ses deux filles, après que l'idée de prostitution n'y a pu être soufferte dans la personne d'une sainte qui en fut garantie.[17]

> [Scédase was only a peasant from Leuctra, and I would not take his [story] to be unworthy of appearing there [onstage] if the purity of our stage could suffer that we spoke on it of the actual rape of his two daughters, after even the idea of prostitution could not be suffered in the person of a saint who was spared from it.]

In referring to *Scédase*, Corneille underscores the gulf between acceptable tragic representations in the early seventeenth century and those of the mid-century. While audiences once accepted, nay, expected, graphic sexual violence onstage, they come to reject as improper and entirely offensive even the mention of a rape that never takes place, as in Corneille's own *Théodore vierge ou martyr* (1646). In this logic, Hardy represents for Corneille and his contemporaries an earlier, freer, model of the French tragic aesthetic, synonymous with a time when audiences understood tragedy to be shocking, morbid, spectacular, and bloody. *Scédase* stands, therefore, as both a point of reference for playwrights and as an anti-model, a distinct illustration against which to judge changing French tragic norms.

Upon an initial reading, *Scédase ou l'hospitalitée violée* seems to be a conventional example of the "Tragedies of the Scaffolds" genre: the royal character is depicted primarily as an all-powerful judge who will assess the innocence or guilt of the accused; the plot revolves around a crime – the killing of Scédase's two daughters – followed by a trial that the sovereign heads in search of a juridical resolution; the trial ends in a graphic display of the violence the royal decision provokes since the eponymous father commits suicide onstage in response to the king's decision not to seek punishment from the Spartan soldier-culprits. In *Scédase*, then, the sovereign's exercise of justice emphatically fails to bring about a cathartic reaffirmation of the dominant social order. Instead, spectators watch as the royal judge intentionally strays from the explicit legal norms he has himself laid out; lacking clear-sightedness, the king's verdict leads to the most dire of consequences – unpunished crime and the death of a virtuous father. In this play, therefore, the result is not an affirmation of royal judgment, but a severe indictment of the sovereign's decision. By the close of *Scédase*, the royal judge appears vulnerable and illegitimate, directly responsible for the death of the tragedy's hero.

As the seventeenth century advances, the sovereign's decision will occupy different positions within the theatrical narrative, moving from the dénouement to the tragic knot of the play. By including Hardy in our analysis of this fluctuation, we come to understand the political and theatrical motivations behind the structural shifts in the presentation of royal judgment. We will see how Hardy's concept of what a tragedy should do – the feelings it should generate in the audience and the moral values it should promote – is bound up in his development of tragic structure. Exploring Hardy's legacy as a distinctive, and distinct, example of royal judgment enables us to gain insight into the changing face of sovereignty and the sovereign's changing relationship to the law on the French tragic stage.

2 *Scédase ou l'hospitalité violée* – Royal Judgment as Calamity

Because they showed hospitality to a pair of Spartan soldiers, the two beautiful daughters of the virtuous peasant, Scédase, were raped and killed. All signs point to the two young Spartan men whom the spectators have seen commit these crimes. And yet, the play's final scene presents Scédase's desperate suicide as a consequence of the Spartan king Agésilas's failure to condemn the men. Although the king's presence is marginal to the overall plot, and the trial scene itself is short (spanning only 34 verses within a 1,368-verse play), the royal decision pinpoints the king's power to determine the outcome of the legal and theatrical argument. At the close of *Scédase ou l'hospitalité violée*, the audience is left with a bitter sense of the expediency of royal judgment and the tragedy it can provoke.

The king's hasty and politically practical decision serves the plot the-matically and structurally. On the one hand, Agésilas's refusal to try the Spartan men underscores the upsetting and unjust nature of his judg-ment, while on the other hand, its expediency enables the plot to come to a sudden end by rapidly closing the criminal case and the play. This suddenness highlights the absence of a divine intervention or, in theat-rical terms, the absence of a *deus ex machina*, which would reverse the wrong-headed royal decision. Scédase's tragic destiny lies in the fact that no one – human nor divine – arrives to impede the royal decision and bring about the longed-for reversal of injustice.

Initially, the aggrieved Scédase turns to the king hoping for a trial to punish the barbaric actions of the men towards his daughters. Specta-tors familiar with the structure of the "Tragedy of the Scaffolds" genre might anticipate that the royal judgment will reverse the tragic situation in which the father finds himself. The opening of Act V where the king appears onstage addressing Scédase kindly and professes a deep concern for equity seems to foreshadow an *in extremis* castigation of the guilty men. Agésilas assumes the role of the supreme judge, announcing that he will show no favouritism in the judicial procedure that he prepares to undertake:

> Ton équitable plainte a beaucoup d'apparence.
> Thémis aux yeux bandés n'admet la préférence
> Que l'on observe ailleurs, tenant avec les lois
> Sur toutes qualités toujours un même poids.   (vv. 1097–100)

> [Your equitable complaint possesses great appearance of truth. / Thémis whose eyes are veiled does not admit the favouritism / That we observe elsewhere, holding with the laws / That we regard all conditions always with equal measure.]

The king's reference to the blind justice of the goddess Thémis, as well as his assurances that all who come before him are judged according to an "equal measure" draws on commonplace images of justice associated with impartiality. The use of the present tense to speak of Thémis's re-gard for justice – "does not admit favouritism" – implies that the goddess is present in guiding the king's judgment.

Yet, Agésilas's justice is quickly separated from the realm of divine jus-tice, and instead firmly situated in socio-political and economic realities. Exposing a view at odds with the ideals embodied by the blind goddess

Thémis, the king undermines his pledge that all who come before him should be judged equally when he insists on the particular punishments he would dispense to criminal noblemen:

> Fusses-tu de fortune encore plus infirme,
> Cela n'amoindrit pas l'atrocité du crime
> Tant plus l'extraction relève ses auteurs,
> Moins doit-on modérer le supplice, fauteurs;
> La vertu suit le sang, quiconque dégénère,
> Qui noble du seul titre a l'âme roturière,
> Mérite double peine, exemple à l'avenir
> De qui ne se sait pas en son sort maintenir.   (vv. 1100–7)

[Were you of even smaller fortune / That would not lessen the atrociousness of the crime / Especially since their extraction elevates its authors, / Even less so must we be moderate in the punishment of the criminals; / Virtue follows blood, and whoever degenerates / He that is noble only in title but has a common soul, / Deserves a doubled sentence, an example for the future / For those who do not know how to maintain themselves in the condition given to them by fate.]

Rather than a spectacular demonstration of the king's power to intervene, the "hyperbolic" retaliation against the guilty which would change the course of the dramatic action for the better, Agésilas articulates a convoluted vision of punishment. This passage reveals the acute distinctions the king makes between the peasant who comes before him, asking for justice, and the accused noblemen. The king's insistence that even if Scédase were of an "even smaller" (*infirme*) status, he would still protect him, emphasizes his awareness of the father's lowly social condition and the underlying social clash underpinning the case. The special punishment the king reserves for noblemen who have the "souls of commoners" puts into doubt the equity of Agésilas's ultimate decision to not even attempt to locate the Spartan men.

The king's refusal to take on the role of the wise judge ends the trial scene with the disconcerting conclusion that the accused will never be made to answer for their actions. Hardy's dénouement diverges from the scaffolds genre and from the spectacular *coups de théâtre* of the period's increasingly popular tragicomedies where the swift and effective royal decision acts as a transformative means of rectifying the injustice at the heart of the dramatic plot. In contrast, the dominant feeling at the close of *Scédase* is a sense of halted justice, as if something or someone *should* have intervened to bring the trial to a satisfying end. Hardy does not share Aristotle's view that tragedy should produce particular emotions in its spectators, the "pity and fear" that constitute the desired "distinctive mark of tragic imitation."[18] In displaying the punishment of a virtuous father and the support of the wicked, the French tragedian equates tragedy with injustice and catastrophe, a mindset the *doctes* of the latter seventeenth century will increasingly insist on countering through the presence of an admirable royal judge.

In *Scédase*, the king's decision not to judge the accused men extends the peasant's misfortune, confirming his fall from happiness to unhappiness, and offering no inkling of hope to a wronged father who is "pauvre, simple, étranger, sans crédit, sans moyens" (v. 1123) [poor, simple, foreign, without credit, without means]. Hardy's dénouement vividly illustrates the gulf separating this early seventeenth-century conception of tragedy from the poetic precepts and practices that will take hold less than two decades later. Furthermore, attention to Hardy's early model allows us to grasp the ways in which the conventions of tragicomedy will shape the tragic genre's *bienséant* tragic dénouements, especially when they are brought about by royal decisions.

In 1639, La Mesnardière rejects tragic endings like those of Hardy, claiming that authors should have recourse to dramatic reversals or providential punishments that transform the dire trajectories of tragic plots. The critic recommends sudden reversals, especially when they serve to undo injustice: "L'agnition est mieux appréciée lorsqu'elle est bien placée et qu'elle intervient pour mettre fin à la persecution de ceux qui étaient affligés sans mériter leurs malheurs"[19] [Recognition is most attractive when it is well placed and when it intervenes to bring to an end the persecution of those who are afflicted without deserving their sufferings.] La Mesnardière urges an embrace of positive endings through the adoption of Aristotelian models of reversal and recognition in an effort to quell the disturbing effects of misery-provoking royal decisions. Firmly anchored in the political-poetic turn of the 1630s, the French critic recommends a demonstration of justice that saves the day in contrast to Aristotle's preference for tragic scenarios that take a turn for the worse.[20]

In a poetic twist of irony, despite the increasing focus on *vraisemblance* in neoclassical tragic poetics, recognition scenes – those cornerstones of the tragicomedic genre – are viewed as ideal means of mitigating morally disturbing tragic endings. This is clearly the case when Jean Chapelain, writing the critique of *Le Cid* in the name of the Académie Française, goes so far as to suggest that Corneille should have revealed against all expectation and historical accuracy that Don Gomès was only Chimène's putative father. The sudden discovery of Chimène's true identity, he argues, would have served to nullify the troubling morality of *Le Cid*'s closing royal decision. In imagining this bizarre recognition scene, Chapelain seeks to edit out the king's responsibility for a distasteful and illogical judgment. Better, he argues, to resort to non-linear effects of surprise and stage a discovery that would show the king in a positive light, than to end the play with a disturbing depiction of royal injustice.

How different from Hardy's dénouement! Scédase's death results from the royal failure to judge accurately and set things right. No surprise ending, no miraculous reversal will salvage Scédase's sorrowful fate: his daughters were raped and killed and no one will punish the men who did it. Agésilas's judgment rests on an excessive reliance on procedure, a bureaucratic response to a most tragic matter as the trial scene dwells on the formality of the judicial hearing. The Spartan king asks for the details of the case to be presented to him. In response, the distressed Scédase provides evidence against the men: he brings forth witnesses who testify to having heard the screams of the young women and to soon afterwards seeing the Spartans near the scene of the crime. The royal judge hears this compelling testimony but once the witnesses have spoken, he rules that he will not question the Spartan men. Insisting on the lack of proof of their guilt and on his concern for sullying the good names of their aristocratic families, the king announces: "Condamner toutefois les absents sur l'indice / Ne se pratique point où règne la justice" (vv.1109–10) [Condemning the absent, however, on suspicion / Is not practised where justice reigns]. The trial ends, quite simply, in a royal refusal to intervene – the king dismisses the case. The opposite of a *coup*, the royal decision arrives in a whimper, a ruling by technicality that nevertheless leads to catastrophe. The king is unwilling even to help the bereaved father locate the men so they can be brought to testify before the court. Agésilas remains oddly untouched by the plight of the father before him. No hope emerges in Hardy's creaturely world when life is dominated by an all-too human sovereign, a cold and remote character, overly tied to prosaic concerns of rank and political influence.

The king's power in *Scédase* remains limited to his ability to close the case, rather than transform the situation through an awe-inspiring gesture. The evasive Agésilas attempts to dispense with Scédase by admitting that the crime remains unsolved but that there may come a day when justice will be served. Offering vague assurances, the king speaks of this

vengeance in a passive voice, evoking no intentionality on his part, so
that all Scédase can cling to is his own "patience."

> Tu seras plus vengé, plus que tu ne l'espères.
> Reste que ta douleur sensible tu tempères
> D'un peu de patience.   (vv. 1221–3)

> [You will be more avenged, more than you hope for / There remains only
> your acute grief that you will temper / With a little patience.]

The king's open-ended promise of an indefinite, eventual reward, as opposed to a sovereign action in the here and now to produce change,
underscores not only Agésilas's unresponsiveness to Scédase's plight, but
the extent to which Hardy's tragic royal judge is entrenched in a world of
failure and failed decision-making. If in *Le Cid*, for example, the Spanish
king, Don Fernand, similarly temporizes, his call for a future reconciliation is accompanied by an active promise to ally himself with the nobleman hero, Rodrigue, in bringing about a happy outcome:

> Espère en ton courage, espère en ma promesse,
> [...]
> Pour vaincre un point d'honneur qui combat contre toi
> Laisse faire le temps, ta vaillance, et ton Roi.   (vv.1863–6)

> [Have hope in your courage, have hope in my promise.
> …
> And, if her sense of honour still resists,
> Leave it to time, your valiance and your king.]

Agésilas's deferral simply reflects the king's wish to wash his hands of the
crime and to rid himself of the responsibility to punish the guilty. There
can be no hope for a transformative outcome stemming from royal action when the king embraces expediency over an allegiance to a sacred
dignitas.

Although Agésilas articulates the final verdict himself, Hardy surrounds
the king with councillors who shape his view. This depiction of judgment
through consultation resembles ancien régime judicial practice where it
was not uncommon for the king's principal ministers to advise him on
legal matters. Playwrights of the later seventeenth century, however, will
tend to present their sovereign characters as the sole decision-making

authority within the kingdom, leaving advisors to appear only when the dramatic plot directly addresses the subject of the corrupt influence of self-interested ministers, as in Tristan's *La Marianne* (1637), Corneille's *La Mort de Pompée* (1644), or Racine's *Britannicus* (1669). In *Scédase*, by contrast, the royal councillors, Androclide, Xantippe, and Léonide are unequivocally biased towards the absent noblemen. Their prejudice does not stem from an expectation of reward or a clear Machiavellian leaning; it simply attests to the ordinary proceedings of the court – a favouritism of nobility and privilege. Hardy's realistic depiction of biased judicial-political dynamics and the court's indifference to the peasant father's sorrow makes flagrant the absence of a *coup de théâtre* to overturn the appalling injustice of the court and to relieve Scédase. Tragedy, according to Hardy, means chronicling the steps in the path towards an inevitably dire end. The courtroom scene stands as the decisive moment when the tragic outcome is sealed.

3 The Monarchical-Marvellous Aesthetic

Scenes such as Scédase's experience before the royal judge will become foils for the seriousness and dignity neoclassical tragic poetics demand. The memory of Hardy's early tragedy shapes the development of a monarchical-marvellous aesthetic, a portrayal of the king's decision as inherently transformative and awe-inspiring. In *Scédase*, rather than a hoped-for reversal of the main character's fate, the king's judgment decidedly lacks transcendence and verges on the grotesque, especially in the extent of its callousness towards the peasant father's suffering. After the ruling, one of the king's councillors unceremoniously commands the royal guards to "throw out" Scédase from the courtroom:

LÉONTIDE: Huissiers! Holà, quelqu'un! Jetez-le-moi dehors!   (v. 1231)

[Guards! You, there, someone! Throw him out!]

Far removed from the domain of Spartan law, the term "huissier" refers to ancien régime ushers who opened and closed doors within the royal residence.[21] By linking the hero's tragic end to a mundane French servant of royal power, Hardy ties the brutality of the king's decision to the seventeenth century in a manner all spectators would recognize. The councillor's crass insensitivity accentuates the absence of a marvellous intervention to save Scédase and gives his plight a flavour akin to the "pure joke" Benjamin describes as the counterpart to the German mourning play: "Comedy – or more precisely: the pure joke – is the essential inner side of mourning, which from time to time, like the lining of a dress at the hem or lapel, makes its presence felt."[22] To have turned to the king in a desperate search for justice and to wind up expelled from the physical space of judgment is at once harrowing and ridiculous. The scene accentuates Scédase's solitude and powerlessness, but also displays the comically feeble and contemptible exercise of justice within the king's court.

Chapelain, in response to such unreservedly non-marvellous scenes as Scédase's ejection from the courtroom, will define a conception of *vraisemblance* dependent on provoking feelings of awe:

> Ce qui fait désirer une si exacte observation de ces lois [celles de la vraisemblance] est qu'il n'y a point d'autre voie pour produire le Merveilleux, qui ravit l'âme d'étonnement et de plaisir, et qui est le parfait moyen dont la bonne Poésie se sert pour être utile.[23]

> [What makes one desire such an exact observation of these laws (those of verisimilitude) is that there are no other means to produce the Marvellous, which fills the soul with astonishment and pleasure, and which are the perfect means that good Poetry employs to be useful.]

While commentators of this passage usually view it in light of discussions of the sublime, which will occupy poetic debates in the second half of the seventeenth century, we should also attend to its demarcation of "good Poetry" from bad, an effort to eliminate troubling and overly realistic scenes from French theatre. As we saw earlier in our study, Chapelain disapproved of what he deemed to be an unflattering – and therefore implausible – royal decision in Corneille's *Le Cid*: "le dénouement de l'intrigue n'est fondé que sur l'injustice inopinée de Fernand, qui, comme un dieu sortant d'une machine vient ordonner un mariage que raisonnablement il ne devait pas seulement proposer"[24] [The dénouement of the intrigue is founded only on an inexplicable injustice by Fernand, who, like a god from a machine, comes to order a marriage he could not reasonably even propose]. Either too realistic or too implausible, Hardy's *Scédase* and Corneille's *Le Cid* stand as contrary to the ideals of *vraisemblance*, a concept which will generate the vein of the "monarchical-marvellous" when it comes to royal portrayals, and serve to contest the "indignation and horror" of these plays.[25]

Thus, in reaction to unsettling dramatic representations and in response to the randomness of tragicomedy's endings, Chapelain theorizes a poetic stance described by Forestier as, "la poétique de la merveille sans merveilleux"[26] [a poetics of the marvel without the marvellous]. Building on Forestier's analysis, John D. Lyons has aptly summed up the *doctes'* desire to create a form where a "visible and rationally traceable causality" dominates the events of the plot.[27] As Lyons writes:

> Aristotle's *deus ex machina* is abhorrent to early-modern theorists precisely because such a device is a *deus extra-machina*, a god that comes from outside the machine that is itself the play. Writers, or at least theorists, have nothing against machines themselves, but they want to build a certain kind of closed, textual machine.[28]

In understanding the theorists' preference for the *intra-machine* plot, we must recognize it as a politically anchored stance. A signature feature of the French neoclassical aesthetic – the self-contained plot and narrow structure – develops in response to the distressing effects scenes of royal judgment produce, especially in the emotional moment of the tragic intrigue's dénouement. Instead of searching beyond the borders of the plot for an unanticipated and random intervention, the monarchical-marvellous approach emerges to present the royal judge as the perfect blend of a rational causality and surprise. The king's unique capacity to restore order via a decisive judgment becomes the "marvel without the marvellous" and replaces the "overwhelming sense of fortuitousness" that governed tragicomedy.[29]

In the 1623 "Preface à l'*Adonis*," a critical work composed more than a decade before the *Sentiments de l'Académie*, Chapelain insisted that the "Marvellous" was a common factor across literary genres, although manifested differently according to each genre:

> Ainsi non seulement les interventions divines dans une épopée ou une tragédie, mais une péripétie provoquée par un valet dans une comédie, mais la richesse d'une image dans une ode, sont du Merveilleux. Le Merveilleux est tout ce qui suscite l'admiration par la surprise.[30]

> [Thus not only the divine interventions in an epic poem or in a tragedy, but also an incident provoked by a lackey in a comedy, or the richness of an image in an ode, stem from the Marvellous. The Marvellous is everything that provokes admiration through surprise.]

In his mediations on surprise in literature, Chapelain reserves divine interventions for the serious genres of the epic and the tragic, and allocates the lowly lackey to comedy, but he couples these seemingly antithetical outside agents in their ability to produce a similar type of unexpected change within the plot. In the wake of *Les Sentiments de l'Académie*'s critique of Fernand, the monarchical character develops as the intra-plot solution, a powerful agent capable of resolving the intrigue through his decision-making. In other words, the royal judge, operating in a realm situated somewhere between the divine and the domestic, manifests his *in extremis* ability to produce marvellous reversals. Far from a walling off of genres, the role allotted to the royal judge stems from a rejection of Hardy's realistic portrayals and the embrace of the marvellous as taken from the intersection of dénouements from French tragedy, tragicomedy, and comedy.

This cross-genre appropriation and critical push for adherence to the "monarchical-marvellous" influences ongoing discussions of royal portrayals onstage. Molière's *L'Impromptu de Versailles* (1663) attests to the combination of efficiency and awe that playwrights will seek to attribute to their monarchical characters, especially at the moment of the dénouement. In *L'Impromptu*, Molière manages to endow the royal character on the comedic stage, in fact Louis XIV, with grandeur and strength by making the king present in the wider frame but never having him actually set foot on the stage. The plot begins in a realistic mode as a theatrical troupe gathered at Versailles prepares to put on a play ordered by Louis, a generous patron, but also a demanding spectator of comedy whom the actors must promptly satisfy. The actors are not ready to perform and they run the risk of failing in their enterprise. Ultimately, Louis XIV resolves the actors' dilemma, and the dramatic intrigue, through his display of the most princely of virtues – clemency. He sends an emissary, his "*nécessaire*," who arrives to announce that the monarch has decided to give the unprepared actors a reprieve in the form of more time to rehearse their new play. This announcement is met with great relief and cries of gratitude for the royal decision, which is described as "la plus grande grâce du monde" [the greatest pardon of the world] and praises for the king who "nous redonne la vie" [gives us new life].[31]

Molière's sovereign intervenes efficiently and magnanimously to bring about a happy outcome – precisely what the monarch fails to do in *Scédase* but what the authors of *Les Sentiments de l'Académie sur Le Cid* will encourage tragedians to portray. In *L'Impromptu*, Molière is simultaneously adhering to poetic fashion and poking fun at the by-then well-established tragic conventions of royal judgment onstage. *L'Impromptu*'s dénouement blends tragicomedy's fortuitous closing royal judgments with the tragic topos of sovereign clemency. Louis's emissary offers a more prosaic version of the emperor Augustus's sublime "grâce," thus making the scene a perfect parody of ideal tragic dénouements but also providing an impeccable end to his play. Molière draws on what have become clichés of theatrical royal representations by the 1660s. Since the comedy's action unfolds in a time contemporary with the audience, staging the king would entail an actor's impersonation of the historical monarch – an unthinkably dangerous proposition, which would egregiously lack *bienséance*. Instead, Molière resorts to the presence of the king's delegates – four lackeys – who serve as manifestations of an off-stage king. As Molière's comedic example attests, respect for the royal person has become a necessity, and acceptable representations entail a demonstration of the king's ability to dispense justice in what are at once marvellous and predictable ways (because they have become conventional by this point).

We can measure the distance separating Molière's dénouement from the one devoid of salvation in Hardy's *Scédase* where the title character finds only silence and a royal refusal to take action to alleviate his suffering. A peasant though he may be, the afflicted father is the admirable character whose anguish at the murder of his daughters brings him more dignity than either the violent Spartans or the royal judge possess. When Scédase sees the king's patronizing attitude for what it is – inaction – he implores the gods to intervene against such "artifices":

O juges immortels,
Ne laissez impunis des artifices tels!
J'appelle devant vous de pareille remise,
Grâce à ces assassins exécrables promise.   (vv. 1223–6)

[Oh, immortal judges / Do not let such artifice go unpunished! / I appeal such exoneration / A pardon promised to these hated murderers.]

Scédase beckons a *deus ex machina* to replace the *rex ex machina* the king has failed to embody. For a brief interval, then, as the father laments his plight just before he stabs himself, the play hints at the possibility that a higher authority will swoop down and render justice in the sovereign's place. However, the hoped-for reversal of the royal decision never occurs. The play remains tied to the logic of cause-and-effect, in accordance with other "Tragedies of the Scaffolds," with a dénouement that rests on the royal decision and its responsibility for a bloody death. The onlookers plead with the elderly father not to take his life, but, without hope, the desperate Scédase stabs himself and dies onstage.

4 The Silence of Kings and Gods

For most of the play, *Scédase* aligns with the conventional plots of "Tragedies of the Scaffolds," in particular with its depiction of the various episodes that constitute the criminal process – from the first inkling of a crime, to the conditions that allow it to be committed, to its action, discovery, and trial. Hardy's play is remarkable, however, in its refusal to provide closure for the murder, especially after staging the step-by-step depiction of the crime. This deviation from the more typical outcome serves to reinforce the relationship between *Scédase*'s tragic ending and the king's injustice. As is usually the case in the "Tragedy of the Scaffolds" genre, the intrigue progresses in a crescendo as violated hospitality turns into a violation of the women, and then expands to their murder. In Act I, the Spartan soldiers openly premeditate their crime. The men are told by an elderly mentor not to put their honour at risk by paying a visit to the Boetian women, but they ignore these warnings and declare themselves incapable of resisting the urge to possess such beauties. Then they carry out their plan, killing the women to ensure their silence. In an emphasis of their cold-blooded mindset, they decide to throw the bodies down a well to allow themselves time to escape before the murders are discovered. Finally, having accomplished what they set out to do, they leave the stage, never to reappear. The disappearance of the perpetrators closes a parenthesis of unrestricted violence and gives way to a judicial process which ultimately proves to be equally violent by not only refusing to condemn the criminals, but also by leading to their accuser's suicide.

When the play shifts to the father's pursuit of justice, it also shifts from the domestic sphere of country hospitality to the public domain in which a subject calls upon the king to articulate a judgment. The king's court replaces the peaceful peasant-world of filial obedience glimpsed at only in the play's opening scene when the father bid farewell to his daughters. The French audience watching this action unfold can only hope that the king will behave as the virtuous father of his kingdom, that Agésilas's care for his subjects will parallel Scédase's love for his daughters. Instead, the king appears far removed from Scédase in more ways than one, since the lack of adherence to the unity of location emphasizes the distance separating the crime from its locus of judgment. The change in setting deepens the chasm between the respect for the ancient custom of hospitality and the impersonal juridical process in which the elderly Scédase finds himself mired.

The king's indifference or inaction regarding Scédase's "plainte" (v. 1097) [complaint] and the lack of a reversal of his plight are accompanied by a heightened involvement of the French audience in the drama. Spectators are initially called upon to react when the first of Scédase's daughters is attacked. She shouts, "A la force! Au secours! A l'aide, mes amis!" (v. 767) [Send help! To the rescue! Help, my friends!"], as if to enjoin the audience to intervene. Her sister calls on the gods and then prays for her neighbours to save her: "A la force! Voisins, hé! De grâce, accourez, / Et contre ces brigands notre honneur secourez" (vv. 779–80) [Help! Neighbours, there! I beg of you, come, / And from these rogues rescue our honour]. Given these desperate appeals, the audience's mixed sense of powerlessness, emotional investment, and indignation towards the king's judgment must have reached its climax in Act V. The staging of a formal trial scene presses them to take part in the proceedings they see onstage, and yet the king dismisses the case on the simple basis that there were no eyewitnesses to the crime. Agésilas asks his courtroom audience: "Lequel ce meurtre vu précisément dépose? / Lequel fut spectateur et ne l'empêcha pas" (vv. 1166–7) [Who having seen this murder can precisely attest to it? / Who was a spectator and did not prevent it?]. As the only persons capable of answering this question affirmatively, Hardy's spectators are condemned to remain silent and watch on as the king's demands for irrefutable proof lead Scédase to suicide.

Despite the dénouement's lack of closure when it comes to solving the murders of Scédase's daughters, Hardy's final scene parallels more conventional "Tragedies of the Scaffolds," such as Jean de Bretog's *Tragédie française* where witnesses gather to discuss the outcome of the trial they have observed. In *Scédase*, onlookers join together in a final reflection on the fate of the father. Though Scédase was not, strictly speaking, executed, he dies in response to his "plainte repoussée" (v. 1312) [complaint dismissed] and because he has lost all faith in royal justice – "le misérable père qui de toute justice humaine désespère" (vv. 1309–10) [the miserable father who despairs of all human justice]. The "coup" he gives himself, "C'en est fait à ce coup" (v. 1340) [It is done at this blow] designates all at once the physical *coup* that extinguishes his life,

the metaphysical marker of his tragic destiny – the "*C'en est fait*" of fate
sealed – as well as the absent "*coup de théâtre*" that would have reversed
his plight. In Hardy's play, nothing will prevent Scédase's suffering: he
can find no escape from the injustice inflicted upon him, and, therefore,
becomes complicit in the crime as the "coup" he inflicts upon himself
makes him "un homicide" (v. 1343) [a killer].

The tragedy comes full circle, from the presence of the happy family
glimpsed at ever so briefly in the opening scene when the loving father
bid his daughters farewell, to the father's death in the last scene of the
play. These deaths, all three depicted before the spectators' eyes, reinforce what Rousset identifies as the particular aim of early seventeenth-
century tragedy: "l'écrasement de l'homme"[32] [the crushing of man]. As
Rousset describes, the aim of this genre is to "faire porter tout l'accent
dramatique sur le Malheur, un Malheur physique, visible, envahissant,
un fatum viscéral, sanglant et spectaculaire"[33] [to place the entire dramatic emphasis on Misfortune, a physical misfortune, visible, invading,
a visceral fatality, bloody and spectacular]. Unremarked upon by Rousset, however, but important to Hardy's vision and to our understanding
of the post-*Sentiments de l'Académie* concept of tragedy that will counter
it, the "crushing of man" is inflicted by the king's judgment. Scédase's
misfortune contains an important secular dimension since the monarch
could have reversed his tragic fate but the judge's inability, or unwillingness, to intercede to make things right, culminates in the hero's death.

Coupled with the king's inaction, the silence of the gods also weighs
heavily on *Scédase*'s dénouement. The absence of a divine intervention,
despite the beckoning pleas of the king's victim, highlights in contrast
the allied response of the Boetians to the tragic hero. After witnessing
Scédase's death, the villagers band together in their promise to honour
the elderly father. Implicitly condemning the royal decision, the Boetian
chorus depicts Scédase as an innocent man executed for his defence of
a just cause. The onlookers, whom Hardy designates as the "chœur de
Leuctriens" [a chorus of Luctrians], elevate the aggrieved father to the
level of a "guardian saint" (v. 1361), as they vow to shower his tomb annu-
ally with offerings of flowers, tears, and sacrifice, turning the lowly rest-
ing place of a deceased peasant into a sacred altar where the faithful will
come to commemorate a holy action. Moreover, in this portrait of the
public's response to Scédase's plight, Hardy implicitly alludes to Spartan-
Theban political history. Spectators familiar with the demise of Lacedae-
monia would have known that the battle of Leuctra, waged between the
two city-states, was the famous site of a bloody Spartan defeat in 371 BC,

under Agésilas's reign, spelling the end of Sparta's political and military ascendency over the Greek peninsula. By indirectly referencing the defeat of the great military nation, a Spartan failure situated beyond the frame of the present tragedy, Hardy hints at the advent of a long-delayed and indirect punishment. The world where Scédase will be avenged is offstage, removed from this plot, as if the playwright were asking spectators to look beyond the tragedy of Scédase to find an answer to the injustice they have observed. As the Leuctrians insist, Scédase belongs to those "héros" who will be buried, "après le cours fatal de leurs trames finies" (v. 1362) [after the fatal course of their finished plots].[34] An all-too-faint glimmer of justice lies beyond the dire end of Scédase's "trame."

Indeed, within the cadre of Hardy's plot, no balance is re-established between crime and punishment. The royal judge compounds societal violence since his refusal to punish the murderers leads to another death, and Hardy insists on the recognition of the individual's powerless response. Tracing the differences between Hardy's model and the poetic precepts of the "regular" tragedy to come allows us to gauge the extent to which favouring a well-prepared, i.e., logical and justified dénouement, constitutes a political stance. The call for closure to become a new tragic norm stems from a willingness to have the royal authority within the play reclaim the final judicial narrative, thereby turning the focus on the king's actions, not towards the victims' lamentations nor those of their sympathizers.

This new poetic vision parallels Richelieu's efforts to dictate the political narrative produced at the sight and moment of a public execution of the condemned. As the historian Hélène Fernandez-Lacôte describes in her study of political executions under Richelieu, the sight of a man on the scaffolds and the spectacle of his punishment were a means of expressing the sovereign's ability to provide closure for the disorder wrought by the criminal:

La force, mais aussi les ambiguïtés des messages dont les derniers instants du condamné sont porteurs, font de l'exécution un moment clé du processus politique et du règlement du conflit; ils en font aussi le moment qui sera, par excellence, raconté et remémoré, et dont le récit peut aisément prendre un sens politique précis.[35]

[The force, but also the ambiguity which the last moments of the condemned contain, make of the execution a key moment in the political process and in the settlement of the conflict; they also make of it the moment

which will be, par excellence, retold and remembered, and whose narrative
can easily take on a precise political meaning.]

Although writing pre-Richelieu, Hardy is nonetheless attuned to the
dramatic possibilities generated by the ambiguous meaning of the condemned man's last moments. In accordance with the common structure
of the "Tragedy of the Scaffolds," the playwright constructs his dénouement around the onlookers' reaction to Scédase's public death. As the
villagers' mournful promise to remember Scédase demonstrates, his
death – an indirect execution but an execution nonetheless – carries a
message centred on the individual, his drama, his fate, his tragedy. The
condemned man's final actions articulate an ultimate truth about the judicial process: the royal decision is both the source of Scédase's tragedy
and its resolution: a realization markedly out of alignment with what will
become the primary edificatory purpose of the public judicial ceremony
under Richelieu.

In describing the objectives of the ancien régime public trial, Biet
insists on the judicial authorities' aim to pacify the conflict between the
sovereign and the condemned by restoring order through a display of
punishment. He calls the public trial, "un rituel destiné à d'une part
représenter la punition de la loi, et d'autre part à célébrer le passage du
condamné contrit à l'espérance d'un salut, via l'expiation et la réintégra-
tion"[36] [a ritual designed to, on the one hand represent punishment by
law, and, on the other hand, to celebrate the condemned man's passing from contrition to the hope of salvation, via expiation and reinte-
gration]. Hardy's tragedy undermines such a process. Scédase insists on
provoking the public's sadness, sense of loss, and frustration by stressing
the law's – and, therefore, the king's – failure to punish the guilty. The
darkness that reigns at the play's close underscores the despair, rather
than the hope of salvation and reintegration, that emerges from the judicial process. Hardy offers a dénouement that beckons spectators to pass
judgment on the royal judge – to decry his decision and lament its consequences. Ultimately, the audience is asked to formulate its own condemnation of a royal verdict that has led to such bitter violence.

5 Monarchical Poetics: How to Rid Tragedy of Guilty Kings

The negative reaction to the king in Scédase is just the sort of ignoble or
unkingly behaviour that d'Aubignac deplores in La Pratique du théâtre
when he turns to the vraisemblable to insist that a royal character must

uphold his royal function and speak above all "as a king."[37] In accordance with Chapelain's prescriptions for the king to be a solemn lawgiver and teacher of moral lessons, d'Aubignac asserts that the circumstance of being a king is the dominant trait of a theatrical sovereign and must shape everything he does. "Speaking as a king" entails ensuring that the royal character receive the respect and authority his status (or *dignité*) demands. In short, a king must be recognizable as possessing all the qualities – in both senses of the word – of a king; he cannot simply make a terrible decision without the reasons for that behaviour being explicitly justified.

In *Scédase*, as we have seen, Hardy offers no explanation for why the sovereign judge decides not to allow the trial to proceed, except in its responsibility for sealing Scédase's tragic fate. The audience gains no insight into the king's interiority – no royal monologue, no prolonged scene of consultation with the royal ministers, no complaint of the weight of royal power. Spectators are left to draw their own conclusions about the king's motivation: perhaps Agésilas's judicial pragmatism results from his political interest in resisting the accusations of the peasant against the noblemen. Or might it be that he believes subjects have greater privileges than foreigners – the complaints of Scédase, a Boetian, carry less weight with the king than does the reputation of the Spartan soldiers. Yet another possibility could be that the king seeks to uphold juridical procedure at all costs and his unwillingness to proceed with a trial of the suspects stems from a rejection of circumstantial evidence, as when he insists that only eyewitnesses can provide positive proof of guilt. This theory would confirm the supposition surrounding Scédase's invalidating social status. As Andrea Frisch has shown, the early modern concept of eyewitnessing was primarily related to the notion of giving evidence – of testifying *to* someone – instead of the modern definition of seeing or hearing an event first hand.[38] As a peasant, Scédase's personal credibility and standing within the community are subject to doubt and scepticism. In spite of this, since the play's spectators have observed the rape and murder of the daughters, they know the eyewitness testimony of the peasant and his neighbours to be trustworthy and legitimate. Despite all these possibilities, the motivations and circumstances behind the king's decision remain blurry, unlike the misery they cause.

The mournful ending generated by the royal judgment underscores another significant divergence that occurs between Hardy's tragic conception and the neoclassical poetics that follow. The critics writing in Richelieu's theatrical sphere do not just emphasize the need for dramatic

and emotional closure at the end of the plot (an element they found
sorely lacking from *Le Cid*, as we have seen), they also claim that tragic
intrigues should be resolved in a positive way. The simultaneous injunc-
tion to depict the royal figure in a *vraisemblable*, i.e., idealized manner,
to bring closure, and to portray favourable dénouements is not discon-
nected from contemporary royal narratives, to be sure. In *La Pratique
du théâtre*, d'Aubignac insists that associating tragedy with unhappiness
is a misguided assumption: "Je sais bien qu'on le prend [ce terme de la
Catastrophe] pour un revers ou bouleversement de quelques grandes
affaires, et pour un désastre sanglant et signalé qui termine quelque
notable dessein"[39] [I know well that we take it (the catastrophe) for a
reversal or upheaval of some great matters, and for a bloody and known
disaster that ends a noted design]. D'Aubignac specifies that the defining characteristic of tragedy is a reversal of circumstance, and not necessarily a negative reversal, only a transformation of the initial situation
in a surprising way: "Pour moi je n'entends par ce mot, qu'un renversement des premières dispositions du Théâtre, la dernière Péripétie, et un
retour d'événements qui changent toutes les apparences des Intrigues
au contraire de ce qu'on en devait attendre"[40] [As for me, I understand
this word to mean a reversal of the original order of things onstage, the
last incident, and a transformation of events that changes all the appearances of the Intrigue into the opposite of what we expected from it].
Tragic structure and monarchical rhetoric converge as the noble genre's
features must contain reversal, surprise, and change at the plot's end,
echoing absolutist narratives which describe the king's unique capacity to
stop and overturn a seemingly inevitable progression of events through
transformative action. Surprise and good fortune at the dénouement,
once the bedrock of tragicomedy, become the pillars of tragic dénouements and royal propaganda, similarly eager to promote the anticipation
and mystery that surrounds the king's ability to resolve conflicts.

On the one hand, d'Aubignac's refusal to conflate tragedy with negative endings muddles generic differences, erasing the usual markers
between tragedy and tragicomedy. He goes so far as to insist that the
term "tragicomédie" is "inutile" [useless] since all it means is a tragedy
with a happy ending, and by calling a work a tragicomedy, a playwright
foolishly gives away to his spectators that the outcome of the plot will
be positive. In fact, "celui [le terme] de Tragédie ne signifie pas moins
les Poèmes qui finissent par la joie, quand on y décrit les fortune des
personnes illustres"[41] [(the label) of Tragedy means also Poems that end
in happiness, when they describe the fortunes of illustrious persons].

D'Aubignac wishes to take from tragicomedy its surprisingly optimistic demonstration of justice and good fortune, leaving behind tragedy's pessimism and dark fatality. Yet he leaves behind tragicomedy's improbable and illogical endings, setting forth a new understanding of the role kings within a tragic plot should play.

In contrast to Hardy's *Scédase* and the tragicomedies of the first quarter of the century, d'Aubignac narrows the population of tragedy, demarcating its characters based on a hierarchy of social class. Plainly situating tragedy within a political setting, the critic states that the theatrical world is divided between "trois sortes de Vies" [three sorts of lives] and that tragedy tells the stories of "les Grands dans la Cour des Rois" [The Great in Royal courts]. Furthermore, he assigns a more restricted subject matter to the genre:

étant certain que ce terme ne veut rien dire sinon *Une chose magnifique, sérieuse, grave et convenable aux agitations et aux grands revers de la fortune des Princes*; et qu'une Pièce de Théâtre porte ce nom de Tragédie seulement en considération des Incidents et des personnes dont elle représente la vie, et non pas à raison de la Catastrophe.[42]

[being certain that this term means nothing if not *A magnificent thing, serious, grave, and suitable to the agitations and the great reversals of the fortune of Princes*; and that a play carries this name of Tragedy only in consideration of the Incidents and people whose lives it represents, and not because of its Catastrophe.]

The emphasis on "seriousness" and "gravity" departs from the whimsical, often light-hearted and apolitical intrigues of popular tragicomedies. As for the mention of "suitable" activity, Hardy is suggesting a more dignified and exemplary storyline to showcase the status of princes.

D'Aubignac insists that the French have wisely "corrected" ancient tragedies (or those like Hardy's) and rejected the horrors that characterized them: "nous avons rejeté du théâtre, les histoires d'horreur et les cruautés extraordinaires"[43] [we have rejected from the theatre, stories of horror and extraordinary cruelty]. If we compare *Scédase* to Hardy's tragicomedy *La force du sang* (1625), and consider both of these in light of d'Aubignac's precepts, we can better grasp the changes the author of *La Pratique du théâtre* hopes to see within tragic intrigues, but also the elements of justice he wishes to integrate. In *La force du sang*, Hardy once again stages a play where a nobleman rapes a woman of a lower social rank. This time, after the violence, he abandons her. The culprit does not realize that during her ordeal, the young woman managed to steal a portrait which she hid on her person. She becomes pregnant as a result of the rape and gives birth to a son. Seven years later, back in the presence of the nobleman, she uses the portrait as proof of the crime and identifies the father of her son. His family orders him to marry her, and the play closes with the promise of a newly restored family unity. As Jacques Scherer describes it, "Dans cette vue optimiste d'une aventure qui commençait mal, tout le monde est bon, même le faible Alphonse [the nobleman rapist]"[44] [In this optimistic outlook of an adventure that started badly, everyone is good, even the weak Alphonse]. We see how the world of tragicomedy is presented as surprisingly just, and its justice is surprisingly effective at siding with the innocent and making the criminal repent.

While d'Aubignac wishes to see tragedy's universe resemble tragicomedy's, he and his fellow proponents of regularity would prefer to see justice come from within the plot. As Lyons has shown, in tragicomedy the prop is a point of encounter between the inner and the outer world, a repurposed object that propels dramatic actions by somehow resisting human agency.[45] It is the outside elements and objects, the smoking guns, so to speak – the portraits, swords, and hairpins (as in Corneille's *Clitandre*) – which serve as irrefutable evidence and ultimate identifiers of guilt, making judgment easy. Instead of these *invraisemblable* props, the royal judge, capable of "serious" and "grave" judgment becomes the ideal character to decipher good from evil and replace the randomness of tragicomedy's salutary objects. What better way for spectators to contemplate the royal character in the exercise of his *dignité*, and for the plot to reach a positive end?

In the chapters that follow, we will continue to trace the evolving portrayal of the royal judge onstage, and we will often find him not making admirable judgments. One need only think of Agamemnon's and Thésée's flawed judgments to be persuaded that d'Aubignac's theories remained just that – theoretical. Not all tragedians jumped onto the happy-outcome bandwagon, although they will take pains to explain in prefaces or paratexts why such portrayals were justified. As my chronological detour from the reception of *Le Cid* in chapter 1 to Hardy's tragic model in chapter 2 attests, I do not wish to argue for a teleological progression of tragedy where the imperfect model of Hardy culminates in ideal theatrical kings at the antipodes of the flawed early seventeenth-century version. Nor do I suggest there is a finality or point of arrival where the judge presented onstage is perfectly aligned with the "monarchical-marvellous" aesthetic of the French king. Rather than establish a clear-cut genealogy that moves from one point to another, I hope the discussion of Hardy's portrayal of royal judgment has brought to light how, under the increasing weight of respect for royal judgment, *Scédase*'s tragic model recedes but does not entirely disappear. The courtroom procedural of the "Tragedy of the Scaffolds" gives way to portrayals of royal judgments in the seemingly less historically referential space of the royal cabinet or chambers. Or else, playwrights will situate the evil judgments of their kings explicitly within the tyrant's court such as in Tristan L'Hermite's *La Mariane* (1637) or *La Mort de Sénèque* (1645), making their royal judges explicit counter-examples to the contemporary ideals of kingship.

We have seen that although Hardy's *Scédase ou l'hospitalitée violée* and Corneille's *Le Cid* occupy very different positions within the canon of French literary history, they share strong commonalities in their presentation of a sovereign deemed threatening and antithetical to the narratives of monarchical justice set in place in the Richelieu era. Beyond their shared status as foils against which to measure the portrayals that will be advanced in contrast, they represent important reference points for the way French tragic production – the theory and the practice – evolves. The dramaturgy known as French neoclassical theatre, an aesthetic associated with stringent codes and a clarity of form, arises from a resistance to dramatic models often considered antithetical to the great French genre: the dénouements of the "Tragedy of the Scaffolds" or the "Marvellous" surprises of tragicomedy. By experimenting with these established structures, reconfiguring, and smoothing over the elements deemed unflattering to the monarchical *dignité*, critics and playwrights gradually inaugurate new norms for the portrait of sovereignty on the French stage.

Chapter Three

The Ceremony Unravels: Tragedy's Comedic Turn

Nous sommes tous rivaux dans la passion de contribuer quelque chose à la gloire d'un si grand prince: chacun y emploie les différents talents que la nature lui a donnés.

> Jean Racine, "Discours prononcé à l'Académie Française
> à la réception de M. l'abbé Colbert"[1]

1 When Tragedy Fails to Persuade

Starting in the 1630s when Richelieu turns his attention to the stage, he understands tragedy to be a promising means to promote pro-absolutist principles and political lessons. Its traditional focus on matters of state and the affairs of great men allow it to become a privileged space to stage vivid examples of admirable royal behaviour. According to theorists working close to Richelieu, the persuasion that occurs via tragedy should no longer arrive through heavy-handed use of *sentences* and the delivery of virtuous maxims interspersed in characters' speeches; instead, the critics recommend presenting theatrical characters as models of conduct for the audience to admire.

For instance, when La Mesnardière details the qualities demanded of a theatrical king and his minister, his description reads like a royal panegyric and a wish-list for the French kingdom:

> Un Roi sera grave, jaloux de son autorité, mêlera la rigueur de Maître avec la douceur de Père, et punira généreusement les manquements de respect que l'on commettra devant lui. Un Grand Ministre d'Etat sera soigneux, vigilant, courtois et officieux envers les gens de mérite, adroit, fidèle et

courageux; ne considérera jamais que les intérêts de son Maître, entrepren-
dra toutes choses honnêtes et légitimes pour lui conférer le repos pour
augmenter la puissance, et pour accroître sa gloire.[2]

[A King will be solemn; he will jealously guard his authority, blend the
rigour of a Master with the tenderness of a Father, and severely punish the
lack of respect shown towards him. A Great Minister of State will be meticulous, vigilant, courteous and diligent towards persons of merit, adroit, faithful, and brave; he will only ever consider the interests of his Master, will
undertake all honest and legitimate things to give him peace of mind, to
augment his power, and to increase his glory.]

Published in 1639, when Louis XIII's authority and Richelieu's respect
for his master and the "persons of merit" of the kingdom were under
fire, La Mesnardière's *La Poétique* is replete with passages that attempt
to negate contemporary criticism of the king and his minister. The critic
instructs playwrights to make their characters conform to an ideal of
government where the exercise of power is perfectly defined, prudently
delegated, and productively employed for the good of the king and his
kingdom.

Scholars of French tragedy have too often taken this kind of poetic
prescription for royal portraits as a cornerstone of French neoclassical
tragedy, as if playwrights immediately generated and always achieved
the intended persuasion – or mystification – of their audiences through
brilliantly effective dramatic portraits. In parallel to the ways in which
monarchical images and rhetoric of the period are thought to have
forcefully executed political-artistic aims, critics have resolutely believed
in the success of classical rules and authors in creating their intended
effects. The tragedies of Pierre Corneille and Jean Racine in particular have been viewed as testaments to the authors' masterful ability to
negotiate between the demands of the various spheres (theatrical, cultural, political) in order to create lasting works which could dramatize
absolutist ideals while also subtly conveying their individual perspective
and ethos.[3]

Such precepts are interesting especially when read alongside the early
seventeenth-century model of tragedy we considered in chapter 2, for
the poeticians' endeavour to sever so drastically with the Hardy tradition
comes into full view. Their eagerness to polish the royal image and to
propose flattering examples of royal behaviour exposes the investment
of Richelieu's political vision in tragic poetics in the decades ranging

from the 1630s all the way to the 1660s. We should not take these prescriptions, however, as more than revealing efforts to change the standards of a changing genre. In practice, such formulas proved far less
efficient to apply, and Hardy's model far more tenacious than is usually
assumed. Playwrights, even the most talented among them, struggled
with the balance of the new demands and the practice of placing monarchical characters onstage.

Louis Marin stands out as one of the most sophisticated readers of
royal iconography of the seventeenth century, offering complex analyses of how the Crown mobilized art, historiography, medallions, and
architecture to proclaim the king's power, to the point where the king
himself was absorbed in the glory of his own image. Such interpretations, however, leave little room for attention to the splinters, cracks, and
divergences in a royal discourse whose dominant feature, according to
Marin, is its persuasiveness. He is as convinced as the historians known
as the "ceremonialists" of the "readability" (*lisibilité*) of royal representations and therefore, as they do, he places excessive faith in the effectiveness of royal productions.[4] Marin artfully deciphers the strategies behind
monarchical productions, yet his conviction that the artists were in full
control of their enterprise obscures how the carefully constructed "*récits*"
may have spawned images and narratives at odds with those envisioned
by the very producers of the works. Marin places too much faith in the
unity and lucidity of such royal "texts." In contrast, social historians like
Alain Boureau have convincingly argued that the theory of the king's two
bodies was first and foremost an aesthetic elaboration, what he calls "une
série de fictions articulées" [a series of articulated fictions] that were not
necessarily received as authoritative or plausible by the public.[5] Spectators experienced royal ceremonies in diverse ways; they could participate
in or receive the event, which itself was subject to alterations, mistakes,
and omissions, depending on the specific context in which it took place.

The same is true for tragedy where the increasing focus on the prominence of the royal body and the fixity of the genre's structure has led
readers to regard it as participating in a solemn monarchical ritual. With
its embrace of decorum, strict conventions, a rigid tempo, and its tone of
pomp and grandeur, tragedy has often been considered by critics to be
one more ancien régime ceremony. Recent scholarship has pushed back
against this view, exposing how the celebratory perspective of the order,
harmony, and rationality that French neoclassicism brought to the stage
was often inflected with chauvinistic accents.[6] John Lyons's careful analysis of the contradictory and ambiguous poetic precepts that informed

tragic productions has opened the door for a revised understanding of
the diversity of neoclassical artistic codes.[7] Other critical efforts have cast
light on the varied audience reception of theatrical representations, and
on the wide-ranging role of the actor in communicating dramaturgical
messages and emotions.[8] Scholarly attention has turned towards the dis-
crepancies between absolutist rhetoric and theatrical fictions, focusing
on what is erased or sublimated when absolutist rhetoric is transposed
to the stage.[9]

Even though critics acknowledge the complexity and multiplicity of
practices shaping the artistic, material, and political ideologies advanced
through tragic plots as they coalesce into persuasive dramatic works,
neoclassical tragedy has not been able to shake its status as a monarchical ritual – mystical, majestic, and transcendental. To see tragic fictions
as rehearsing monarchical rituals, however, neglects the ways in which
such narratives so frequently veer off course. It is this notion of tragedy
that I wish to address. My analysis will focus on moments when playwrights and their critics grapple with tragedy's failure to maintain the
plot's intended decorum. In examining how the seriousness and grandeur associated with the genre so easily collapse into comedy, we will
understand how critics and playwrights sought to forestall such moments
by instituting prohibitions on the subjects of tragic fictions, in particular in relation to the royal character. In other words, beneath the playwrights' intended laudatory fictions of tragedy, lies a strong tension that
discredits or contradicts the royal portrait the plays sought to advance.
Countering neoclassicism's aura of mastery and the tendency to read
these tragedies as reflecting the playwrights' expert grasp of the codes,
formulas, and prohibitions of the genre, this chapter will accentuate the
notion of a troubling and inadequate, even a "failed," royal portrayal: it
offers a study of the fissures when the ceremony comes apart and persuasion collapses into farce.

In an often-cited passage on the nature of Racine's tragic conception,
Michel Foucault turns to the vocabulary of ceremony to describe the
playwright's presentation of the royal figure. He defines tragedy as undo-
ing and then reconstituting a monarchical ritual. In a theatre noted for
its complex psychological examinations, Foucault underscores the political scope of Racine's representations and intriguingly ties them to "les
problèmes de droit public" [problems of public law]:

La tragédie classique, la tragédie racinienne que fait-elle? Elle a pour
fonction – c'est en tout cas un de ces axes – de constituer l'envers de la

cérémonie, de montrer la cérémonie déchirée, le moment où le détenteur de la puissance publique, le souverain, se décompose peu à peu en homme de passion, le roi-souverain pourra renaître et se recomposer: mort et résurrection du corps du roi dans le cœur du monarque. Et c'est là le problème juridique, beaucoup plus que psychologique, qui est posé par la tragédie racinienne.[10]

[Classical tragedy, Racinian tragedy what does it do? Its function – or at the very least one of its axes – is to constitute the reverse of the ceremony, to show the torn ceremony, the moment when the person who holds public power, the sovereign, decomposes little by little into a man of passion, the king/sovereign can be reborn and recomposed: death and resurrection of the royal body in the heart of the monarch. And therein lies the juridical problem, much more than the psychological one, which is posed by Racinian tragedy.]

Foucault adopts here an overly optimistic view of tragedy's ability to "recompose" and "resurrect" the king, and, like Marin, describes a perfect correlation between Racine, the tragic playwright, and Racine, the royal historiographer; he considers both roles as working in tandem to affirm the king's supremacy:

[Louis XIV] demandait [à Racine], au fond, d'écrire, comme historiographe, le cinquième acte d'une tragédie heureuse, c'est-à-dire la remontée de l'homme privé, de l'homme de cour et de cœur, jusqu'à ce point où il devient chef de guerre et monarque, détenteur de la souveraineté.[11]

[(Louis XIV) was asking Racine, essentially, to write, as historiographer, the fifth Act of a happy tragedy, in other words, the rise of the private man, the man of court and of love, to the point where he becomes war chief and king, the bearer of sovereignty.]

In this view, the controlled and orthodox basis on which tragic playwrights build their fictions seems to allow disorder, or the portrait of the "torn ceremony," only long enough to make the positive ending more meaningful and to demonstrate more clearly the masterful conclusion the playwright has engineered to showcase the triumph of the dominant order. Foucault's comments follow in the tradition of Thierry Maulnier and Jacques Scherer whose readings drew out to varying degrees the ceremonial elements of (Racinian) tragedy.[12]

In contrast, seventeenth-century playwrights and critics were acutely aware of the potential for the dramatic staging to come up short, fall flat, or, simply, fail. At different junctures in their theoretical reflections Chapelain, d'Aubignac, La Mesnardière, Corneille, and Racine all express an awareness of how theatrical representations can take on a life of their own, unexpectedly tarnishing or undermining what should have been a source of admiration. La Mesnardière emphatically articulates the dangers of a portrait's "degeneration": "dans les Ouvrages de Théâtre [...] la plus grande beauté peut dégénérer en laideur et paraître monstrueuse, quand elle n'est pas bien placée"[13] [in Theatrical Works ... the greatest beauty can degenerate into ugliness and appear monstrous, when it is not well placed]. A simple mistake in placement can transform something beautiful into something horrifying: the stakes of such an error in judgment prove particularly high for royal characters where a faulty portrayal can denigrate and tarnish the dignity one should most seek to protect.

Thus, in contrast to Peter Burke's analysis of the "the reverse of the medal," in which he separates official monarchical productions from illicit "alternative" writings (pamphlets, caricatures, parodies, and overt attacks on the king), I agree with Christian Jouhaud's refusal to pit one side of "the medal" against the other, for fear that either side should be taken as a coherent and unified whole.[14] Carefully constructed tragic portrayals of the king regularly degenerated into a mix of comedy and threatening brutality, taking on all at once an air of ridicule and an air of danger. Our faith in tragedy to execute its intended effects – a faith honed by our trust in poetics and by literary history's singling out of tragedy – obscures the shakiness of the genre's parameters and the difficulties in conveying the anticipated portrayal onstage.

Playwrights, all too aware of the political-cultural hazards of such flawed representations, were forced to rethink and justify what had seemed like a coherent tragic structure. Corneille's experience with Œdipe (1659) provides a vivid example of such a thwarted theatrical monarchical portrait.

2 Œdipe's Farcical Saga

Despite Aristotle's praise of Sophocles's Oedipus Rex as the crowning achievement of Greek tragic production, for French playwrights the Theban king proved to be a disconcerting monarchical figure. Writing Œdipe at a defining moment of his career, shortly before the publication of his most sustained poetic reflections, the *Trois discours sur le poème dramatique* (1660), Corneille grappled with the challenge of staging the Theban king's disgrace, including the tragedy's defining scene where the bereaved Œdipe, guilty of parricide and incest, gouges out his eyes in a brutal act of self-disfigurement:[15]

> Je ne déguiserai point qu'après avoir fait le choix de ce sujet, sur cette con-
> fiance, que j'aurais pour moi les suffrages de tous les savants, qui le regar-
> dent encore comme le chef-d'œuvre de l'Antiquité, et que les pensées de
> Sophocle et de Sénèque, qui l'ont traité en leurs langues, me faciliteraient
> les moyens d'en venir à bout, je tremblai quand je l'envisageai de près. Je
> reconnus que ce qui avait passé pour merveilleux en leurs siècles pourrait
> sembler horrible au nôtre; que cette éloquente et curieuse description de la
> manière dont ce malheureux prince se crève les yeux, qui occupe tout leur
> cinquième acte, ferait soulever la délicatesse de nos dames, dont le dégoût
> attire aisément celui du reste de l'auditoire.[16]

> [I will not hide that after having chosen this subject, with the confidence
> that I would have for myself the support of all our scholars, who look upon
> it as the masterpiece of Antiquity, as well as the thoughts of Sophocles and
> Seneca, who treated it in their languages, which would make it easier for
> me to achieve this task, I trembled when I looked at it closely. I recognized
> that what was considered to be marvellous in their centuries could seem
> horrible to our own; that this eloquent and curious description of the way
> this miserable prince pierces his eyes, an action that takes up all of their
> fifth Act, would repulse our ladies whose disgust so easily drives the disgust
> of the rest of the audience.]

As Corneille tells it, surprise dominates his discovery of a work held up as exemplary by tradition. Upon rereading the play, he recognizes its potential to shock and appall the French public, in particular French women, those staunch arbiters of good taste. He regards with dismay what the Oedipus plot actually entails. Corneille viscerally reacts – "I trembled" – at the anticipated disgust his audience would feel for the staging of the "miserable prince," and he describes his awareness of the inherent danger of such a portrayal on a French stage. Self-servingly, perhaps, Corneille insists on the challenge it was to bridge the aesthetic and political chasm separating Greek tragedy from ancien régime norms. Intriguingly, Corneille must confront the "*dangereux spectacle*" [dangerous spectacle] of failed royal judgment because he took up the Oedipus subject at the behest of Louis XIV's soon-to-be-condemned minister of finances, Nicolas Fouquet, who is said to have first suggested he write a new version of the Theban saga.[17] Turning to Oedipus and his egregious self-mutilation at a time when discussions regarding the protection of the royal image raged amounted to raising the stakes on making a scene of failed royal judgment acceptable to French audiences.

The potential for a negative reaction to his play leads Corneille to circumvent the most troubling elements of his source text and insert a parallel plot entirely extraneous to the original: "Ces considérations [la volonté de gagner la voix publique] m'ont fait cacher aux yeux un si dangereux spectacle, et introduire l'heureux épisode de Thésée et Dircé"[18] [These considerations (the desire to win public support) made me hide from their eyes such a dangerous spectacle, and introduce the happy episode of Thésée and Dircé]. The odd invention of a sister for Œdipe, in the person of Dircé, and the inclusion of her lover, Thésée, whose presence has struck many readers as bizarre, stems from a willingness to dampen the scandal of the leading royal character's vulnerability. First, he adds a strong female lead to please the women in his audience, and, second, he inserts Thésée into the plotline to diminish the image of a weak king by countering it with a figure for admirable sovereignty linked to the grandeur of Athens rather than the decadence of tragic Thebes.[19]

Corneille's impulse to dilute the "danger," as he puts it, of theatrical portrayals coincides with d'Aubignac's perspective. In *La Pratique du théâtre*, the critic forcefully lays out the impossibility of obtaining a favourable audience reaction to a display that transgresses a cultural-political taboo. D'Aubignac holds conformity to social practices and beliefs to be the fundamental tenet of theatrical representations:

> Il ne faut pas oublier (et ce n'est peut-être pas une des moindres observations que j'ai faites sur les Pièces de Théâtre) que si le Sujet n'est conforme aux mœurs et aux sentiments des Spectateurs, il ne réussira jamais, quelque soin que le Poète y emploie et de quelques ornements qu'il le soutienne [...] Nous ne voulons point croire que les Rois puissent être méchants, ni souffrir que leurs Sujets, quoi qu'en apparence maltraités, touchent leurs Personnes sacrées, ni se rebellent contre leur Puissance, non pas même en peinture; et je ne crois pas que l'on puisse faire assassiner un Tyran sur notre Théâtre avec applaudissement, sans de très signalées précautions.[20]

[We must not forget (and this is not one of my lesser observations on theatrical works) that if the Subject does not conform to the customs and feelings
of the Spectators, it will never succeed, no matter how much effort the Poet
puts towards it and no matter how many ornaments accompany it [...] We
do not want to believe that Kings can be cruel, nor can we stand to think that
their Subjects, although seemingly mistreated, could ever attempt anything
against their Sacred Person nor rebel against their Power. Not even would
this be acceptable in a painting; and I do not think that a Tyrant assassinated
on our stage would meet with approval, without very careful precautions.]

In this passage, d'Aubignac equates royal praise and tragic poetics. This
view testifies to how far theatrical customs have shifted since Hardy's in-
differently cruel king in *Scédase ou l'hospitalité violée* (circa 1615), since by
insisting on the imperative of showing the royal figure in a positive light,
d'Aubignac rules out all expectation of success if spectators cannot respond positively to the monarch onstage. The notion of *bienséance* takes
on a distinctly political hue as "precautions" must be taken to ensure that
the royal portraits presented to audiences "conform" to their "customs."
The notion that the affection of French subjects for their sovereign pre-
vents them from even imagining him capable of cruelty or of supposing
a rebellion could ever be justified is distilled into a new imperative of
tragic poetics.

Despite Corneille's modifications to his source text, in a climate where
critics sought to dilute negative royal portrayals, the Oedipus saga was
always going to be viewed by the post-1637 *doctes* as a terrible choice
for the French public. The playwright's intention of making a version
more palatable to his audiences backfires and is received as misguided
because of the futility of finding success in a theatrical representation
not grounded in a society's beliefs. Responding to Corneille's play,
d'Aubignac emphasizes the perilous unintended consequences of portraying a faulty sovereign:

Il me semble aussi que M. Corneille devait considérer qu'il mettait son
Œdipe sur le Théâtre français, et que ce n'est pas là qu'il faut manifester
les grands malheurs des familles Royales, quand ils sont mêlés d'actions
détestables et honteuses, et que les sujets se trouvent enveloppés dans le
châtiment que le Ciel impose à la Terre. A quoi bon faire voir au peuple,
que ces têtes couronnées ne sont pas à l'abri de la mauvaise fortune, que
les désordres de leur vie, quoique innocente, sont exposés à la rigueur des
puissances supérieures?[21]

[It also seems to me that Mr Corneille should have considered that he was putting his Œdipe on the French stage, and that it is not there that one should manifest the great misfortunes of Royal families when they are linked to dreadful and shameful actions, and that their subjects find themselves enveloped in the punishment that the Heavens impose on Earth. What is to be gained from showing the people that these crowned heads are not safe from misfortune, that the disorder of their lives, however innocent, exposes them to the rigour of superior powers?]

In this condemnatory passage of *Œdipe*, the societal perils posed by negative royal portrayals outweigh d'Aubignac's earlier concerns regarding the spectators' distaste for flawed monarchs. For the critic, *Œdipe* threatens France's political stability. He hones in on the upheavals that can accompany the "manifestation" of the monarch in the precarious position of experiencing "great misery." The risks are high since, according to d'Aubignac, such portrayals can lead spectators to question the very basis for divine-right monarchy and prompt them to reconsider the relation between monarchical errors in judgment and divine retribution. Far from performing a work of persuasion that will buttress the established social order, such presentations undermine the foundations of the French kingdom:

C'est donner [au peuple] sujet, quand il arrive quelque infortune publique, d'examiner toutes les actions de leurs Princes, de vouloir pénétrer dans les secrets de leur cabinet, de se rendre juges de tous leurs sentiments, et de leur imputer tous les maux qu'ils souffrent, et qui ne doivent être que la punition de leurs propres iniquités.[22]

[It means giving (the people) grounds, when any public misfortune occurs, to examine all the actions of their Princes, to want to penetrate the secrets of their cabinet, to make themselves judges of all their feelings, and to impute to them all the pain that they suffer, and which should only be seen as punishment for their own iniquities.]

With *Œdipe* comes a real fear that the "the people's" judgment will suddenly feel empowered to usurp the place of royal judgment, or that the audience will judge the judge. In voicing this concern, d'Aubignac's critique has left the domain of successful theatrical composition and entered into a discussion of the very real social turmoil the portrayal of a faulty sovereign onstage can provoke.

According to d'Aubignac, playwrights must embrace the greater project of preserving spectators' admiration for royalty. The first element of such an endeavour should be to eliminate portraits that could upset the public's confidence in royal judgments and lead to threatening reflections on royal power:

Il faut les [les spectateurs] entretenir dans cette pieuse croyance que les Rois sont toujours accompagnés d'une faveur particulière du ciel, qu'ils sont partout innocents, et que personne n'a droit de les estimer coupables [...] En France il n'y faut jamais joindre l'horreur des incidents, ni le crime des Princes malheureux: il y faut tant d'innocence quand on veut que nous y compatissions, que je conseillerais toujours à nos Poètes d'éviter ces sujets comme trop difficiles et presque toujours dangereux.[23]

[It is necessary to preserve their pious belief that Kings are always accompanied by a particular favour of the heavens, that they are always innocent and that no one has the right to deem them guilty ... In France one must never include the horror of incidents nor the crimes of unfortunate Princes: so much innocence is required when one hopes to inspire compassion that I would always advise our poets to stay away from such subjects as too difficult and almost always too dangerous.]

D'Aubignac cannot conceive of the Oedipus story except through the lens of how it will affect the monarchy of his century. Subjects must be chosen strategically to ensure that dramatic plots serve the greater purpose of social stability and monarchical glory, always reinforcing spectators' faith in royal preeminence. Theatre should serve as yet another locus for pro-monarchical praise.

Tellingly, the tone of respect d'Aubignac adopts when describing tragedy's prestigious role in promoting admiration for the king and compassion for royal struggles quickly turns to disparaging humour when he moves to the specifics of the Oedipus plot. His sense of alarm for French society gives way to a mockery of the comical aspects at the heart of the play as he reduces the tragic *Œdipe* to a farcical tale:

Qu'un père et une mère sur le trône, où l'on sait que la passion d'avoir un légitime héritier règne autant que l'ambition, aient eux-mêmes fait exposer un fils aux bêtes féroces, cela contredit tous les sentiments de la nature et de la raison. Mais quand il faut s'imaginer le fils d'un Roi courir à pied comme un gueux, sans aucun valet qui porte son bissac, et qui lui puisse donner son bonnet de nuit et ses pantoufles aux hostelleries, cela paraît plus propre à faire rire le petit bourgeois dans une farce qu'à plaire aux honnêtes gens dans une tragédie.[24]

[That a father and mother on the throne, where we know that the passion for having a legitimate heir reigns as much as does ambition, would have exposed their own son to ferocious beasts, surely contradicts all feelings of nature and reason. But when on top of that, we have to imagine the son of a King running on foot like a beggar, without a servant to carry his bags or hand him his night-cap and bedroom slippers at the inn, all that seems more likely to make the lowly bourgeois laugh at a farce than to please honest audiences in a tragedy.]

D'Aubignac refuses to consider the myth except in relation to the norms of seventeenth-century French society. Drawing on contemporary anxiety regarding Bourbon monarchical succession, a fear that only the birth of Louis XIV – *dieudonné* – had momentarily quelled, d'Aubignac's mockery of *Œdipe* demonstrates how a tragic premise, even one whose source is as respected as this one, can veer off into comedy when it does not match French royal customs. Much like the criticism Don Fernand in *Le Cid* received for being at once tyrannical in his illogical decisions and foolish like a court jester, d'Aubignac's reading distorts Œdipe into a comical character; the Theban prince's archetypal tragic action at the fated crossroads suddenly turns into a scene of parody wherein he becomes a lonely vagabond roaming the streets. Although the critic belonged to a milieu that wished to erect tragedy as a genre of unique gravity and prestige, on the one hand, he insists on its terrible perils for French society, and on the other, he is quick to belittle its plots and ridicule an author who has failed to deliver on the promise of distinction. The same critic who heralds tragedy as a vehicle to foster admiration for French princes also allows himself to laugh at and denigrate tragic royal characters.

In order to protect the unstable dignity of the sovereign onstage, playwrights must think in accordance with the habits of seventeenth-century royalty. If Louis XIV would not venture alone on the roads of his kingdom, Œdipe should not do so either. From this observation, playwrights seek to devise practical solutions to escaping the potential for comedy: Corneille limits the physical actions and exertions of royal characters. His *Sertorius* (1662) and *Suréna* (1674) reflect the strategy of depicting sovereign authority through forceful commands that involve little mobility from the sovereign figure; Sertorius is defined by his great speech and negotiations with Pompée, while *Suréna*'s king, Orode, distinguishes himself by his decisive command – a cold-blooded order to kill the eponymous hero who threatens his preeminence. These "men of authority," to use Corneille's term, conserve their aura of strength through the force of their speech, not their physical actions.[25] The same goes for Racine's depiction of Titus in *Bérénice* (1670) and Agamemnon in *Iphigénie* (1674) where the wait for the sovereign's momentous judgment, not his physical undertakings, underscores how the solution to the plot rides on his decisions. Too much emphasis on the royal body in action threatens to reveal the latent comedy beneath the tragic portrayal.

Racine, whose sovereigns have a fallible side, nonetheless understands how to protect the dignity of characters who are supposed to possess a divine quality. In *Iphigénie*, the playwright chooses never to show Calchas, the oracle-pronouncing priest, onstage. In the absence of a physical form, Racine manages to preserve Calchas's sacred dignity and menacing aura by confining him to the spectators' imagination. The playwright thus avoided having to call on an actor capable of reciting dialogue in a way that would satisfy the audience's high expectations of the elusive religious figure. How would he have found someone capable, in sum, of conveying oracular power? The wise decision not to place Calchas before the audience's eyes allowed Racine to avoid the comedic effect, or outright ridicule, that might have come with trying to stage the priest's physical appearance, described only in Ulysse's hypotyposis as, "l'œil farouche, l'air sombre et le poil hérissé, / Terrible et plein du dieu qui l'agitait sans doute"[26] [wild-eyed, with a somber air and bristling hairs, frightening and full of the god who moved him undoubtedly].

In contrast, many years later Voltaire suffered the consequences of failing to inspire respect for the divine because he opted to have the royal ghost in *Sémiramis* (1748) make an onstage arrival. Finding the stage too crowded by spectators' chairs, the actor playing the spectre was not able to proceed forward, so a stagehand shouted out: "Place à l'ombre!" [Make way for the ghost!], giving way instead to the audience's jeers and taunts.[27] Despite Voltaire's investment in exploring new forms of special effects for the theatre, his decision to stage the spectre revealed how easily an unanticipated event or reaction can make the tragic "ceremony" deviate into a comical action deprived of all solemnity.

3 Tragedy and the Everyday

La Mesnardière shares d'Aubignac's sensitivity towards the potential for tragedy to lose its seriousness and swerve into a territory of laughter and derision. In *La Poétique*, as he reflects on what should and should not appear onstage, the critic insists on eliminating objects with vulgar connotations, prone to provoking jeers. Specifically, he argues that in order to maintain a sense of tragic dignity, any apparatus of torture should be removed from the stage:

> On ne met point au Théâtre les épées, les gibets, les roues, le feu, ni les autres supplices dont on punit les criminels, à cause qu'il font horreur, et qu'il est très difficile d'imiter ces bourrelleries sans que la feinte en soit grossière, & par conséquent ridicule. Outre que l'infâme attirail de ces Punitions odieuses, et les gens qui les exécutent choquent par leur seule présence les yeux des personnes bien nées, et sont absolument indignes de la majesté de ce Poème.[28]

> [We do not place on the Stage swords, gallows, wheels, fire, nor the other modes of torture with which we punish criminals because they inspire horror, and it is very difficult to imitate such objects without the imitation being vulgar and therefore ridiculous. Other than the fact that the vile paraphernalia of these odious Punishments, and the people who execute them, shock by their simple presence the eyes of the well-born, they are absolutely unworthy of the majesty of this Poem.]

The "vile paraphernalia" is ill-suited to tragedy because it incites a range of negative emotional reactions in the spectators, none of which coincide with the sense of dignity and grandeur the genre should inspire. Much like Corneille's recognition that spectators would be "shocked" by Œdipe's terrible mutilation, La Mesnardière thinks that to simply view objects of torture onstage will inspire feelings of repulsion, antithetical to the genre. To make props out of crass means of inflicting pain, reduces the monarchy's tools of punishment even further to their material form: they become vulgar imitations of vulgar equipment, whereas royal judgment and punishment should belong to an elevated sphere. The will to rid tragedy of torture devices constitutes an attempt to detach theatrical scenes of judgment from quotidian contexts, especially in a period when the sight of noblemen executed on public squares was a familiar experience.[29]

Based on such critical precepts, literary historians have designated neoclassical tragedy as an emblem of French "high culture" and "high literature," defining the genre according to its distance from the everyday. Tragedy comes from a distant tradition; apart from some rare exceptions, it is set in a far-removed past, and presents characters of elevated status with lofty ambitions. Tragedy belongs to what Bakhtin describes as "a valorized past of beginnings and peak times [...] this past is distanced, finished and closed like a circle."[30] Such features lead to its differentiation from the comedic genre, set in a contemporary time frame with familiar protagonists of humble origins in its main roles. As Bakhtin explains, contemporaneity is seen as belonging to a lower order, antithetical to the prestige of the "classical forms" – the epic and the tragic.[31] In this view, contemporaneity equals crudeness and comedy, and where there is laughter, there can be no distance: "It is precisely laughter that destroys the epic, and in general destroys any hierarchical (distancing and valorized) distance."[32] To retain its ceremonial aspects, tragic royal judgment must be situated beyond the materiality of the instruments royal authorities resort to for obedience. Audiences must not think of Henri III hiding behind a curtain while his *bourreaux* torture a poor soul; instead, tragedy should compel audiences to admire the dignity of the divinely inspired justice of the royal judge.[33] This ideal, however, is persistently undermined by unexpected connections within tragedy to unflattering elements of royal justice which provoke comedy or vulgarity, despite efforts to cut the genre off from such inappropriate resonances.

In theory, *bienséance* is devised as a way to ensure the tragic ceremony can continue on unimpeded by awkward reactions that would derail the tragic formality intended by the playwright. In the same passage of *La Poétique* where La Mesnardière discusses the "vulgarity" of torture devices, he dwells on the related necessity of eliminating bloody spectacles from the stage, which are too appalling and distracting to audiences. He defines the new vein of tragedy developed in the 1630s against the "Tragedy of the Scaffolds" of the first quarter of the century known for its violence, graphic content, and recourse to props.

As we saw in Hardy's *Scédase ou l'hospitalité violée*, royal judgment in early seventeenth-century tragedy often took place in a formal trial setting with witnesses asked to testify and present proof in evidence of crime. While not going so far as to present scenes of torture and dismemberment common to the most violent "Tragedies of the Scaffolds," Hardy's tragedies reference the bodily suffering that comes from contemporary modes of royal punishment. In his *Mariamne* (circa 1615), for example,

the tyrant-sovereign, Hérode, escalates his threats against his eponymous
wife, whom he suspects has betrayed him, by listing the precise modes
of torture he will use against her. Hérode calls on two witnesses to testify
against Mariamne, but despite his assurances that they can speak freely,
when their answers counter his certainty of his wife's guilt, he calls on
guards to apply various modes of torture to the witnesses:

Prévôt, que de ce pas on le livre aux bourreaux;
Qu'ils recherchent parmi le fer, le feu, les eaux,
De quoi le tourmenter, le presser, le contraindre
A nous notifier ce qu'il a voulu feindre.   (Act III, vv. 1087–90)

[Officer, immediately give him over to the executioners;
That they search among irons, flames, and water,
For what they need to torment him, press him and force him
To tell us what he wanted to hide.]

The striking enumeration, first of the elements (iron, fire, water), and
then of the actions (torment, press, force) stresses Hérode's intent to literally crush the individual: it vividly and unnervingly evokes the arsenal
of torture available to the contemporary king to cause his subjects to suffer in ways horrifyingly recognizable to the audiences.[34] When Hérode
repeats his threats to a second witness whom he suspects has had an adulterous relationship with Mariamne, the audience is confronted again
with a disturbingly realistic portrait of royal brutality:

Possible que tantôt les gênes apprêtées
T'induiront à accepter mes offres rejetées.
Chargées de fers, trainez-le au creux d'une prison;
Que faute d'en vouloir tirer autre leçon
Faites (car je le veux) que mourir il se sente.   (Act III, vv.1183–7)

[It is possible that soon when the instruments of torture are applied
They will induce you to accept the offers you reject.
Burdened with irons, drag him to the corner of a cell;
That having failed to learn a lesson
Ensure (for I desire it) that he feels like he is dying.]

The king's command to drag a man in chains to his cell, and his call
for the *prévôt* – the royal prison officer – to torture him so extensively

that "he feels like he is dying" offers a frighteningly graphic portrait of just the sort La Mesnardière will seek to limit. By the mid-1630s, the *doctes* will call for tragic fictions to distance the king from the dirty work of the executioner. Even in Hérode's case, the threats of a corrupt and tyrannical ruler should transcend the practicalities of punishment in order to reside in a realm of abstract terror. Only abstraction can preserve the dignified aura that must be associated with sovereign commands.

This understanding leads playwrights to incorporate more *coups de théâtre* as a way of providing a jolt of excitement without the need to delve into the specifics of a brutal action. Tragic dramatists replace instruments of torture and bloody displays with implicit scenes of judgment: such measures provide a sense of danger and fear for the audience who is faced with the sovereign's overwhelming power, but eliminates the risk that the stage will devolve into a grotesque display of force. Auguste's surprising announcement of clemency at the close of Corneille's *Cinna*, or Roxane's "Sortez" (V.4, v. 1573) [Leave] in Racine's *Bajazet*, which reads as a chilling death sentence, as well as ominous scenes like the ones in Act II of *Britannicus* when the tyrannical Néron slips behind a curtain and announces to his victim, Junie: "Caché près de ces lieux, je vous verrai, Madame" (v. 679) [Hidden near here, I will see you, my lady]. Such eerily menacing verses attest to the turn away from the material tools of judgment towards an unsettling tone that highlights the dangerous potential of a supremely powerful judge.

Paradoxically, then, as French tragedy becomes explicitly theorized as political – that is, as dealing with matters of state and the portrayal of sovereignty, not as synonymous with miserable outcomes and the downfall of princes – overt allusions to the legal process and to the apparatus of justice, including prisons, executions, and scaffolds, disappear. Only comedy and tyrant drama, and the latter mostly in relation to martyr tragedies, continue to refer openly to the "paraphernalia" of the judicial process and its role in enforcing royal judgment.

Far from a fixed ceremony, the changing conventions, language, and imagery shaped a genre always in flux. Playwrights searched for sure ways of protecting their characters' dignity and standing, despite their awareness of the lack of a set formula. Even with the intense critical focus on dramatic imperatives, even in the period considered to be the noble genre's heyday, the partition between tragedy's idealized world and the world of the everyday proved thin. While in principle the *doctes* sought to separate and preserve "regular" tragedy from the supposedly inferior forms of comedy and tragicomedy, they simultaneously drew from their structures and dénouements, an enterprise especially evident in relation to royal judgment. Indeed, when we consider these genres together from the perspective of the king as judge, the porousness between them comes into focus. Tragedy and comedy overlap, offering intersecting scenes of judgment, and often turning a supposedly grave king into a comedic figure.

In becoming attuned to the corresponding difficulties of staging sovereignty within the purportedly contrasting genres, we gain a better sense of the challenges embodying legal authority posed for the theatre, *tout court*, not just for tragedy. To draw out the tensions that surround the royal judge in comedy and tragedy, the discussion will move now to consider two plays by Racine – a comedy, *Les Plaideurs* (1668) and a tragedy, *Britannicus* (1670) – in which the playwright addresses the problem of an illegitimate exercise of legal power in congruent ways. Certainly, the register for presenting the issue of judicial authority differs between the two works; however, they both accentuate the threat an improper embodiment of justice constitutes for the state. Furthermore, a juxtaposition of *Les Plaideurs* and *Britannicus* allows us to see how in writing his comedy and tragedy Racine combines tropes of judgment from both genres as part of his reflections on the exercise (political and theatrical) of justice.

4 Improper Performances of Judgment: Racine's *Les Plaideurs* and *Britannicus*

Eight years after Corneille published his proscription of royal judges from the stage in the "Examen de *Clitandre*," arguing that the "que comme juge" [only as judge] royal character projects insufficient éclat for the monarchical *dignité* [office], Jean Racine wrote a comedy, *Les Plaideurs* (1668) that satirizes French judicial culture.[35] The play focuses on an obsessive bourgeois magistrate, Monsieur Dandin, who is so wedded to his profession that he compulsively judges day and night. In order to remedy this destructive mania, his son organizes the trial of a dog accused of having stolen a rooster from the kitchen. Over the course of the legal inquisition held within Dandin's home, complete with witnesses and speeches by the defence and prosecution, the French judicial system and French conventions of theatrical royal judgment are ridiculed. The long-winded and pedantic speeches of lawyers, whose incompetence is surpassed only by the judge himself, follows a well-established tradition of poking fun at the predilection of most *plaideurs* for hearing themselves speak, not for defending their clients. But this demonstration of the vacuous rhetorical exercises that their speeches have become also alludes to the contrived nature of judgment scenes on the theatrical stage. By 1668 playwrights and critics alike condemn the recitation of set pieces of judicial eloquence that serve no greater purpose than to demonstrate a playwright's skill in versification and rhetoric, especially if they are included at the expense of bored audiences. Still early in his dramaturgical career, Racine engages in *Les Plaideurs* with the poetico-political questions of representing monarchical justice onstage. Through the lens of comedy he ridicules a magistrate who distorts the absolutist ideal of royal judgment. The playwright reflects on how a delegation of legal power necessarily alters and misrepresents the will of the absent king. On a metatheatrical level, he explores the question of representation: what separates a comedic royal judge from a tragic one onstage? And what is the relationship between these dramatic characters and the supposedly omnipotent and omnipresent contemporary royal judge – Louis XIV?

The comedy mocks a wide spectrum of French judicial customs: the slow legal process, arbitrary judgments, and pretentious judges and lawyers. Above all, the plot turns on the father/judge who has gone mad with the folly of compulsively handing out verdicts. Judge Dandin's farcically undignified behaviour, lamentable blindness, and shameful abuse of authority vividly assert how flawed his performance of justice is, despite his claims of authority. Dandin's every comment can be taken either as a dig by Racine towards the seventeenth-century legal context in which the aristocracy finds itself belittled by unseemly bourgeois judges, or as a way of poking fun at the traditional French tragic structure that opposes a sovereign-judge to a nobleman hero.[36] Given the sustained scorn the comedy shows towards the judicial process, it is no wonder Racine takes pains to insist that *Les Plaideurs* is a mere translation of Aristophanes's *Wasps*.[37]

Sounding like a tyrant who has lost all sense of proportion regarding the limits of his position, the blustery and prideful judge Dandin mocks the nobility's dependency on his decisions. He unreasonably asserts his superiority over the needy *marquis* who turns to him for help:

> Compare prix par prix
> Les étrennes d'un juge à celles d'un marquis:
> Attends que nous soyons à la fin de décembre.
> Qu'est-ce qu'un gentilhomme? Un pilier d'antichambre.

Combien en as-tu vu des plus huppés,
A souffler dans leurs doigts dans ma cour occupés,
Le manteau sur le nez, ou la main dans la poche,
Enfin pour se chauffer, venir tourner ma broche.[38]   (vv. 93–100)

[Compare cost to cost / The stockings of a judge to those of a marquis: / Just wait until we're at the end of December. / What is a gentleman? A pillar of antechambers. / How many have you seen among the most chic / Busy blowing into their hands in my court, / Their coat over their nose, or their hands in their pockets, / Who, finally, to stay warm, come turn my meat spit.]

Dandin alludes here to the precarious financial position of the impoverished seventeenth-century aristocracy, whose gloomy prospects often stemmed from failed lawsuits. The passage also evokes a typical tragic dynamic where a nobleman, in the position of supplicant, turns to the sovereign for protection. The comical image of the winter-battered *marquis* resorting to the judge's phallic "meat spit" to stay warm parodies the dominance the sovereigns of tragedy exert over noblemen in their court. At the close of Corneille's *Cinna ou la clémence d'Auguste*, for example, the conspirator-aristocrats are reduced to no more than "piliars of antechambers," forced to rely on the sovereign/judge Auguste to keep what remains of their noble flame burning.

Poking fun at tragedy's stilted respect for unity of place, Racine presents judge Dandin's son, Léandre, convincing his father not to leave their home and to rule instead within the walls of their basement where he hopes to keep the father/judge locked up:

Hé! Doucement,
Mon père. Il faut trouver quelque accommodement.
Si pour vous, sans juger, la vie est un supplice,
Si vous êtes pressé de rendre la justice,
Il ne faut point sortir pour cela de chez vous:
Exercez le talent et jugez parmi nous.   (vv. 601–6)

[Hey, not so fast, / My father. We must find a compromise. / If for you, without judging, life is a torment, / If you are in a hurry to render justice, / It isn't necessary for you to leave your home to do so: / Exert your skill and judge among us.]

In alluding to the judge's rush to render justice, Racine jabs at the artificiality of judgment scenes, as, for example, in Corneille's *Horace* (1641).

The elder playwright was criticized for his awkward adherence to the unity of place in the tragedy's fifth act when the Roman king, Tulle, implausibly arrives at the home of Vieil Horace. Tulle comes to congratulate the Horace family for the heroic son's military victory over the Alban fighters, but no sooner has the king done this than the celebratory royal visit turns into a trial of young Horace for the murder of his sister. In *Les Plaideurs*, Léandre's recommendation that his father stay put evokes the contrivance of a scene such as *Horace*'s. It mocks the swiftness with which sovereigns are "in a hurry to render justice" and pronounce verdicts that conform to the unities of time and place in order to bring the plot to an end. Moreover, in setting the basement where Dandin judges in Lower Normandy, Racine references a provincial world, far from the grandeur of Paris or the royal court, removed from the elevated spheres of tragic judgment and cut off from proximity to the legitimate sovereign in whose name justice should always be rendered.[39]

While the relationship between Corneille and Racine is often viewed through the prism of a rivalry, the playwrights engage with each other and reference earlier scenes in dialogue with their own. For example, when judge Dandin answers his son – "Ne raillons point ici de la magistrature: / Je ne veux point être un juge en peinture" (vv. 607–8) [Let us not poke fun at magistrates, / I do not wish to be only a painted judge] – he references a famous verse of Corneille's *Nicomède* (1651). In that tragedy, the eponymous hero and his beloved Laodice lament King Prusias's lack of authority over both the meddling Romans and his second wife, Nicomède's cruel step-mother. In verses renowned for their audacious flair, Laodice states:

> Puisque le Roi veut bien n'être Roi qu'en peinture,
> Que lui doit importer qui donne ici la loi.
> Et qui règne pour lui, des Romains, ou de moi?   (vv. 1736–8)

> [Since the king is willing to be no more than a painted king, / What does it matter to him who makes law here? / And who reigns in his name, be it the Romans or I?]

The "painted king" fails because he cannot impose his law and thereby command his kingdom. The passage underscores the difference between being the law – actually possessing power – and delegating law, i.e., *posing* as a sovereign but doing so only so long as that performance goes unchallenged. In *Nicomède* and *Les Plaideurs*, ineffective judgment comes to the fore, whether in the person of a king who delegates his power to a Roman ambassador, himself a delegate of the Roman emperor whose authority he represents, or in the father/judge's impersonation of a king who is seemingly no more present in Normandy than in a painting. Both plays ask how sovereignty can be imposed from a distance, and how to differentiate between the source of authority and the mouthpiece for that source.

In theatrical terms, the "painted judge" and the "painted king" pinpoint the difficulty of conveying a prestigious dignity through appearance and gesture. By the time Antoine Furetière publishes the first edition of the *Dictionnaire Universel* in 1690, a "roi en peinture," is an attested expression: "On dit aussi qu'un roi n'est roi qu'en peinture, lorsqu'il ne gouverne pas son Etat par lui-même. Lorsqu'il en laisse à d'autres le soin et l'autorité"[40] [We also say that a king is only a painted king when he does not govern his State himself. When he leaves its care and authority to others.] The painted kings and judges of comedy and tragedy are defined by their poor imitation of a distinguished role; they reveal themselves incapable of fitting the bill, so to speak, and therefore come up short in their performance of sovereignty in analogous ways.

Les Plaideurs highlights the discrepancy between the ideal of royal justice propagated in encomiastic monarchical narratives of the period and the reality of a flawed system overseen by incompetent judicial actors. Richelieu, and later Colbert's, determination to transform the French judicial system led them to limit the power of local authorities detached from the Crown, especially in regions distant from the royal court.[41] The comedic basis of *Les Plaideurs* lies in the distance separating Dandin's justice from Louis XIV's. Yet, the inadequacies of the wayward father and harsh judge from Normandy make the Crown vulnerable because of the deformed version of justice performed in the king's name, just as the conduct of Racine's tyrants in the tragic genre threatens the foundations of the state.

The parody of justice in *Les Plaideurs* is not, therefore, just an inverse portrait of the historical king's justice, a negative portrayal meant to highlight the glory of Louis XIV's judgment. Instead, by staging Dandin's hopelessly failed mediation of monarchical justice, *Les Plaideurs* wrestles with the shared political and theatrical challenges of embodying an absent sovereignty. If the king is truly exceptional, how can he ensure that when he delegates his power to his representatives they will live up to his standards? If the symbols, vocabulary, and images of royal justice can be misappropriated, how can the king ensure their control and limit their meaning? In short, how can the Crown safeguard against judges like Dandin who make a mockery of royal legal authority?

The brutal and uncouth judge of comedy, humiliator of the *marquis* who are hostage to his judgments, looks like a parody of Néron, the tyrant at the centre of *Britannicus*, a tragedy which Racine wrote only a few months after *Les Plaideurs*. In understanding the proximity of Racine's comedy – including his satire of justice – to his tragedy, we see that the long-held assumptions about the high genre's inherent superiority and its airtight register of dignity fades as the loftiness of its characters becomes more a matter of context than content. In their shared mania of judgment and their loss of limits grounding their relationship to the law, Dandin and Néron are theatrical royal judge cousins, both ridiculous and tragic in their perversion of justice.

Over the course of four scenes of Act II in *Britannicus*, Néron confronts his captive, Junie, in a scene of judgment. Without calling on explicit objects of torture, the confrontation between the innocent Junie and the perverse commands of the emperor provoke a chilling sense of dread in the young woman, as well as in Racine's spectators. Forced to stand before him like a criminal, the innocent woman's trial seems as absurd as trying a dog for stealing a rooster from the kitchen. Junie is unaware of her crimes and yet feels acutely the threat of punishment hanging over her:

> Et quel autre, Seigneur, voulez-vous que j'implore?
> A qui demanderai-je un crime que j'ignore?
> Vous qui le punissez, vous ne l'ignorez pas.
> De grâce, apprenez-moi, Seigneur, mes attentats.   (II.3.vv. 535–8)

> [And who else, my Lord, would you want me to implore?
> To whom will I ask about a crime of which I am ignorant?
> You who punish it, you must not be ignorant of it.
> I beg of you, tell me, my Lord, what crimes I have committed.]

Junie's desperate questioning of her "Lord," the judge, master of her fate, signals the volatile and quasi-ludicrous situation of being called before the emperor in judgment. Néron, like Dandin, orchestrates a senseless prosecution as part of a judicial process that obeys neither limits nor reason. Junie expresses bewilderment at the situation in which she finds herself: "Seigneur, avec raison je demeure étonnée. / Je me vois, dans le cours d'une même journée / Comme une criminelle amenée en ces lieux" (vv. 603–5) [My lord, with good reason I remain stunned. / I find myself, over the course of the same day, / Like a criminal brought here]. Racine takes to farcical extremes the inability of the accused to understand the prosecution, much less the verdict, making the tragic Junie resemble in this respect Citron the dog in *Les Plaideurs*, although this time the dynamic of the obsessive judge is played out on a pathetic register because the life of a noblewoman is at stake.

In the sort of repetition usually reserved for comical effect, Junie will be forced to duplicate Néron's cruelty. Just as the emperor refused to disclose his reasons for arresting her, she cannot reveal to her lover why she is cold and distant towards him. Her encounter with Britannicus, a torture scene which we should place in the tradition of early French tragedy, constitutes the structural centre of the plot. As Néron disappears behind the curtain, he transfers to Junie the command to pronounce the "arrêt si sévère" (v. 675) [the so severe ruling] he has decreed. She must break the young man's heart by telling him she no longer loves him. The cruelty she displays is not simply an effect of Racine's preference for the psychological jousting of his characters, but a portrayal of the brutality inherent in the judicial process. In the realm of comedy, the problem of delegation resided in the king's inability to know, or control, how inept judges misappropriate his authority in distant parts of the kingdom; in *Britannicus* the absolutist model of royal all-knowingness becomes the driving force behind the sovereign's perversion and abusive control, as exemplified by Néron's vicious surveillance: "Caché près de ces lieux, je vous verrai, Madame" (v. 679) [Hidden near here, I will see you, my lady].

Les Plaideurs and *Britannicus*'s portrayals of judgment stem from a corresponding travesty of a monarchical ideal by characters supposed to represent (first, in the sense of displaying, and second, in the sense of acting in the name of) legitimate legal authority. In contrast to the absurd inefficiency of the comical judge Dandin, Néron's judgment appears frighteningly ingenious because of its exceedingly personalized and targeted basis. Earlier in the play, Néron had articulated his plan for judicial delegation in these terms: "Je ne veux point le [Britannicus] perdre. Il vaut mieux que lui-même / Entende son arrêt de la bouche qu'il aime" (vv. 667–8) [I don't want to be the one to kill him. It is best that he hear the verdict himself / from a mouth that he loves]. The emphasis on Junie's "mouth," as opposed to Junie herself, accentuates her role as a mouthpiece for conveying Néron's words and judgment, much as Dandin was a mouthpiece unfit to represent royal justice. The act of ventriloquism performed by a pure maiden who utters the lines given to her by Néron, whose very name symbolizes moral decadence, sketches a fine line between the horror of such an act of delegation and its comedic potential.

That Junie must articulate Néron's command ("take upon yourself the offence," v. 669) underscores the bizarre relationship wherein she who is so averse to Néron's immoral behaviour becomes an extension of the emperor's will. Evoking the celebratory occasions of comedies such as *Tartuffe* or *L'Impromptu de Versailles* when the royal *émissaire* speaks in the king's name to reveal good news and save the day at the play's end, Junie becomes the king's messenger. But in this case, the delegated announcement sets in motion the tragic outcome that will lead to her lover's death. This time, rather than proclaim the sovereign's message, she must hide her role as his emissary. Racine has taken a convention of comedy – that the king must be absent from the stage and represented through delegation – and turned it into a means of reinforcing the appalling perversity of the sovereign in *Britannicus*.

Furthermore, not only does the chilling portrait of Néron making Junie his messenger distort a comedic convention that leads to happy dénouements, it also warps the royal closeness exemplified by the archetype of virtuous royal judgment – Saint Louis under his old oak tree.[42] The Roman tyrant's proximity to those he judges is not the result of an open-air meeting under a protective tree, but the consequence of the asphyxiating constraints of a corrupt royal court. If Junie is close to Néron it is because he ordered her late-night arrest and now holds her captive. Saint Louis's subjects revelled in the possibility of being able to touch their king, whereas Néron's victims recoil in fear from his lascivious touch. Both Néron and judge Dandin simulate the words, gestures, and practices of seventeenth-century legitimate judgment, but their wayward application of the judicial model results in a perversion of the ideal it should embody.

Racine accentuates the dangers of imitation through Néron, who up until the play's end feigns love for those he hates the most, pretending to embrace Britannicus and his mother, Agrippine, just as he prepares to murder them. The father/judge Dandin, as we have seen, has gone mad endlessly repeating the gestures and pronouncements of justice without care for actually upholding the legal authority on which social order rests. Both men perform justice in such a way that all that remains of the law are its gestures and words – nothing but its outward appearance. They replicate the motions of royal judgment, but the act of copying, rather than in fact being a legitimate judge, pinpoints the artificiality of their performance and devolves into either comedy or tyranny.

Ultimately, the comedic father/judge and the tragic tyrant are similarly defeated by their powerlessness to bring about the judgments they have decreed. Dandin remains prisoner to his mania of judging, which despite the play's happy ending continues to obsess him, as the last words of the play reveal, "Allons nous délasser à voir d'autres procès" (v. 910) [Let's go unwind by watching more trials]. For Dandin, judicial ceremonies remain a source of entertainment, a pastime, just as a judgment scene on the theatrical stage amuses spectators. *Les Plaideurs* highlights the danger of a judge who only pronounces verdicts out of a love of ruling and is detached from the only legitimate source of justice – the king. Meanwhile, despite Néron's decision to kill Britannicus and possess Junie, she escapes him by entering the Vestal temple:

Le seul nom de Junie échappe de sa bouche.
Il marche sans dessein, ses yeux mal assurés
N'osent lever au Ciel leurs regards égarés.   (vv. 1776–8)

[Only Junie's name escapes from his mouth. / He walks without aim, his eyes uncertain / Do not dare raise up to the Heavens their disoriented gaze.]

The emperor's trial of Junie and condemnation of Britannicus results in the escape of the person he most wants to dominate. Incapable of upholding a model of blind justice, his injustice has left him blinded. Both the sovereign who had dictated such harsh judgments and the obsessive comedic judge have become irreversibly "*égarés*" [adrift].

Dandin and Néron's distortions of judgment are acceptable onstage because they can be attributed to either the comic domain, defined by exaggeration, or enclosed within the vein of tyrant drama, dependent on egregious behaviour. One can either see Néron at the close of *Britannicus* as fully entering into the frightening tyranny he is known for, or else as devolving into folly, giving in to a comical mania in which he only repeats Junie's name, much like Dandin can only repeat the same judgments over and over. Far from a triumphant ceremony that ends with the redemption of a royal figure who had been under the threat of his passions, the tragic sovereign character disintegrates into a comedic version of himself. Although the authors of tragic poetics of this period painstakingly erected barriers to separate "high" works from their "low" counterparts, guarding the tragic label as a means of promoting

royalty and monarchical narratives, upon closer analysis even a canonical French tragedy such as *Britannicus* shares a strong proximity to a
comedy based in Lower Normandy. The historical-cultural contexts presented within *Les Plaideurs* and *Britannicus* differ, as do the expectations
surrounding how the audience will receive the characters. Yet, Dandin
and Néron overlap in fundamental ways in their alarming distortion of
a contemporary monarchical ideal of justice, thereby revealing how the
performance of justice is so readily usurped and so prompt to become a
caricature of itself.

Having examined how Racine enters into an implicit dialogue about
the performance of justice across the genres of comedy and tragedy, we
will turn now to the royal judge's changing face in Corneille's theatre. In
contrast to his younger rival, Corneille's corpus spans a wider time frame
since he begins his career before the preservation of royal dignity became
a high-stakes endeavour. Following the author of *Le Cid* from his early
career to a gradual awareness of the new politico-poetic expectations,
enables us to perceive how he comes to terms with these demands, nego-
tiating between his preference for dramatic surprise and the emphasis
on politically flattering depictions of royalty. The political Corneille that
has stood for so long in opposition to the tender Racine turns out to be
similarly engaged in a cross-genre conversation, trying out different formulas and drawing heavily from the comedic tradition to invest his royal
judges with an indispensable, but always fleeting, authority.

Chapter Four

Learning from Experience:
On Corneille and Coherence

Whereas tragedy ends with a decision – however uncertain this may be – there resides in the essence of the *Trauerspiel*, and especially in the death-scene, an appeal of the kind which martyrs utter.

> Walter Benjamin, *The Origin of German Tragic Drama*[1]

1 *Clitandre ou l'innocence délivrée*

In tracing the entanglement between political theories of royal judgment, tragic poetics, and seventeenth-century theatre, we may begin to grasp how the royal trial scene, far from being a static convention or a simple reproduction of monarchical ideals, is continually reinvented by French playwrights. Scholars of the seventeenth century have too easily assumed that tragedy's sovereigns are figures for absolutist order, the unified and all-powerful entities we imagine Louis XIV to have been.[2] As I hope the analysis of the correspondences between tragic and comedic portrayals has revealed, sovereigns of serious drama are never immune to the intrusion of comical tropes into the tragic register. The potential for overflow from one genre to another undoubtedly shaped how playwrights imagined the behaviour and actions of their monarchical characters.

The focus returns now to Pierre Corneille in an exploration of the playwright's uncertain and uneven fashioning of theatrical kings. The playwright's long-held reputation for being the most nuanced political thinker among the French tragedians and his lengthy theatrical career make him an ideal subject for tracing the vivid changes his royal characters undergo. The exploration of his corpus will draw out the lessons he

learns as he moves from play to play in a piecemeal search for a successful tragic formula, pleasing to spectators and critics.

A commonplace of Cornelian studies consists in distinguishing
between a pre- and a post-*Le Cid* Corneille. The consensus seems to be
that the playwright's earlier works have little to do with the great *œuvres*
that follow. The gist of such a stance is that only with his Spanish play
does the playwright adopt the Cornelian "ethos" as an aesthetic-political
framework unique to him which cements his status as the literary genius
generations of French students have known and loved.[3] Reading Corneille through the grid of the "*éthique du héros cornélien*," stresses the consistency and homogeneity of the playwright's theatrical vision and has
determined for decades how spectators and readers have encountered
his works.[4] In contrast, when we follow the transformations of kings in
the act of judgment from play to play, we are able to debunk the notion
that the playwright steadily applied a coherent concept of power or heroism in his theatre. He was, rather, constantly shifting in his presentations, seeking out new ways of refining his plots and characters to satisfy
the changing demands of critics, spectators, and potential patrons, while
hoping not to alienate monarchical authorities.

Certainly, *Clitandre* (1631) differs from the more "regular" tragedies
that follow, for, as Corneille freely admits in *Clitandre*'s "Examen" (1660)
of the three unities, only the twenty-four hours of action are respected.[5]
Moreover, whereas the specificity of the historical settings in *Le Cid* and
Horace – Spain and Rome, respectively – define those plots and characters, in *Clitandre*, Corneille accentuates the ahistorical, that is, imaginary, premise for his play: "Ma scène est donc en un château d'un roi,
proche d'une forêt; je n'en determine ni la province ni le royaume; où
vous l'aurez une fois placée, elle s'y tiendra"[6] [My scene is therefore in
the castle of a king, near a forest; I designate neither the province nor
the kingdom; where you will have placed it once, that is where it will
remain]. This fictional emphasis explains, perhaps, the scholarly reluctance to read *Clitandre* alongside Corneille's later works, but it also demonstrates how profoundly the terms of poetic discussion differed only
a few years before the quarrel of *Le Cid*.[7] Corneille's tongue-in-cheek
comment that the king will be where the spectator/reader decides to
place him, confirms the levity with which he considers such questions
of setting and reveals his overall attitude of jest in his critical analysis
of the play. Yet, as early as *Clitandre*, Corneille stages a king rendering a
legal decision: the royal judge evaluates the guilt of a nobleman, restores
order, and closes the play.

Recognizing the similarities between *Clitandre, Le Cid, Horace,* and *Cinna*'s structures and plot confirms Walter Benjamin's theory that minor authors – or, in this case, minor works – more readily reveal the intricacies of a genre's form.[8] With regards to royal representations, *Clitandre* makes explicit the phenomenon that critics will most vocally reproach Corneille for in *Le Cid*: the king's silly antics. *Clitandre* lays bare how the king can serve a predominantly structural role, i.e., he has the authority to make a judgment that determines the fate of all the characters onstage and ends the play.[9] That he is situated outside of history, bears an ostentatiously fictional name (Alcandre), appears onstage only twice over the course of the play, and then merely to pardon or condemn, confirms the king's status as a *rex ex machina* – a sovereign who arrives *in extremis* to resolve the dramatic conflict.[10] The king's marginal presence throughout the majority of the plot generates a degree of humour, especially as he tries to rule on matters he does not understand, to the point that it is not inconceivable that Corneille intended for these elements to be received as downright comical. In a plot line that echoes ancient recognition plays, as well as tragicomedy's fondness for surprise, all evidence of crime falsely points to one culprit until an incredible turn of circumstances reveals the actual guilt of another. The spectators, themselves in the know, watch as *Clitandre*'s king, far from being an all-seeing monarch, relies on faulty reasoning and circumstantial evidence – a letter supposedly written by Clitandre and the presence of Clitandre's servants – to erroneously convict the nobleman. The king undermines his own royal dignity all the more so since his mistaken verdict is accompanied by claims that he owes the public "l'exemplaire justice" (v. 798) [exemplary justice], all the while demonstrating an inexplicable brashness and refusal to listen to the nobleman Clitandre's pleas for clemency. It is only once the actual events have been sorted out, which happens not by the king's doing but through a combination of astonishingly improbable events, that "l'innocence [est] delivrée" [innocence is freed] as the subtitle to the play announces.[11] Then, the king – "honteux" (v. 1721) [ashamed] and with "une âme confuse" (v. 1721) [an embarrassed soul] – admits he was fooled by appearances.

The play's final scene brushes aside what could be troubling questions surrounding royal injustice and the king's failed judgment. In providing the tragicomedy with the necessary closing reconciliation, Corneille's monarchical figure loses all semblance of gravitas. At its initial staging in 1631, the balance was still in favour of tying up the play's loose ends; by 1660, when Corneille writes the "Examen," the balance has tipped the other way, towards a political shielding of royal characters, and preserving the royal image has become the primary concern.[12]

Neither the humiliation of the nobleman-hero, whom the audience saw lament his unjust incarceration from within his onstage prison, nor the issue of royal responsibility for misjudgment are explicitly broached at the dénouement. Instead, *Clitandre* embraces a novella fantasy of marriage for all the characters that remain. The king blithely admits to the challenges inherent to judging: "Qu'il est peu de lumière en nos entendements, / Et que d'incertitude en mes raisonnements! (vv. 1709–10) [There is little light in our understanding / and so much uncertainty in my reasoning]. He yearns to erase the memory of his error and orders his wrongly accused subject to forget the past: "Perds-en le souvenir" (v. 1725) [Forget it ever happened] and "Ne nous arrêtons plus sur la reconnaissance / Et de mon injustice, et de son innocence" (vv. 1741–2) [Let us not dwell on the recognition / Of both my injustice and his innocence]. The king's surprising readiness to move on, here explained by the apolitical and scarcely plausible universe of tragicomedy, will be repeated in *Le Cid*, but in that play it becomes an infamous instance of shocking royal behaviour because Rodrigue's military service ratchets up the plot's political setting and increases the sense that by eagerly calling for Chimène to "essuyer [ses] larmes" (v. 1821) [dry her tears], Don Fernand is coercing her into forgetting her father because of his own political debt to Rodrigue.

To consider the closing scenes of *Clitandre* and *Le Cid* in parallel enables us to place Don Fernand's concluding judgment of Rodrigue's innocence and an impending marriage in perspective since the dénouement of Corneille's most famous play repeats almost exactly the final reconciliation scene of *Clitandre*. In the earlier play, the king's decision to unite the young couples – Rosidor will marry Clarise and Clitandre will marry Doriste, despite the lack of affection between the last pair and their avowed love for other people – reads like a light-hearted and optimistic act of paternal pride, rather than a tyrannical and illogical stance, as critics will deem Fernand's uniting of Chimène and Rodrigue to be. *Clitandre* stages a comedic ending with no other design than to wash away remaining tensions from the plot. Certainly, the royal decision feels like wishful thinking, especially since the audience has witnessed false imprisonment and attempted rapes and murders, but above all the closing scene evokes the standard paternal confidence conventional of the genre, and therefore elicits spectator willingness to accept such a far-fetched reconciliation.[13]

Beyond the light-heartedness intrinsic to tragicomedy, deficiencies in the plot's structure cast the king in a comical role. We encounter a distinct sense of monarchical clowning when it comes to the royal judgment of Pymante, the man guilty of murder and rape. Rather than articulate a forceful punishment himself, the king entrusts the aristocrat's fate to his royal council: "Dites à mon conseil que pour le châtiment / J'en laisse à ses avis le libre jugement; / Mais qu'après son arrêt je saurai reconnaître / L'amour que vers son Prince il aura fait paraître" (vv. 1779–2) [Tell my council that for the punishment / I leave them free to judge; / but that according to their decision I will know / how much love they have shown to their Prince]. The odd delegation of the royal decision avoids a structurally awkward dramatic repetition since the king had already pronounced a strong judgment earlier, in Act III, when he mistakenly condemned Clitandre. In the initial misguided passionate verdict, the king insisted on the personal offence the crime represented:

> Aussi n'est-ce qu'à moi de punir ces forfaits
> Et de montrer à tous par de puissants effets
> Qu'attaquer Rosidor c'est se prendre à moi-même:
> Tant je veux que chacun respecte ce que j'aime!
> Je le ferai bien voir.   (vv. 791–5)

[Indeed, it is only up to me to punish these crimes. / And to show all by these powerful effects / that to attack Rosidor is to attack me: / so much do I want everyone to respect what I love! / I will make it known.]

A second staging of a royal condemnation would have turned the king into a tiresome, farcical figure of endless impassioned judgments. From *Clitandre*, Corneille will learn to better measure the weight of the royal verdict within the dramatic plot in order to more subtly turn to a judgment to generate maximum excitement and suspense from the theatricality of its announcement. In *Clitandre*'s case, when the king entrusts the final decision about Pymante's future to another judicial body, he appears inconsequential – reduced to celebrating marriages – and so fails to uphold the dignity of his royal position.

The royal council in *Clitandre*, a behind-the-scenes legal entity to which the king turns to execute his justice, confirms that despite the common assumption that "le théâtre cornélien rejette toute pratique consultative" [Cornelian theatre rejects all consultative practices], in the playwright's tragicomedy the *conseil* does not necessarily entail a corrupt manipulation of royal justice.[14] In alluding to a secondary judicial body, the playwright drew on a contemporary authority, a legitimate entity to which the king could turn to delegate his decisions. During the reigns of Henri IV, Louis XIII, and the early years of Louis XIV's rule there was a supreme *Conseil* – known as "*le Conseil de Cabinet*" which constituted the king's inner circle and advised him on the most crucial political matters. Beginning in 1629, Louis XIII openly referred to Richelieu as "le Principal Ministre de nos Conseils d'Etat" [the Principle Minister of our Royal Council].[15] Accordingly, in *Clitandre* we do not yet see the suspicion and political cynicism surrounding the *Conseil*'s ability to carry out royal decisions; we only see its theatrical limitations. This absent body, an indistinct appendage to royal power, lessens the weight of the king's judgment and his unique position to judge, which therefore diminishes the spectacular effects associated with that distinctiveness. Corneille will soon choose to present royal ministers and councils as untrustworthy, most notably in *Cinna* and *La Mort de Pompée*. This shift away from royal councils places the power of judgment back in the hands of the sovereign and makes him alone bear the responsibility for deciding wisely. In separating the king from the faulty advice of advisors, the relationship between the sovereign and his ministers becomes suspenseful, creating tension surrounding his response to them.

In looking back at *Clitandre* nearly three decades after its initial publication, Corneille was keenly aware of the feeble demeanour of his sovereign judge. In response, as we have seen, in the play's "Examen" he goes so far as to introduce a rule forbidding the depiction of the king solely as judge:

> Le roi et le prince son fils paraissent [dans *Clitandre*] dans un emploi fort en-dessous de leur Dignité: l'un n'y est que comme juge, et l'autre comme confident de son favori. Ce défaut n'a pas accoutumé de passer pour défaut: aussi n'est-ce qu'un sentiment particulier dont je me fais une Règle, qui peut-être ne semblera pas déraisonnable, bien que nouvelle.[16]

> [The king and his son the prince appear (in Clitandre) in a role far beneath their Dignity: one is there only as a judge, and the other as the confidant of his favourite. This defect is not customarily identified as a defect: therefore it is only from a personal feeling that I make this a Rule for myself, which might not seem unreasonable despite its newness.]

By 1660, the playwright recognized the need to reconcile plot dynamics and cultural expectations surrounding the royal role. The Corneille of the second half of the seventeenth century can clearly articulate that being *only* a judge or *only* a confidant fails to maintain the prestige of a royal character who must be more than a peripheral presence. But even in 1637 when Corneille embarks on his next tragicomedy, he has already grasped that he must deliver a more prestigious royal role and create more tension surrounding the monarch's actions. The model generated by *Clitandre*'s mediocre king explains the enigmatic character of Don Fernand. The Spanish king will play a more important and politically active part within *Le Cid*'s plot, but his profile still closely resembles Alcandre's. From Fernand's comedic aspects, to which Corneille's critics proved so sensitive, to his role within the dramatic structure in which the dénouement by royal judgment brings about a troubling and oddly contrived happy ending, the playwright's most famous work is in many ways but a fine-tuning of an imperfect dramatic formula.

2 The *Médée* Interlude

In between Corneille's tragicomedies of dénouement by royal judgment, the playwright tried his hand at composing a tragedy for the first time, settling on what many have deemed to be the surprising choice of *Médée* (1635). In fact, close attention to the first work the playwright labelled a tragedy confirms the influence early seventeenth-century models of the tragic genre had on him: he picks a subject associated with a dire ending, monstrous spectacles, and criminal behaviour. Elsewhere I have argued that from his first tragic endeavour Corneille's tragic vision rests on a heroic transgression of law, a theme he will perpetuate in many of his tragedies including *Horace, Cinna, Rodogune,* and *Nicomède.*[17] Through *Médée*, we encounter a Corneille writing prior to the *doctes*' calls for demonstrations of a virtuous king punishing crime onstage. The very grandeur of the playwright's first tragic heroine lies in her powerful criminality, which makes her so blatantly superior in strength and courage to her treacherous husband, Jason, and to the powerless king, Créon, whose marginality, blindness, and inconsistent character resembles both Alcandre's from *Clitandre* and Don Fernand's from *Le Cid*.

In contrast to important readings by Michèle Longino and Mitchell Greenberg who view the "witch of Colchis" as the ultimate outsider, the Oriental Other and diabolical female who threatens French classical order, my understanding of Médée is closer to Christopher Braider's.[18] He sees her as a source of dramatic inspiration for Corneille – a "muse" – whose energy, resistance, and self-assurance are at once a reflection of the playwright's ethos and a prototype for his female characters to come. I wish to go one step farther, however, and suggest that Médée offers a mould not only for Corneille's heroines, but also for his sovereigns in particular.

Médée's infanticide, as appalling as it may seem, constitutes a violent response accomplished in the name of an ideal. Like many of the noblemen executed on Richelieu's scaffolds, Médée perpetuates a crime in opposition to the lowly politics and pathetic figures of monarchical authority who have declared themselves her judges. To understand why seventeenth-century audiences could have admired a character as guilty as Médée, we must place her in the context of aristocratic resistance to what they saw as the illegitimate judgments and public executions ordered by the king's minister. Certainly, as Corneille states, his portrait of the witch of Colchis is that of "le crime en son char de triomphe," [crime on its chariot of triumph] but at this early juncture in his career, he saw such conquering heroism as a means of commanding the public's respect for his main character.[19]

The playwright establishes a clear-cut contrast between Médée's dignity versus Jason and Créon's mediocrity. Jason is an unfaithful husband, a man of "accommodement" (v. 28) [compromise], "maxime d'Etat" (v. 28) [maxims of State] and "âme légère" (v. 134) [flighty soul].[20] He incarnates cowardice, an insult Médée will proffer repeatedly and that will always remain contrary to Corneille's sense of heroic grandeur. As for the royal character, Créon is aligned with Jason and cast from the same mould as the feeble kings of tragicomedy: he fails to exert authority over his subjects. King Créon's preoccupations lie with finding a husband for his daughter since his role consists mostly of siding with Jason over Médée – a decision that will lead to his death, as well as his daughter's. He is never the eponymous heroine's worthy adversary or a legitimate authority. Créon's volatile judgments enable Jason to abandon Médée, but since the king continues to change his mind regarding what to do with her, his character proves incapable of generating admiration. He promises first to protect Jason and Médée; then he chooses to defend only Jason, agreeing to return Médée to King Acaste, who is in search of the guilty couple. Créon finally withdraws from that position as well, deciding to simply banish the dangerous woman. Faced with another decision of importance – the choice between Jason or King Ægée as a husband for his daughter – he again judges erroneously, favouring Jason and thereby denigrating his own royal status by disrespecting a fellow prince, the king of Athens no less.

Faced with an inconsequential monarch, Médée becomes the justice figure of the play who condemns him to die with the verdict that she will "l'ensevelir dessous sa propre cendre" (v. 265) [bury him beneath his own ashes]. In short, Corneille's first tragedy embraces the spectacle of vengeance and dire dénouements, with little concern for the dignity of royal characters. By the end of the play, Médée has accomplished a one-woman *fronde*; having rejected her status as the accused, she takes on instead the role of judge, prosecutor, and executioner of her adversaries: she triumphantly rises above all the other characters in the plot.

Three decades later, in the analysis he offers of the tragedy, Corneille expresses particular regret for his failure to present the royal character in a more dignified light. His critique stems from an awareness of theatrical *bienséance* and a recognition that the stage must display a more general respect for the royal character. He deems that no one in *Médée* shows enough deference towards the king: "Ægée étant dans la cour de Créon, ne parle point du tout de le voir"[21] [Ægée although in Créon's court does not even speak of seeing him]. He faults Euripides and Seneca (whom he has followed in this regard) for having made the kings speak in a public place in the name of unity of location, rather than in the more dignified settings of the court or royal cabinet. Finally, echoing d'Aubignac's assessment of *Œdipe*, Corneille notes that, all things considered, it would be inconceivable for Médée to publicly announce her intention of killing Créon before a chorus of fifteen Corinthian women, "sans qu'aucune d'elles ait la moindre pensée d'en donner avis à ce prince"[22] [without any one of them having the idea of warning the prince]. He explains that he presented Ægée as in love with Créuse, "pour donner un peu plus d'intérêt à ce monarque dans l'action de cette tragédie"[23] [to produce a little more interest in this monarch in the action of this tragedy], but he reproaches himself for having staged the imprisonment of this same king. He admits: "la prison où je mets Ægée est un spectacle désagréable, que je conseillerais d'éviter"[24] [the prison where I place Ægée is an unpleasant spectacle, that I would advise one to avoid]. Thus, reading *Médée* in light of Corneille's subsequent critical review of his own work, allows us to gauge how greatly his concern for the royal figure has grown over the course of time. So much of the playwright's analysis of his first tragedy in the "Examen" written twenty-five years later is dedicated to explaining why he portrayed the king as he did, and how his understanding of royal portrayals has changed since he began writing tragedies.

With the hindsight of his theatrical experience and an increased understanding of the political-poetic emphasis placed on showcasing the king's superiority, Corneille adopts a position contrary to his early mind-set. While the playwright will never go so far as to fashion wholly idealized images and scenarios of royal justice exactly in line with those promoted by La Mesnardière or d'Aubignac, Corneille does become sensitive to the particular demands of royal portrayals in the genre. In *Médée's* "Examen," the playwright admits that Créon and Créuse's lamentions at the play's end "importunent plus par leurs cris et par leurs gémissements qu'il ne font pitié par leur malheur"[25] [bother more by their shouts and wails than they cause pity for their misfortune]; such cries therefore neither provoke compassion nor stir the interest of the spectators. He realizes that when those who should represent order and stability lack the dignity of their office, they appear insignificant, especially in comparison to the vigorous and commanding heroine.

According to Corneille, spectators prefer the guilty Médée, the "âme criminelle" (v. 1554) [criminal soul] because they respect the source of her indignation and consider it justified. The collective degradation of Créon, Jason, and the princess Créuse leaves the audience with little sympathy for them and great sensitivity towards the injustice Médée has faced. Corneille explains:

> La raison [qu'ils ne font pas pitié] en est qu'ils semblent avoir mérité [leur malheur] par l'injustice qu'ils ont faite à Médée, qui attire si bien de son côté toute la faveur de l'auditoire qu'on excuse sa vengeance, après l'indigne traitement qu'elle a reçu de Créon et de son mari, et qu'on a plus de compassion du désespoir où ils l'ont réduite que de tout ce qu'elle leur fait souffrir.[26]

> [The reason (that they do not cause pity) is that they seem to have deserved (their deplorable fate) by the injustice that they caused to Médée, which attracts entirely to her side the favour of the audience so that they excuse her vengeance, after the undignified treatment she received from Créon and her husband, and that we have more compassion for the despair to which they have brought her than for everything that she makes them suffer.]

Corneille bases his evaluation of the play on watching spectators' reactions to his tragedy. Wavering and puny royal characters inspire neither interest nor admiration, and such "unpleasant spectacles" as the "undignified treatment" of Médée leave audiences unmoved. He has become aware that because of both theatrical and political demands, he must take measures to uphold monarchical dignity onstage.

In 1660, the same period when he reviews *Médée*, Corneille redefines the terms of tragedy, articulating a new definition that accentuates the centrality of the monarch's political role:

> Lorsqu'on met sur la scène un simple intrique (sic) d'amour entre des rois, et qu'ils ne courent aucun péril, ni de leur vie, ni de leur Etat, je ne crois pas que bien que les personnes soient illustres, l'action le soit assez pour s'élever jusqu'à la tragédie. Sa dignité demande quelque grand intérêt d'Etat, ou quelque passion plus noble et plus mâle que l'amour, telles que sont l'ambition ou la vengeance; et veut donner à craindre des malheurs plus grands, que la perte d'une maîtresse.[27]

> [When we stage a simple love story among kings, and that they risk no danger, either to their life or to their State, I do not think that although the characters are illustrious, the action is elevated enough to be a tragedy. Its dignity demands some great interest of State, or some passion more noble and more male than love, such as ambition or vengeance; and it should provoke fears greater than the loss of a mistress.]

Corneille has reached the conclusion that kings should no longer just be match-makers, concerned with bringing together couples in marital union as in *Clitandre* or *Médée*, nor should they be principally invested in their own love life, as is the infatuated Ægée, whose amorous investments eclipse his status as king of Athens, leaving him to resemble a *barbon* of comedy. Having eliminated the category of the king present *only* as judge, Corneille eliminates the category of the king present *only* as man. What remains is the king as king: the tragic fiction must offer the portrait of a sovereign in the act of governance. The "noble" and "male" passions the king should display are the same passions that had guided Corneille's vision of Médée's ambition and vengeance, revealing, perhaps surprisingly, that the model of tragic dignity originally conceived for his "witch of Colchis" will guide his conception of royal representations in the second half of the seventeenth century.

In 1662, only two years after the playwright publishes his poetic treatise, the "Discours sur le poème dramatique," Corneille presents the character Sertorius, who in famous verses asserts that, "Rome n'est plus dans Rome, elle est toute où je suis" (v. 936) [Rome is no longer in

Rome, it resides entirely where I am]. This mindset aligns the Roman general with Médée. Sertorius proclaims that beyond a throne, beyond a title, or even beyond a space of power, sovereignty constitutes a way of being, a demand for respect, and a demonstration of unparalleled dignity. Certainly, Sertorius is a general, not a king, but he is undeniably a man of authority, the sovereign figure within the play, a role Corneille is, by then, invested in protecting.

The insight Corneille gains from the experience of *Médée* is evident in the particular blend of brutal authority and guilty dominance that characterizes many of his sovereign characters, including Cléopâtre (in *Rodogune*), Œdipe, Attila, and Orode (the king in *Suréna*). These are all sovereigns whose judgments distinguish their power over others and propel the theatrical plot. In his last tragedy, *Suréna* (1674), Corneille returns to the rivalry he first displayed in *Médée* between the king and the hero, with a similar focus on their competition for respect and preeminence within the kingdom. In the conflict between Orode and Suréna, the latter is undeniably the more virtuous character, but in a reversal of Corneille's inaugural tragedy, the king is now the ultimate judge, prosecutor, and executioner of the nobleman. Suréna, whose virtue and heroism are antithetical to Jason's, will be deemed guilty of royal disrespect by Orode because of his refusal to marry the king's daughter. When Suréna turns down a marriage Jason was so quick to accept, he does so in the name of an immutable allegiance to the woman he loves. This time, however, heroic faithfulness proves naive and it is brutally countered by a superior power – the king's. Despite the obvious royal injustice, Suréna cannot vanquish its force, just as Jason and Créon were powerless before Médée. With Suréna's assassination, the tragedy ends on the recognition of a profound guilt linked to the sovereign, but also with a demonstration of the independence and supremacy of royal action, which none can rival.

Suréna's death is accompanied by the proclamation that the noblemen's death stems from a royal verdict which declares that whoever, "dédaign[e] les rois" (v. 1720) [disrespects kings] will face a similar fate. Corneille closes his dramaturgical career with a work that still hinges on royal judgment, with a dénouement by royal decision, but by the 1670s his overwhelming concern is to show the political dominance of the sovereign, at the expense, even, of his virtue and morality. It's not a "demolition of the hero" so much as a demonstration of the indisputable superiority of royal judgment.[28]

In returning now to Corneille's early career, we will dwell on the way the announcement of the royal decision within the tragic plot gradually becomes a central structural and thematic concern. Although the role of king as judge is a consistent trope for Corneille, he increasingly shifts the tone and register of his judgment scenes. He searches for the right method to endow a fictional king with a recognizable royal dignity that will strike spectators and critics as actively powerful and worthy of respect. Corneille's kings were not focal points of his drama from the outset, nor were they flawless symbols of authority and law. Only through continuous practice, not an all-encompassing vision, does Corneille imagine new roles for his tragic kings.

3 *Le Cid*: Why Corneille Misjudges

For some time now, critical commentary on *Le Cid* and *Horace* has viewed the plays' dénouements through the prism of the Cornelian *éthique du héros* when, it is claimed, the monarchy validates the play's central aristocratic protagonist, recognizing his vital support to the Crown. Don Fernand's pardon of Rodrigue and the Roman King Tulle's pardon of Horace represent a portrayal of the advantageous alliance between the monarchy and the nobility in contrast to the "demolition" the hero will undergo in Corneille's later plays as absolutism gains ground historically.[29] Defined by the strength of their resolve (*volonté*) and courage, the heroes of *Le Cid* and *Horace* incarnate values antithetical to the Machiavellian politics of morally corrupt kings. In such readings, Don Fernand and Tulle's pardons become the measure by which to judge Corneille's impending turn towards the dark dominance of the monarchy, which will seek to snuff out the hero's *éclat*. In an influential account, Thomas Pavel describes an axiological division within Corneille's plays where characters are opposed according to their moral and political principles. On one axis, he says, we find kings preoccupied first and foremost with the well-being of the state; they are caught up in political considerations which surpass their devotion to moral principles. In Corneille's early theatre (meaning *Le Cid, Horace*, and *Cinna*) the political expediency of the kings does not oppose the moral sense of the spectators: the kings arbitrate in favour of the embattled hero and side with him. The tragedies following *Cinna*, however, belong on another axis where sovereigns side against the nobleman hero. Corneille's later tragedies dwell on the impossible divide between morality, heroism, and politics.[30]

The difficulty of such readings, I believe, lies in their assumption that Corneille was ideologically invested from the start of his career in a clear-cut political stance. In this perspective, he sides with the aristocratic

ethos, a position demonstrated by his emphasis on the hostile monarchy's stranglehold of the hero whose world view of feudal grandeur is at
odds with "reason of state" politics. From what we might call the "demolition perspective," Corneille imposes a provocative partisan attitude in
his works and exhibits a sharp grasp of the period's monarchical-noble
conflicts. According to this framework, *Le Cid*'s 1648 edition, when the
playwright composes substantial *variantes* to the 1637 version and re-
labels the play a tragedy, not a tragicomedy, becomes the authoritative
version on which many of these readings rely.[31] This critical vein devotes
surprisingly little attention to how the playwright grappled with specifically theatrical concerns regarding his dramatic portrayals. Such an
omission seems glaring since, in his commentary of the plays, Corneille
dwells almost exclusively on issues of theatrical practice and theory. By
favouring the tradition of Corneille as a political thinker, scholars have
minimized the playwright's investment in comedy and tragicomedy.[32]

Moreover, as we saw in chapter 1 regarding critical reactions to *Le Cid*,
Corneille's contemporaries scarcely saw Don Fernand as a consensus-
making figure of arbitration, acting for the good of the state and hero.
They lashed out at his strangely conceived role, his lack of authority,
his curiously immoral decisions, and what they deemed to be his farcical antics. To read *Le Cid* before the quarrel, but after *Clitandre*, enables
us to better grasp Corneille's dramaturgical mindset in 1637. Considering that between *Clitandre* and *Le Cid*, he wrote four comedies, and
that *L'Illusion comique* (1636), written immediately before *Le Cid*, turns
on the mixing of genres and pleasures of illusion, it is no wonder we find
a strong sense of light-heartedness and humour in Corneille's Spanish
play.[33] Even before its polemical reception, *Le Cid* was not immune to the
growing influences of "regular" tragedy, but, as the *Lettre à Ariste* (1637)
attests, Corneille espoused a principle of freedom of creation, preferring
a blending of genres at the poet's whim to strict codes of practice. By
taking our eyes off the nobleman hero and focusing them instead on the
king as judge, we can better perceive the continuities between *Clitandre*
and *Le Cid*, especially in their common dénouements by royal judgment.
From there, we come to better understand how the challenges and
failures of those plots influenced the structure and characters of what
would become Corneille's first political tragedy, *Horace* (1641). Read in
this light, the playwright's political concerns stem neither from a deeply
anchored *parti pris* for a noble ethos nor from the defence of a staunch
political point of view, but from the need to concoct a more coherent –
and less polemical – royal portrayal.

Le Cid picks up where *Clitandre* left off with the announcement of an impending marriage. Indeed, the Spanish play starts where comedies usually end, since from the opening scene the audience learns that, happily, the daughter's and the father's preference for her husband match.[34] This joyous occasion turns sour only when the king makes a decision based on what values to impart to his son. He chooses Don Diègue, the father of Rodrigue, Chimène's suitor, to be the *dauphin*'s governor at the expense of Don Gomès, Chimène's father.[35] Hence, although similar to the king in *Clitandre* because Don Fernand is marginal to the intrigue for most of the play up until the dénouement, royal judgment nonetheless drives *Le Cid*'s plot from the outset. Furthermore, despite the shift in dramatic focus towards the lovers' difficult choice between love and honour, Chimène's tenacious "*poursuite*" [prosecution] of Rodrigue after he kills her father in a duel sets in place the royal verdict that will close the play. That *Le Cid* will ultimately end where it began, with the announcement that the couple will wed, gives the plot the surprising yet providential-like outcome typical of tragicomedies. As Merlin-Kajman notes, despite Chimène and Rodrigue's initial fears, "le dénouement va pourtant infirmer cette vision tragique et pathétique tout à la fois: les pères vont leur coûter bien moins de pleurs et de maux qu'un spectateur du XVIIe siècle n'est en droit d'attendre. Et nos héros vont pleurer peu"[36] [The dénouement will invalidate this at once tragic and pathetic vision: the fathers will cost them far fewer tears and headaches than a seventeenth-century spectator might have expected. And our heroes will only cry a little]. *Le Cid*'s closing happiness should not come as a surprise, though, since we know that within Corneille's joyous framework of tragicomedy, social and amorous reconciliation win the day to make marriage possible, and even the death of fathers can be forgotten.

In *Le Cid*, Corneille still shows little preoccupation with theatrical royal prestige. He remains more invested in the Romance tradition of tragicomedy where gallantry, adventure, and surprise trump the seriousness of judicial debate and monarchical portrayals. The benefits of idealized chivalric action are opposed to the ineffective and slow justice dispensed by the monarch. The king's deficiencies open the door for Chimène to turn to another source to avenge her father's death, thereby fostering a sense of suspense regarding the source of Rodrigue's punishment. For example, Don Sanche, Chimène's second suitor, offers himself to settle the case against Rodrigue: "Employez mon épée à punir ce coupable; / Employez mon amour à venger cette mort" (vv. 788–9) [Use my sword to punish this guilty man; / Use my love to avenge this death]. In response, Chimène expresses faith in the king's justice: "J'offenserai le Roi, qui m'a promis justice" (v. 783) [I would offend the king who has promised me justice]. Showing little concern for the offence he might cause to the king by so thoroughly disparaging royal justice, Don Sanche asserts that royal justice is inept. The events of the plot eventually prove that he was not fully mistaken:

> Vous savez qu'elle marche avec tant de langueur,
> Qu'assez souvent le crime échappe à sa longueur,
> Son cours lent et douteux fait trop perdre de larmes.
> Souffrez qu'un cavalier vous venge par les armes:
> La voie en est plus sûre, et plus prompte à punir.   (vv. 793–7)

> [You know that it works with so much languor
> That all too often crime escapes its slowness,
> Its slow and uncertain course makes too many tears fall.
> Suffer that a knight avenge you through weapons:
> This means is more certain, and more prompt to punish.]

In contrast to *Clitandre*'s king who was undeniably and (tragi-) comically too "prompt to punish," *Le Cid* presents a monarch characterized by his "languor" and "slowness," whose justice follows a "slow and uncertain course," flaws confirmed by Chimène's repeated reminders throughout the play for Don Fernand to exercise his judicial duties. A few scenes after Don Sanche's exortations, Don Diègue criticizes Fernand for failing to uphold the law when the king excuses Rodrigue from fighting in the duel.[37] While the heroic leading men are always ready to swiftly execute actions, the king stands as a foil to their bold spirit. Rounding out the list of characters unimpressed by royal justice, Rodrigue himself reiterates how slowly the king's justice works, urging Chimène to make herself judge in Fernand's place:

> Ne diffère donc plus ce que l'honneur t'ordonne:
> Il demande ma tête, et je te l'abandonne;
> Fais-en un sacrifice à ce noble intérêt:
> Le coup m'en sera doux, aussi bien que l'arrêt.
> Attendre après mon crime une lente justice,
> C'est reculer ta gloire autant que mon supplice.   (vv. 933–8)

[Do not defer any longer what honour orders you to do:
It asks for my head, and I abandon it to you;
Sacrifice it to this noble interest:
The blow will be soft, as well as the verdict.
Waiting for a slow justice after my crime,
Is to delay your glory as well as my punishment.]

In a manner typical of the *galanterie* of tragicomedy, Rodrigue mixes judicial vocabulary with chivalric discourse in designating Chimène as his judge. In so doing, he pinpoints the importance of her judgment over the king's. Her verdict is more capable than the monarch's of punishing Rodrigue who excludes the king from the play's dominant dynamic of love and honour.

Although Chimène resolutely refuses to relinquish her belief in the primacy of the king's justice, a position that leads to the play's dénouement, the plot remains focused on the lovers and their seemingly insoluble division. As Corneille describes in his analysis of *Le Cid*, despite the immorality the critics targeted in the play, crowds of spectators came to see the star-crossed lovers, and they reacted emotionally and excitedly to their encounter in Chimène's home after Rodrigue has killed her father:

tous Presque on souhaité que ces entretiens se fissent; et j'ai remarqué aux premières représentations, qu'alors que ce malheureux amant se présentait devant elle, il s'élevait un certain frémissement dans l'assemblée, qui marquait une curiosité nouvelle et un redoublement d'attention pour ce qu'ils avaient à se dire dans un état si pitoyable.[38]

[Almost everyone wanted this exchange to take place; and I noticed from the first staging, that when the miserable lover presented himself before her, there rose up from the audience a certain stirring that marked a renewed curiosity and focus for what these lovers had to say to each other in such a pathetic state.]

The spectators who came to see Corneille's tragicomedy were interested in matters of the heart, the touching moments between the lovers, not in a discussion of the forms justice can take, or in the nature of royal law and its consequences. To be sure, *Le Cid* offers more serious judicial considerations within its plot than do *Clitandre*'s or *L'Illusion comique*'s brief prison scenes. In *L'Illusion comique* (1636), for instance, the hero bemoans

his impending execution (Act IV, scenes 7–10) only to be saved by his
beloved, whose friend has convinced the jailer to set him free and escape
with them. In contrast, *Le Cid* stages a forceful portrayal of royal judgment, including an explicit courtroom dynamic with the passionate and
extended *plaidoyers* of Chimène against Don Diègue in Act II, scene 8, as
well as the noblewoman's straightforward articulation of the key dilemma
she faces: "Va je suis ta partie, et non pas ton bourreau. / Si tu m'offres ta
tête est-ce à moi de la prendre ?" (vv. 940–1) [Go, I am your prosecutor
nor your executioner. / If you offer me your head is it my place to take it?]
Nonetheless, in *Le Cid* Don Fernand still remains secondary to the other
characters onstage, and the play's resolution calls for an erasure of the
troubling legal matters in favour of an optimistic embrace of the future.

As Corneille shifts to the genre of tragedy in *Horace* (1641), *Cinna ou la
clémence d'Auguste* (1642), *Polyeucte* (1643), and *La Mort de Pompée* (1644),
he will accentuate and push farther his staged debates on legality, reflecting more deeply on the monarch's role in performing justice. The more
versed he becomes in the practice of tragedy, the more decisive the royal
judge becomes.

With Don Fernand, as Corneille's critics lamented, the king walks too
fine a line between comedy and tragic tyranny. This unsuitable blend
leads to disconcerting effects where the Spanish king is all at once
unknowable, feeble, cruel, and unimportant. He belongs to the same
category of uninspiring judge-monarchs of the first quarter of the seventeenth century, those pale kings in *Clitandre* and *Médée* or in Hardy's
Scédase. Chimène's complaints of the king's disregard for her case and its
ultimate dismissal echo the reckless royal judgments of the earlier plays.
The noblewoman laments:

> De ma juste poursuite on fait si peu de cas
> Qu'on croit m'obliger en ne m'écoutant pas!
> Puisque vous refusez la justice à mes larmes,
> Sire, permettez-moi de recourir aux armes.   (vv. 1395–8)

> [To my just pursuit so little attention is given
> That he thinks he obliges me by not listening to me!
> Since you refuse to give justice to my tears,
> Sire, permit me to have recourse to weapons.]

Chimène's realization that Don Fernand will not help her comes late in
the play (Act V), a sign that the hope she had held onto that the king

would finally perform the role of judge she so passionately asked of him has finally vanished. In Chimène's desperate turn to another form of justice – the arm of Don Sanche in a duel – the play swerves away from tragedy and situates itself fully in the genre of romance and adventure where the focus lies with the valiant knight's battle for the affections of the noblewoman. Fernand's odd announcement that he authorizes the duel between Rodrigue and Don Sanche but not in his presence confirms that the spotlight belongs to tragicomedic action, not to the solemn politics of tragic royal decision-making.

Ironically, among all the characters of *Le Cid* it is Chimène who most staunchly believes in Fernand's justice and authority. Yet, she is the person the king takes least seriously, despite his promises to her.[39] His behaviour consists of a strange blend of comedy verging on tyranny, especially when Fernand tries to get a laugh out of his courtiers at the expense of Chimène's grief. The king announces to the court his intention to trick her into believing Rodrigue has died in battle. Everyone is in on the joke except for her, and Fernand asks all who are present to feign sadness: "On m'a dit qu'elle l'aime, et je vais l'éprouver. / Contrefaites le triste" (vv.1346–7) [I am told she loves him and I will test her./ Show a sadder face]. Echoing the language of "Tragedies of the Scaffolds," the term "éprouver" takes on a dual meaning, suggesting that the king will put her through an ordeal, a type of "*épreuve*" [challenge] akin to a "supplice" [torture] or he will simply test her feelings. Either way, the royal actions assume the guise of a punishment that consists in revealing her painfully true affection for Rodrigue. The episode serves no dramatic purpose except to confirm what the audience already knows: Chimène loves the man who killed her father. The king's joking encounter with the noblewoman contrasts so deeply with her passionate pleas for justice that the scene seems intended to lessen the tragic intensity surrounding her character. Swinging the pendulum of genre into a lighter category, the false announcement that Rodrigue has died in battle becomes a moment of joviality rather than sadness. As if watching a comedic play within a play, Fernand comments to the onlookers: "Voyez comme déjà sa couleur est changée" (v. 1352) [See how already her colour changes], and Don Diègue, similarly entertained by what he sees, responds: "Mais voyez qu'elle se pâme" (v. 1353) [But see how she swoons]. In making a spectacle of what otherwise could have been presented as Chimène's tragic suffering for her ill-fated passion, the pain of her situation is distanced, suddenly viewed as less serious and weighty than she believes it to be; this dissolves the tragic register that had characterized her position and turns the serious tone into a playful scene of tragicomedy where mistakenly thinking someone is dead is commonplace.[40] Even the *Infante*, herself a tragic figure of hopelessly unrequited love who seems to have gotten lost within the play's intrigue, tells Chimène to change her perception of things: "Ce qui fut juste alors ne l'est plus aujourd'hui" (v. 1185) [What was once just no longer is so today]. The time to mourn has passed. "Today" heralds the embrace of chivalry and reconciliation proper to dénouements of the cheerful genre of tragicomedy. As the princess sees it, Rodrigue's valiant efforts on the battlefield have negated the tragic division between the two lovers, and the *Infante* articulates a view in line with tragicomedy's formal conventions: a rapid change has occurred, suddenly eliminating a peril because of the intervention of unforeseen circumstances.

The speed at which things change – actions accumulate and positions shift – signals that the world of *Le Cid* runs on the picaresque time of tragicomedy, not on the slow and deliberate unity of tragic time. The frenetic rush of heroic achievements, the cascade of improbable events such as Rodrigue's defeat of Don Gomès, followed by the assembly of Don Diègue's five hundred friends to fight the invading Moors, culminating with Don Fernand's judgment that "Les Mores en fuyant ont emporté son crime" (v. 1424) [The Moors in fleeing have taken with them his crime], all reveal that *Le Cid*'s breakneck rhythm remained similar to *Clitandre*'s action-packed plot. In this case, however, the rapidity and surprise of *Le Cid*'s final outcome leave critics upset with the moral picture such celerity entails. Fernand's straightforward assessment, "J'excuse ta chaleur à venger ton offense; / Et l'Etat défendu me parle en ta défense" (vv. 1263–4) [I pardon your lust to avenge your offence; / And the State defended speaks to me in your defence] too easily forgives a weighty crime and unites a couple who should not be reconciled.

The moral disapproval Scudéry and fellow censors directed towards Chimène underscores the attention critics began to place in the late 1630s on the relationship between dramatic tempo and the moral-ethical positioning of the play – a concern absent at the start of the decade. The pace of action implies a concatenation of events and a compression of time that makes reconciliation impossible, illogical, and immoral. Suddenly, rather than a swift tying up of loose ends, the alacrity with which the dénouement comes together is cause for a serious moral crisis.[41]

The Corneille of 1637 still operated on a different conceptual time frame from the strict demands of the twenty-four-hour unity of time, which would soon dominate poetic discussions. The rapid and surprising

dénouement, the elevation of the hero, the celebratory union of two lovers, and the image of a wider societal consent, as embodied by Fernand,
attest to Corneille's predilection for conventionally comedic endings.
The definition Northrop Frye provides of "New Comedy" impeccably
describes the dénouements of both *Clitandre* and *Le Cid*, thereby high-
lighting their common framework in a way that has too often been
overlooked:

> In all good New Comedy there is a social as well as an individual theme
> which must be sought in the general atmosphere of reconciliation that
> makes the final marriage possible. As the hero gets closer to the heroine
> and opposition is overcome, all the right-thinking people come over to his
> side. Thus a new social unit is formed on the stage, and the moment that
> this social unit crystallizes is the moment of the comic resolution. In the
> last scene, when the dramatist usually tries to get all his characters on the
> stage at once, the audience witnesses the birth of a renewed sense of social
> integration.[42]

Once the (tragi-)comedy arrives at its closing scene, there is little need
for further discussion, or so Corneille thought when he composed
Le Cid's first version. Rodrigue's social status has been elevated and the
Moorish kings recognize him as "Le Cid"; Chimène goes along with the
royal decision, following the general mood of reconciliation, just as
Dorise and Clitandre did in *Clitandre*. In 1637 Corneille failed to grasp,
or simply refused to accept, the new moral-political weight attached
to dramatic portrayals by those in monarchical circles. In situating
Le Cid outside of a purely fictional world, beyond *Clitandre*'s nameless
forests and pastoral lands, the new poetico-political vision of theatre
demanded that the dénouement by royal decision be centred on a
moral lesson.

In reading *Le Cid*, I have sought to show how the play most often considered today to reflect the genius and unique aesthetic of Corneille lies
at the heart of a dramaturgical misunderstanding regarding the application of changing genres and codes. Rather than a principled engagement on the side of the heroic aristocrat's struggle or a depiction of
the emerging conflict between a feudal and a centralized state, *Le Cid*'s
dénouement reveals to us a Corneille swimming against the tide, hanging onto generic conventions that had ceased to be applicable. With
Le Cid he fails to heed the growing dramaturgical-political calls for
more dominant and dignified monarchical displays of power. Corneille

certainly addresses political themes in *Le Cid*, but they are secondary to his preoccupation with adventure and romance. This preference never disappears for Corneille, but he is forced, at least for a time, to seek ways of reframing these qualities within a more serious – and slower-paced – dramatic structure.

4 *Horace*: The Art of Slowing Things Down

Given the uproar over what critics of *Le Cid* saw as Chimène's immoral behaviour and Don Fernand's antics, one would think that Corneille would steer clear of such an explosive combination in his next play. Not so: in *Horace* (1641), Corneille's first Roman tragedy, rather than elimi-nate the upsetting elements of his previous play, he explicitly addresses them by making the relationship between crime, legality, and royal judg-ments the cornerstone of the plot.[43]

After the bitter polemics sparked by *Le Cid*, two theatre seasons passed before Corneille returned to the stage with *Horace* at the Théâtre du Marais.[44] Many saw Corneille's readiness to choose a Roman subject as an implicit acceptance of the Académie Française's dominance and an honest attempt to conform to the rules of tragic poetics for which he had been so harshly taken to task.[45] With *Horace*, Corneille revises *Le Cid*'s frantic pace towards the royal judgment dénouement by creating an Act V entirely dedicated to an extended legal discussion. This change in structure provides a steady build-up towards the king's final judgment and places the closing announcement of his verdict in a clear logic and concatenation of events.

In *Horace*, as in *Le Cid*, the king does not need to parse evidence and witness accounts to uncover who is guilty of the crime in question. It is known from the inquiry's outset who committed the murder.[46] The title character and Roman hero single-handedly ensured Rome's future by defeating the three Curiace brothers on the battlefield, but he followed this military feat with the killing of his own sister within the Horace home. By the end of Act IV, Horace stands before the king who must determine an appropriate punishment for him. He, who had returned home triumphant, at the pinnacle of his glory, brutally stabbed Camille when she admonished him for killing her Alban lover, one of the Curi-ace brothers, and refused to celebrate the Roman victory. In a structure of pro and contra arguments, those who would punish and those who would forgive Horace mount their cases in an Act V judgment scene. The Roman king, Tulle, hears from these different parties, one after the other, four in all, each presenting a different view of the crime. Ultimately, Tulle ends the discussion and decides to forgive the Roman nobleman.

Despite the unambiguous acknowledgment of Horace's guilt over the course of Act V, scholarship on the play has often focused on a moral debate of Horace's action: one side sees him as a heroic defender of the state at the expense of his personal self, while the other sees him as an irredeemably dishonoured tragic protagonist. The critical disagreement has turned on Horace's character – how should one reconcile his initial heroism and his later crime? As Marc Escola argues in an insightful recent edition of *Horace*, to settle the matter scholars have often tried to rehabilitate Horace through psychological interpretations of his personality, even at the expense of Corneille's own commentary on the play.[47] My reading will not attempt to justify Horace's actions in the name of patriotism, Roman virtue, inflamed passion, etc. Quite the opposite: it is crucial to acknowledge Horace's guilt – for which the text leaves little doubt – in order to recognize the role the king plays in pardoning him. The extent to which Horace has committed an unjustifiable crime and sullied his honour heightens the king's remarkable pardon and his important function within the tragedy. None of the characters within the play deny Horace's crime; those defending him seek only to find mitigating circumstances to avert his execution. The certainty of the hero's culpability underscores the dynamic whereby the royal judge alone can clear him, despite even Horace's own wishes.

In stark contrast to *Clitandre* where first the king fails to debate the accused's guilt and then judges erroneously, or in the second instance, where the final judgment will take place within a royal *Conseil* concealed from the view of the spectators, the legal decision in *Horace* stems from a drawn-out, legible, and explicitly divulged basis for judgment. Although Corneille had placed a veneer of "reason of state" politics in justifying the king's verdict in *Le Cid*, Fernand's overly prompt embrace of Rodrigue at the expense of Chimène's tears had struck critics as unfair, unjustified, and precipitous.[48] Further undermining Don Fernand's image, in deciding the fate of his subjects, the over-burdened Spanish monarch turns into a laughable figure as he openly laments his judicial duties. He repeatedly displays an unwillingness to act with gravity, such as when he hears of Chimène's arrival, "Sire, Chimène vient vous demander justice" (v. 1340) [Sire, Chimène has come to ask you for justice] and answers: "La fâcheuse nouvelle, et l'importun devoir!" (v. 1341) [What lamentable news, and what a bothersome duty!]. Far from the ancien régime ideal of the monarch as a "*loi vivante*" or living law, legal authority and royal grandeur in *Le Cid* are hardly intrinsic to the monarchical character.

In comparison, Corneille anchors the royal judgment in *Horace* in a coherent political logic. Dwelling on the explanation of his verdict, the king announces his judgment by addressing each of the four parties directly and calling for a suspension of positive law:

> Cette énorme action, faite presque à nos yeux
> Outrage la nature, et blesse jusqu'au dieux […]   (vv. 1733–5)
> Les moins sévères lois en ce point sont d'accord,
> Et si nous les suivons, il est digne de mort.
> Si d'ailleurs nous voulons regarder le coupable,
> Ce crime, quoique grand, énorme, inexcusable,
> Vient de la même épée, et part du même bras
> Qui me fait aujourd'hui maître de deux Etats.
> Deux sceptres en ma main, Albe à Rome asservie,
> Parlent hautement en faveur de sa vie.
> Sans lui j'obéirai où je donne la loi,
> Et je serais Sujet où je suis deux fois Roi […]   (vv. 1737–46)
> Et de pareils aussi sont au-dessus des lois.
> Qu'elles se taisent donc […]   (vv. 1754–5)

> [This enormous action, committed almost right before our eyes
> Outrages nature and offends even the gods …
> The least severe laws on this point agree,
> And if we follow them, he is worthy of death.
> If, in fact, we want to regard the guilty man,
> This crime, although large, enormous, inexcusable
> Comes from the same sword, and from the same arm
> That today makes me master of two States.
> Two sceptres in hand, Albe subservient to Rome,
> Speak loudly in favour of his life.
> Without him I would obey where I make law,
> And I would be a subject where I am twice king …
> And such men are above the laws.
> Let them be silent then …]

Tulle gives an explanation, a well-defined statement of his political values and concerns, a detailed justification for his judgment in contrast to Don Fernand's illogical verdict. Despite the "enormity" – a word Tulle repeats twice – of the hero's guilt and the certainty of Horace's crime, inexcusable according to natural and divine laws ("outrages nature"; "offends even the gods"), the king makes clear that the nobleman merits a pardon as the future of the state outweighs all other grounds for judgment. Tulle's verdict stems from a consistent line of thought – an understanding of royal favour and gratitude given to a champion of the Crown's cause.

Despite such clear undergirding of the royal decision, however, from the perspective of dramatic composition, *Horace* diverges only slightly from *Le Cid*'s dénouement. The royal judge remains marginal to the overall dramatic action and his decision still entails siding against a young woman whose simple presence is a reminder of the brutality the king condones. In maintaining the dénouement by royal decision, Corneille continues to conceive of the royal character as the structural linchpin of the plot. By making Horace's fate and the play's outcome so dependent on the royal decision, Corneille significantly amends the description of Horace's judgment found in his source text – Titus Livy's *History of Rome*. He clearly intended that these changes be noted since he included excerpts in Latin of Livy's description of the events in the second edition of the play (1647) and in subsequent editions up until 1657.[49] Corneille departs most prominently from Livy's account when he eliminates the participation of the Roman people in Horace's trial. In Livy, King Tullus, out of concern that his sentence would prove unpopular, delegates the judgment of the case to the Roman Diumvirs. Yet, when this commission rules in favour of a condemnation by hanging, Tullus instructs the judges to put Horace's fate in the hands of the people. A public debate ensues and although the Roman people find the warrior guilty, they decide his courage and patriotic service outweigh his culpability. They order Horace to participate in an expiatory ceremony, which will atone for his criminal action. Keeping in mind the account given by the playwright's source text allows us to retain a sense of the surprise Tulle's decisive verdict would have provoked in seventeenth-century spectators for whom the debate surrounding the fate of the Roman warrior was still an open question. Whether in the rhetorical exercises of Jesuit schoolboys or in the course of legal training, French students were regularly asked to side with either Horace or Curiace and to mount a defence of their views in a display of their mastery of eloquence and legal reasoning. To give Tulle the last word in defending the "inexcusable" (v. 1740) is to highlight the role of the sovereign's decision in silencing all other voices – a power reiterated in the play's dedication to Richelieu and one which we know

Corneille experienced personally when the cardinal insisted the Académie Française's judgment of *Le Cid* be the final response on the matter.[50]

Through Tulle's *arrêt*, Corneille simultaneously adheres to the position of contemporary theorists of absolutist power who advocated for the
sovereign's right to make or break laws at will, while also undermining
such views by accentuating how easily the king can bend justice to suit
his needs.[51] Tulle's extensive justification for bypassing the laws of Rome
underscores the troubling morality at the core of the royal decision. The
monarch's repeated use of the first person singular pronoun and pos-
sessive, which appear no fewer than six times in five verses, points to the
advantages the king has gained from Horace.[52] The "sceptres" – material
objects of royal power – speak to Tulle, not the laws of nature nor those
of the kingdom. Moreover, the Roman king justifies his newly powerful
status as grounds for his forgiveness, stressing how Horace doubled his
authority: "two states," "two sceptres," and "twice King." Emboldened by
this new strength, Tulle founds the future of Rome on the triumph of
royal decision-making – "Let the laws be silent" (v. 1755) – although the
triumph is weakened by the force of the politically powerful over the
morally virtuous.

The presentation of competing viewpoints surrounding Horace's
culpability heightens spectator awareness of the king's authority and
his unique ability to put an end to the legal debate (and the dramatic
action), all the more so since, as Couton writes, Tulle's *arrêt* represents a
"mise en vacances de la légalité"[53] [a vacating of the law]. As Greenberg
suggests, the monarch's ability to pardon Horace and to bury the rebellious Camille within the confines of Rome indicate his supreme authority: "The tragedy of origins and difference, of symmetry and State, ends
in the establishment of a new, triumphant order of the same. Camille is
put where she did not want to be, in the same place/grave as Curiace.
The two are made One."[54] Furthermore, the king's ostentatious silencing of opposing views, as when he beckons Valère, the "chevalier romain"
[Roman knight], who speaks in the name of "tous les gens de bien"
(v. 1482) [all the people of virtue], to cease arguing, stresses that Horace's "outrage to nature" is less important than the state's safety.[55] In
a similar gesture of silencing, but this time directed towards the emotional pain and private sense of loss Horace has wrought, the king orders
Sabine to forgive her husband. Yet, in spite of these efforts to demonstrate the monarch's power, the portrayal of sovereignty once again
comes up short. The playwright is able neither to fully satisfy his critics
nor eliminate the troubling feelings of injustice that remain at the close

of the plot. Tulle's silencing of Valère resembles less a clement judge who prepares to make a virtuous decision than a king all too ready to wrap up the debate and draw the curtain on the tragedy, leaving a bitter taste in spectators' mouths.

Indeed, the *doctes* did not greet *Horace* with the enthusiasm Corneille had hoped for. Camille's murder at her brother's hand and the drawn-out prosecution of Act V were focal points of their critique. They advised Corneille to eliminate these even at the expense of historical accuracy. D'Aubignac insisted that the playwright should amend the plot so extensively that Horace's guilt would be erased and the king would not need to pardon him:

> La Scène ne donne point les choses comme elles ont été, mais comme elles doivent être, et le Poète y doit rétablir dans le sujet tout ce qui ne s'accommodera pas aux règles de son Art, comme fait un peintre lorsqu'il travaille sur un modèle défectueux. C'est pourquoi la mort de Camille par la main d'Horace son frère n'a pas été approuvée au Théâtre, bien que ce soit une aventure véritable, et j'avais été d'avis, pour sauver en quelque sorte l'Histoire, et tout ensemble la bienséance de la scène, que cette fille désespérée, voyant son frère l'épée à la main, se fût précipitée dessus: ainsi elle fût morte de la main d'Horace et lui eût été digne de compassion comme un malheureux innocent. L'Histoire et le Théâtre auraient été d'accord.[56]

> [The Stage does not present things as they were, but as they ought to be, and the Poet must reestablish in the Subject everything that does not fit the rules of his Art, as a painter does when working on a flawed model. This is why Camille's death by her brother Horace's hand was not approved of in the Theatre, although it is a true story, and I had advised, so as to save History, so to speak, and also the decorum of the scene, that this desperate girl, seeing her brother sword in hand, would have thrown herself onto it: therefore, she would have died by Horace's hand, but he would have been worthy of compassion like a miserable innocent. History and the Theatre would have been in agreement.]

Much as d'Aubignac dismisses Sophocles's *Oedipus Rex* as unsuitable for French audiences, he saw Livy's famous account as needing to be "saved" ("so as to save History, so to speak") for French spectators. His claim that "Camille's death […] was not approved of" confirms that even King Tulle's drawn-out legitimization of Horace could not quell the uneasy impressions surrounding the young woman's murder. Far from

a resounding affirmation of the king's power to pardon, pace Greenberg, d'Aubignac seeks to turn the blame away from Horace and place it
firmly on Camille's shoulders by imagining her death as a suicide, or as
an accident, rather than a concerted act of force on her brother's part.
Only then would the king's clemency towards Horace have been war-
ranted – "he would have deserved compassion." As it stands, the pardon
invites unwanted focus on the king's political self-interest and cynicism.
Reading along such lines, Harriet Stone has shown how Camille's burial
within the confines of Rome designates a legitimate space of resistance
beyond the frame of the king-hero dialectic: "From her position outside
the law, Camille represents a fuller knowledge [...] For all its efficacy,
therefore, the law that restores political order is separate here from the
order of things perceived by the spectator."[57]

D'Aubignac's reflections on *Hoarce* emphasize the delicate balance
involved in portraying royal judgment onstage. In wanting to display
more explicitly than in *Le Cid* the logic behind the king's verdict, Corneille's theatrical rendering of the royal decision runs up against a
monarchical legal culture increasingly insistent on preventing the public's analysis of the royal decision. Tulle's reasons for pardoning Horace
become too clear, too grounded in political necessity. In displaying the
brutal killing of Camille, followed by the king's pardon of its perpetrator,
Corneille invites spectators to reflect upon and question the validity of
the royal judgment.

As we know, the French monarch judged without a public evaluation
of the testimony, proof, or even the objective facts that made up a criminal case; royal decisions were unhindered by legal commentary, nor
did they need to be accompanied by explanations. Foucault's graphic
descriptions have rendered infamous the spectacular tortured body of
the accused which bore the imprint of torture as the consequence of a
secret administration of royal justice exercised prior to the sentence.[58]
The dramatic punishment of the guilty displayed on the scaffolds was the
result of a decision arrived at outside of public view. Thus, although Tulle
stands as the answer to *Clitandre*'s and *Le Cid*'s illogical and ill-prepared
closing judgments, the bald admission of his verdict as the repayment
of a political debt while a young woman's death goes unpunished beckons spectators to debate and criticize the king's decision. Against state-
centred critical approaches which too rapidly bury Camille and, with
her, the tension that hovers over the stage at the play's close, Stone aptly
suggests that Camille's burial is not an effacement, but a commemora-
tion, of her revolt: "To be recognized after death by the system whose

law threatened her identity – to be ceremoniously honored by society's leader – assures, moreover, Camille's sustained presence in history."[59] In exonerating Horace and honouring Camille, the king's judgment seems to be overly pragmatic in rewarding the powerful arm of the living and satisfying the memory of Rome's victim.

Paradoxically, then, the demonstration of the royal *parti pris* for the state and the political motives behind Tulle's decision jeopardize the king's dignity as much as Fernand's antics did in *Le Cid*. In writing *Horace*'s "Examen" almost twenty years after the first publication of the play, Corneille assesses Tulle in a positive light, viewing him as a distinct improvement over Don Fernand:

> Bien que le Roi n'y paraisse qu'au cinquième [Acte], il y est mieux dans sa Dignité que dans *Le Cid*, parce qu'il a intérêt pour tout son Etat dans le reste de la Pièce, et bien qu'il n'y parle point, il ne laisse pas d'y agir comme Roi.[60]

> [Although the King only appears in the fifth (Act), he is more in his Dignity than in *Le Cid* because he is interested in his State throughout the entirety of the Play, and although he does not speak (before the fifth Act), he never ceases to act like a King.]

Notwithstanding Corneille's stated satisfaction with his progress in communicating the all-important royal dignity to his spectators, the two "bien que" [although] clauses of this passage limit the sense of overall improvement he has achieved in his royal portraits from *Le Cid* to *Horace*. Unmistakably evaluating his theatrical production in terms of a teleology of progress from one play to the next, Corneille compares his royal characters and reflects on the difficulty of reconciling the king's presence within the plot, sustaining the monarchical dignity, and presenting the king in the midst of committing actions worthy of a monarch. Ironically, those plays deemed today to have been among his most successful (and most canonized) are those Corneille sees as so imperfectly executing the poetico-political demands placed upon him.

5 Conclusion: Timing Is Everything

Fundamentally, with *Horace* Corneille still has not resolved the problem that dogged him in *Clitandre* and *Le Cid*: theatrical timing. The faulty aspects of his royal portraits stem in large part from the issue of an imperfect tempo in the distribution and development of action. In the case of *Horace*, from Camille's death to the start of the trial, the dramatic action accelerates into the speedy tempo of tragicomedy as the Roman monarch arrives in person onstage for the first time in Act V, stands in the home of the man he has come to thank for saving Rome, and then orders him tried, then and there, for the young woman's murder. In response to abundant criticism of this scene, Corneille tries to give the hurried action a positive spin:

> Il vient aussi dans ce cinquième comme Roi, qui veut honorer par cette vis-ite un père dont les fils lui ont conservé la Couronne, et acquis celle d'Albe au prix de leur sang. S'il y fait office de juge, ce n'est que par accident, et il le fait dans ce logis même d'Horace, par la seule contrainte qu'impose la Règle de l'unité de lieu.[61]

> [He comes in this fifth Act as a King who wants to honour by his visit a father whose sons conserved the Crown for him and acquired the Alban one at the price of their blood. If he officiates as a judge, it is only by accident, and he does so in the home of Horace, solely because of the constraint imposed by the Rule of the unity of location.]

Corneille is pleased that with Tulle he has gotten away from the royal-judge stock character. No *rex ex machina* in *Horace*, for when the Roman king arrives it is as a political actor, a sovereign who comes to thank a subject for his service. This happens not solely for structural need-to-end-the-play purposes, but for genuinely plot-motivated ones. Unfortunately, as the playwright admits, the constraint of unity of location does him in. The plausibility of the king *qua* king arriving in person to show gratitude in Horace's home, a visit that would be a distinguished honour for the family, is thwarted by his sudden and fortuitous ("by accident") trans-formation into a judge. If in Molière's *Tartuffe* the last-minute arrival of the *Exempt* provides a happy ending by voicing an *in extremis* judgment of the monarch, the arrest of the hypocrite stemmed in the comedy from the king's supernatural ability to discern crime and act in a decisive and timely manner to thwart it.[62] In *Horace*, by contrast, the compression of the royal judgment into an unexpected and unforeseen turn of events, returns the dramatic tempo to the tragi-comedic rhythm of impromptu changes and chance encounters. The scene resembles a structural ploy, yet another *péripétie*, to get the drama to end, rather than a carefully or-chestrated tragic dénouement.

Juggling the shifts in speed and focus, Corneille alters the dramatic rhythm in *Horace* once more with the drawn-out *plaidoyers*, followed by Tulle's deliberate presentation of his reasons for clemency, which slow the place again. But, this time, the action lingers. Corneille states:

> Tout ce cinquième est encore une des causes du peu de satisfaction que laisse cette Tragédie: il est tout en plaidoyers, et ce n'est pas là la place des harangues, ni des longs discours. Ils peuvent être supportés en un commencement de Pièce où l'action n'est pas encore échauffée: mais le cinquième Acte doit plus agir, que discourir. L'attention de l'Auditeur déjà lassée se rebute de ces conclusions qui traînent, et tirent la fin en longueur.[63]

> [All of this fifth Act is another one of the reasons for the lack of satisfaction that this Tragedy causes: it is made up of speeches, and that is not the place for harangues, nor for long discourses. They can be abided at the start of a Play when the action has not yet heated up: but the fifth Act must offer more action than speeches. The Auditor's attention already worn out rejects these conclusions that drag on and extend the length of the play.]

With *Horace*, Corneille struggles, still, in finding and setting a pace of action appropriate to tragedy. Notably, in his analysis of Act V, so clearly defined by the king's judgment, he does not venture to question the validity of the king's decision. He offers no critique of the monarchical position vis-à-vis Horace. He remarks instead on the boredom of his audience. No one wants to hear long-winded speeches by Act V; no one wants the legal debate to drag on. He has learned yet another lesson about timing and dénouements.[64] Despite renewed efforts to please his critics and audiences, Corneille recognizes the sticking points that remain for him in portraying a monarch in the act of judgment onstage.

After these early attempts at staging such scenes, Corneille sought to link the king directly to the dramatic action, to ensure his role would exceed the articulation of a purely judicial verdict, and that the royal action would be a source of "*éclat*" for the character. In juxtaposing Cornelian scenes of royal judgment, we can perceive the challenges – and constraints – related to portraying a king as judge in a century increasingly preoccupied with promoting respect for sovereignty in general and the tragic royal character in particular.

In the wake of *Horace*, Corneille once again alters his dramatic formula in search of an answer to the persistent problem of tragic timing and monarchical dignity. Chapter 5 will consider Corneille's return to the stage after *Horace* with *Cinna ou la clémence d'Auguste* (1642) through the lens of the playwright's experiments in royal judgments. We will see that beyond the portrayal of a generous sovereign action, the act of clemency constitutes an authoritative decision outside of, or beyond, time, precedent, and linear order. The decisive sovereign action in *Cinna,* Auguste's verdict over the conspirators constitutes a progression in the playwright's bid to stage royal judgment in a way that will turn the scene of decision-making into a transformative gesture, allowing the sovereign to appear at once awe-inspiring and central to the theatrical plot.

Chapter Five

Corneille's *Cinna* and Rotrou's *Crisante*: A Search for the Emperor's Judgment

For owing your life to someone is tantamount to losing it.

Seneca, *On Clemency*

1 Clemency and the King

With *Cinna ou la clémence d'Auguste* (1642), Pierre Corneille gains a hard-won victory when he succeeds in satisfying both the tastes of the general public and the demands of his learned critics: "*Cinna* donne de l'admiration à tout le monde: c'est la plus belle pièce qui ait été faite en France, les gens de lettres et le peuple en sont également ravis, elle est aussi belle que celle de Sénèque"[1] [Cinna provokes admiration in everyone: it's the most beautiful play to ever have been made in France, the learned and the people are equally pleased by it; it is as beautiful as Seneca's]. For critics of the seventeenth century and for many today, *Cinna* represents the culmination of Corneille's efforts to master the rules of tragic poetics, which the *doctes* had so vocally accused him of flouting until then.[2] As if grading his composition from the mindset of his critics, the playwright checks off the rubrics he has satisfied in his second Roman tragedy: "Rien n'y contredit l'histoire, bien que beaucoup de choses y soient ajoutées; rien n'y est violenté par les incommodités de la représentation, ni par l'unité du jour, ni par celle de lieu"[3] [Nothing therein contradicts history, although many things are added; nothing is tarnished by the shortcomings of representation, nor by the unity of time, neither by the unity of place]. The last two references seem designed to answer those who had found fault with the timing and location of *Horace*, the play that had immediately preceded *Cinna*, and in particular the dual action brought on by Camille's murder by her brother and the king's judgment of him on the same day in the home of their father, *Vieil* Horace.

From the perspective of the sovereign's portrayal, the illustrious emperor Auguste seems to be an antidote to Corneille's earlier monarchs. Theatrically, the emperor's act of clemency signals a progression, a more refined attempt to depict the sovereign in a more prestigious rendition of the familiar topos of royal judgment onstage. With the Roman emperor's generous decision, Corneille manages to make the sovereign-judge live up to the ancien régime cultural image of an omnipotent – and virtuous – lawgiver whose *arrêts* are explicitly sanctioned by divine authority. The prince's last-minute decision of life over death not only untangles the tragic knot with a triumphant ending, but also portrays royal decision-making as the only basis for the survival of a nobleman-hero.

I wish to argue, however, that the ambiguity surrounding Auguste's gesture has not sufficiently attracted the attention of *Cinna*'s modern commentators. The emperor's clemency seems to be an obvious celebratory disavowal of the tyranny of his earlier reign – the chaotic period defined in the play by references to Auguste's alter ego "Octave." Hélène Merlin-Kajman argues, for example, that the emperor's self-mastery heralds the beginning of an absolutist government, unconstrained by others, but virtuous in its proclamation of self-constraint as exemplified by the famous verses: "Je suis maître de moi comme de l'Univers. / Je le suis, je veux l'être [...]" (vv. 1696–7) [I am master of myself as of the Universe, / So I am, thus I wish to be ...]. In renouncing past excess, Auguste erases Rome's violent legacy and inaugurates a legitimate reign: "Auparavant, [Auguste] détenait, certes, le pouvoir de domination, mais faute d'avoir commencé par se soumettre lui-même à l'exercice intérieur du gouvernement, il n'était qu'un tyran"[4] [Earlier, he had held, to be sure, the power of domination, but without having submitted himself to the internal exercise of government, he was only a tyrant]. Similarly, although Greenberg is attuned to the new hierarchical order instituted by Auguste's clemency, he regards it as exemplary because it ends the traumatic cycle of Roman vengeance:

> Instead of a system of circular exchange that has united all of them along a horizontal axis (Auguste = Cinna = Emilie = Maxime = Auguste) we now have a vertical structure where all meaning flows downward from Auguste, become godlike.[5]

For Merlin-Kajman and Greenberg, Auguste's clemency constitutes an ideal consensus-making verdict insofar as it is politically transformative and morally triumphant. Indeed, a substantial critical corpus has read the portrayal of Auguste as lending support to Richelieu's policies, or at least, as exhorting the cardinal to resemble the emperor in the admirable way he repairs the fractured relationship between the Crown and the most prominent aristocratic families of the state.[6] In this view, the act of clemency is necessarily praiseworthy, victorious, and morally irreproachable, as exemplified by Marc Fumaroli's enthusiastic approval of the emperor's magnanimous gesture: "en faisant grâce aux coupables et à leurs complices, [Auguste] leur rend la vie, et, par ce miracle de générosité, substitue une paternité politique et morale qui les attache à lui par les liens de la reconnaissance"[7] [in pardoning the guilty and their accomplices, he saves their lives, and, by this miracle of generosity, substitutes a political and moral paternity that ties them to him through the bonds of gratitude]. Central to Fumaroli's gloss of Auguste's clemency, however, lies the notion of a new-found debt and attachment to the sovereign who henceforth possesses the ultimate authority over his subjects' lives.

This chapter will reconsider the significance of clemency in *Cinna ou la clémence d'Auguste*, asking why Corneille chooses to portray a sovereign decision that entails moving beyond a traditional framework of crime and punishment. Within the theatrical context of revising scenes of royal judgment onstage and a political atmosphere intent on protecting monarchical images, how does the pardon allow the playwright to reimagine tragic dénouements by royal decision? How does clemency, an action where, in fact, no physical act takes place, become a viable solution to the dramatic impasse Corneille encountered with royal judgments in *Le Cid* and *Horace*?

After a consideration of *Cinna*, the chapter will then turn to clemency's reappearance in Jean Rotrou's *Venceslas* (1647), staged less than four years after Corneille's tragedy and clearly in dialogue with it. In *Venceslas*, once again, a sovereign-judge stands over a man guilty of threatening his personal and political existence, and, again, the royal judge chooses to pardon the accused. The playwrights similarly draw on and intertwine conventions of tragicomedy and tragedy as politically anchored questions surrounding the portrayal of royal judgments explicitly frame their works. Though seldom examined alongside Corneille in a sustained political light, we will explore how Rotrou's tragedy similarly sees clemency as a *vraisemblable* – and politically acceptable – means of recasting the tragi-comedic element of the unexpected into a touching and decisive royal theatrical action.

Finally, in the chapter's third section, I will take a step back in time to focus on the eponymous character of Rotrou's first political tragedy, *Crisante* (1637). In including this earlier tragedy in this chapter, I wish to sketch an evolution parallel to Corneille's. Before Rotrou engaged with clemency as a solution to the cultural-poetic pressures surrounding royal judgment, he was already grappling with the transformations facing tragedy around the time of the quarrel of *Le Cid*. Operating within similar Richelieu-influenced critical circles, Rotrou, I argue, was as invested as Corneille in rethinking the portrayal of royal judgments and trial scenes onstage. Although often categorized as an apolitical "baroque author," the Rotrou of *Crisante* stages a search for legal authority at an interstitial moment when a feeble monarchical regime faces its end, but the invading Roman power has not yet fully established its rule. In this time of flux, the raped heroine of Rotrou's tragedy searches for a sovereign judge. I suggest that through *Crisante* the playwright debates the place of violence, lawlessness, and the staging of legal authority within the newly defined French tragic genre. Before *Venceslas*'s clemency allowed Rotrou to create a dénouement of pathos, surprise, and political efficiency, *Crisante* set the stage for thinking about innovative theatrical portrayals of a sovereign enforcing his law.

Regarding Auguste's clemency, it is essential to not lose sight of how the imperial decision to pardon closely follows *Le Cid* and *Horace* in offering yet another portrait of a sovereign charting new legal territory and testing moral boundaries. In the earlier plays, the royal *arrêt* represented a break in the linearity of the plot; the royal decision amounted to a disruption in communication between the sovereign and his subjects: Don Fernand and Tulle rule against moral expectations and legal precedent. The moral outcry expressed at *Le Cid*'s dénouement is well known due to the ensuing *querelle*. As for *Horace*, at the close of the play, as Lyons has commented, "the audience is left to puzzle over how such an outsized, unyielding protagonist can fit back into the ordinary social world."[8] Despite King Tulle's call for the warrior's return to the private and public communities of Rome, represented respectively by Sabine, Horace's wife, and the Roman nobleman, Valère, reconciliation is not performed onstage. The king pardons Horace, but the play remains silent regarding the reactions of those for whom his guilt was evident. Even in the play's first published version, where the Roman confidante, Julie, reappears after the king's verdict to echo the king's call for reconciliation, the other characters do not respond in agreement; they are not heard from again. Corneille follows *Horace*'s morally questionable closing royal judgment with a sovereign decision in *Cinna* that allows the characters onstage, as well as audience members, to spontaneously embrace the sovereign's verdict. Placing Auguste's clemency in the context of Corneille's dramaturgical evolution enables us to grasp the political dimensions of such a theatrically exciting dénouement.

Corneille shields the royal decision in *Cinna* from attacks regarding its motivations and plausibility by staging a judgment that swerves away from the familiar tragic trial scene, with its cause-and-effect logic, its search for evidence and precedent, and its pronouncement of a clear-cut verdict. Instead, Corneille offers a sovereign ruling, ambiguous in its source and morality, that strikes like a *coup de théâtre* because of the surprising twist in the action it provokes, though it nonetheless adheres to the realm of the possible because of its historically based source.

Drawing on Aristotle's formulation, Corneille describes Auguste's action as belonging to the exceptional vein of the *vraisemblable extraordinaire*, which he defines in the following way:

> L[e vraisemblable] extraordinaire est une action qui arrive à la vérité moins souvent que sa [sic] contraire, mais qui ne laisse pas d'avoir sa possibilité assez aisée, pour n'aller point jusqu'au miracle, ni jusqu'à ces événements singuliers, qui servent de matière aux Tragédies sanglantes par l'appui qu'ils ont de l'histoire.[9]

> [The *vraisemblable* extraordinary is an action that occurs in truth less often that its opposite, but that nonetheless could fairly easily occur, since it does not reach the level of a miracle, nor that of singular events that are the subject matter of the Theatre of Cruelty sustained as they are by the authority of history.]

Bordering on the miraculous, Auguste's clemency stands as a conceivable but exceptional action. Corneille defines the *vraisemblable extraordinaire* precisely in contrast to the "singular events" of "Tragedies of the Scaffolds" whose plots are so far-fetched that they require the legitimacy of history to convince viewers that such actions could ever have occurred. That vein of tragedy tends to present the sovereign-judge as a straightforward punisher of crimes. Indeed, in tragedies of the first quarter of the seventeenth century, those of Hardy, but also of Du Ryer and La Calprenède, trial scenes appear with such frequency that they are a convention of the genre. In this drama, the king is an explicit judge and operates according to a court procedural – questioning witnesses and confronting evidence. Most often, the legal dispute ends in a guilty conviction, with the royal judge ordering a violent death, which may or may not be presented onstage.[10]

By contrast, clemency belongs to a domain situated outside of codified legal action. Clemency operates in its own temporality by eschewing norms in favour of a decision freed from the constraints of procedure. Revealingly, then, Corneille answers the critical attacks directed at Don Fernand and Tulle by drawing on their flaws to depict in *Cinna* a sovereign who ultimately retains power because he rejects legal discussion and diverges from precedent. With *Cinna*, the shift away from expectation is politically beneficial for the sovereign character and dramatically beneficial for the playwright. Politically, Auguste survives because he erases the difference between legality and self-preservation. Theatrically, the sovereign is isolated from criticism because he maintains the aura of power and dignity critics close to the Crown had begun to require of a king on the tragic stage. In peering closely at the portrayal of Auguste's judgment, we may grasp how Corneille has grown more savvy in his art since *Horace*; he deftly criticizes the arbitrary verdicts of a sovereign who bypasses law to redefine a kingdom's legal and moral spheres, while also presenting his audience with a brilliantly suspenseful royal judgment that reinforces the sovereign's *éclat*.

2 Cornelian Clemency: A Dialogue with the Politics of Rome and France

Clemency's status as a seemingly virtuous gesture with a politically efficacious ulterior motive has a complex history. Along with benevolence, temperance, courage, and piety, clemency, a companion to justice, is a conventional princely virtue in both the biblical and classical traditions.[11] In Roman culture it epitomized the virtue of a good leader, although it was first associated with the domain of war where Roman generals would agree to spare the defeated enemy from execution. Yet, even this seemingly honourable behaviour hinged on the adversary's explicit avowal of defeat and capitulation.[12] Although Seneca, in his treatise devoted to the subject, insists that clemency is the unique prerogative of the divinely inspired sovereign, for only the gods can show grace and save a sinner, clemency retains a peculiar status as a virtue because it perpetually binds the guilty to his judge, acting as a relentless reminder of his inferiority.

Seneca illustrates how an inescapable violence belies clemency's admirable character:

> For owing your life to someone is tantamount to losing it: when anyone has been cast down from an eminence to grovel at his enemy's feet and has awaited the other's verdict on his life and realm, his living brings glory to his savior, who gains greater renown by leaving the other unharmed than if he wiped him from the face of the earth. He remains a perpetual showpiece of the other's virtue, whereas he would have passed by in a moment had be been led in triumph.[13]

The sovereign's "power to give life" and turn the guilty into "a perpetual showpiece" of his beneficence entails fostering a sense of debt and loss from the pardoned who, more than diminished, is persistently humiliated.

In staging clemency, Corneille broke with early French tragedy's dynamic of the royal judge's defeat of the guilty man who capitulates under the force of royal judgment. Clemency also allows the playwright to move away from the random, apolitical royal judgments of tragicomedy while nonetheless maintaining the element of surprise, the twist in the plot spectators relish. Finally, although clemency allowed Corneille to retreat from explicit onstage violence, deemed too off-putting for sensitive audiences ever since the imperative of *bienséance* [tragic decorum] began to take hold, he does not entirely eliminate the potential for violence vested within royal judgment.

Corneille was sensitive to the implicit brutality of clemency, referring to its dangers in works written in chronological proximity to *Cinna*. In *Horace*, Valère, speaking in the name of "les gens de bien" (v. 1482) [people of virtue], counsels King Tulle against pardoning the accused nobleman who has killed his own sister, Camille. He emphasizes the subjective, and therefore tyrannical, nature of clemency:

> Faisant triompher Rome, il se l'est asservie;
> Il a sur nous un droit, et de mort et de vie,
> Et nos jours criminels ne pourront plus durer
> Qu'autant qu'à sa clémence il plaira l'endurer.   (vv. 1507–10)

> [Having made Rome triumph, he has subjugated her;
> He has over us the right of death and life,
> And our criminal days will only last
> As long as his clemency agrees to suffer them.]

Valère's view hinges on the dangerous capriciousness of clemency, and he insists that Horace must be punished because he not only usurped the king's role by anointing himself judge, but also because his future behaviour remains arbitrary and unpredictable.

Corneille returns to the perils of clemency in *La Mort de Pompée* (1644), the tragedy following *Cinna*, when he portrays the debate between the king of Egypt, Ptolomée, and his advisors over whether to show clemency by allowing Pompée to seek refuge in his land. In his own analysis of the play, Corneille condemns the discussions between the king and his Machiavellian advisors as "lâche et cruelle politique" [cowardly and cruel politics] but nonetheless displays a keen understanding of the ways clemency can be exploited and abused for the sake of political posturing.[14] Over the course of the debate surrounding Pompée's arrival, one of the advisors anticipates that César will resort to a "fausse clémence" [false clemency] towards his enemy:

> Il lui [Pompée] pardonnera, s'il faut qu'il en dispose,
> Et s'armant à regret de générosité,
> D'une fausse clémence il fera vanité,
> Heureux de l'asservir en lui donnant la vie,
> Et de plaire par là même à Rome asservie!   (vv. 174–8)

> [He will pardon him, if needed,
> And arming himself reluctantly with generosity,
> He will have the vanity of a false clemency,
> Happy to subjugate him by giving him life,
> And to please subjugated Rome by the same token!]

The passage, referring, in fact, to Augustus, makes of clemency a way to "arm oneself," and casts the pardon as a plainly political ploy to impress the public.

The depiction of clemency in *La Mort de Pompée* echoes classical texts that stress its political usefulness. For Julius Caesar, especially in the wake of the Battle of Pharsalus (an important reference in *Cinna* where the eponymous hero is none other than Pompey's grandson), the pardon became a central propagandistic tool. Caesar's policy of clemency was a source of vehement bitterness and indignation on the part of the Roman aristocracy who saw it as a usurpation of power, a factor that classical and modern commentators point to as leading to his assassination.[15] Generally, clemency in the Roman world was thought to tread a fine line between virtue and abuse.[16] Augustus, who for a large part of his reign fashioned himself as Julius Caesar's avenger, rejected clemency in favour of a policy of *severitas*, an exemplary punishment, which saw vengeance as the best expression of justice. In light of Julius Caesar's fate, Augustus is thought to have resisted clemency, as neither efficacious nor capable of leading to stability.

Given the varying accounts of Augustus's propensity to pardon, Corneille portrays the emperor's clemency as a markedly empire-altering gesture. While clemency resolves the fate of each character and puts to rest the demands of Auguste's opponents, it also consecrates a political terminus since the consipiring aristocrats' failure to uphold their defining role – the *devoir de noblesse* – ends their influence on the theatrical and political stages.[17] The female ringleader of the plot, Emilie, specifically articulates the change she experiences as a surrender: "Et je me rends, Seigneur, à ces hautes bontés" (v. 1715) [And I give in, my Lord, to these high graces]. As with her two accomplices, shame and promises of service/servitude accompany their capitulation.[18] For his part, Cinna swears eternal devotion to Auguste and hopes to dedicate his life to serving him; Maxime, meanwhile, expresses only confusion and embarrassment before such grandeur. In a remarkable turnaround, each aristocratic character relinquishes his or her defining characteristic (Emilie's "hatred," Cinna's "offence," and Maxime's "jealousy") as they become undifferentiated, awe-struck subjects silent before a higher presence.

Auguste's renowned judgment speech at the tragedy's end, which is usually read as prototypically conciliatory, emphasizes the new-found separation between the sovereign and his subjects.[19] Despite its veneer of reciprocity, Auguste's new order is based on "un combat" [a battle] where the sovereign always outdoes his subjects. This competition, played out on uneven grounds, is a foregone conclusion – how could Cinna ever possibly match Auguste? – which serves only to highlight the disproportion and distance between the governed and the governor. The "friendship" ("Soyons amis, Cinna") Auguste announces consists of a continual display of his ability to "double" and thereby exceed all attempts made by his subject to repay him. The proclamation of clemency is, then, a not-so-subtle denigration of the nobleman and his "lâche destin" [cowardly destiny]. Not only does Auguste stress his dominance over him, but he also obscures the line between friends and enemies. The enduring message of the verdict of clemency is the sovereign's ability to grant or take away life. Hence Corneille readjusts the old formula of early French tragedy's juridical process in favour of a theatrically pleasing, though more nebulous, zone of judgment.

In *Cinna*, the sovereign still asserts his supreme authority at the play's close, but his means of doing so are no longer explicitly combative nor punitive. Clemency as an exceptional and extraordinary judgment strikes like a *coup d'état* or a *coup de théâtre*, shifting away from linear and legal thinking to transform the order of things. Corneille wrote *Cinna* as France's legal institutions – the *Parlements* – insisted on the importance of relying upon standard procedures of judgment based on custom, ceremony, and legal precedent.[20] They objected to Richelieu's turn towards the judicial process as a weapon in his fight against challenges to the Crown. The jurists, officers, and *parlementaires* who possessed the authority to conduct a trial or weigh in on legal matters, begin to disappear from the seventeenth-century tragic stage, but will seek to reclaim their presence on the juridical stage during the *Fronde*, which will erupt less than a decade after *Cinna*'s publication.[21]

As France's judicial debates grew louder, tragic poetics written in Richelieu's sphere favoured eliminating portrayals of judicial procedure. Corneille follows this turn away from explicit references to the formal process of a trial and to the contemporary legal apparatus such as prisons, henchmen, and the public scaffolds in favour of an emphasis on the weight of the sovereign's decision as central to the plot. Portrayals of prisons and explicit legal actors will increasingly be bound to the comical stage. Certainly, with the accent placed on respect for the unity of location, prison scenes become more difficult to stage, and it is just simpler to allude to threats of incarceration. However, even general allusions to prison fade and are replaced by less graphic mentions of "arrêts" [verdicts], "captivité" [capitivity], or "lieu sûr" [secure location].[22]

In *Cinna*, for example, when Auguste learns of the nobleman's plans to assassinate him, rather than list the many *supplices* he could inflict upon him, the stage directions indicate: "il lui [Polyclète] parle à l'oreille" [he whispers in the ear] of his *affranchi* (between v. 1099 and v. 1100). To which the latter answers: "Tous vos ordres, Seigneur, seront exécutés" (v. 1100) [All your orders will be executed]. The word "executed" highlights the change from a time when tragedy depicted a character's execution and now the new vein of tragedy which depicts "execution" as royal demands to be followed. Not hearing or knowing what Auguste has decided increases the dramatic suspense, of course, but it also pinpoints the judicial scene's transformation from a public hearing, one in which there are numerous listeners, witnesses, and advisors, to a scene viewed and interpreted from the outside, described as mysterious and leading only to speculation as to what the sovereign's intentions are. We see Cinna's arrest from the point of view of Emilie's confidante, Fulvie:

> quand soudain Polyclète,
> Des volontés d'Auguste ordinaire interprète
> Est venu l'aborder et sans suite et sans bruit,
> Et de sa part sur l'heure au palais l'a conduit.　　　(vv. 1277–80)

> [When suddenly Polyclète,
> Usually the interpreter of Auguste's orders
> Came to speak to him without escort and without noise,
> On his behalf immediately led him to the palace.]

Arriving with discretion and quietly approaching the accused underscores the control exerted by Auguste, even without an explicit use of force, to achieve his goal. He swiftly and efficiently arrests a conspirator before he or his allies can grasp what is happening, creating an ominous suspense for the dangers ahead.

The nebulousness associated with Auguste's intentions is repeated in a later scene when the emperor realizes the extent of the conspirators' betrayal and cryptically announces to Emilie and Cinna, "Il faut bien satisfaire aux feux dont vous brûlez" (v. 1660) [I must satisfy the flames for which you burn]. By mixing a commonplace chivalric allusion to romantic passion with an evocation of burning at the stake – a very conceivable punishment for attempted regicide in the seventeenth century but one the emperor will reject – Auguste's judgment takes on the tone of an inside joke he tells himself as he toys with his subjects. The "flames" on Corneille's stage will be limited to a precious imagery of passion.

After *Cinna*, Corneille will continue to move away from overt depictions of *supplices*, prisons, and contemporary legal matters in his tragedies. Nonetheless, as if to underscore the rift between the noble tragic genre and other genres, in *Le Menteur* (1644), the playwright's first comedy following *Cinna*, law and its study are the butt of numerous jokes. The play's main character, Dorante, a young law student, arrives in Paris, determined to "quitt[er] la robe pour l'épée" (v. 1) [leave the robe for the sword], and we learn in the opening verses that he has "fait banqueroute à ce fratras de lois" (v. 4) [bankrupted this mess of laws]. In the play's sequel, *La Suite du Menteur* (1645), the jokes about law increase with Acts I and II staged entirely within a prison-cell, referred to in jest as "la maison du roi" (v. 2) [the king's home]; such devices indicate tragedy's particular burden in upholding royal dignity, especially in matters of justice, and comedy's far greater latitude in treating such matters.

Thus, though prison scenes were popular in early French tragedies of the seventeenth century, and even more so in tragicomedies of the 1630s and 1640s, their presence diminishes markedly in tragedy as the emphasis on protecting the image of the sovereign increases. Reflecting on the difficulties of staging such scenes and on the necessary loss of dignity that accompanies them, Corneille insists on preferring the suggestion of imprisonment over its portrayal:

> Il arrive quelquefois des occasions indispensables de faire arrêter prisonniers sur nos théâtres quelques-uns de nos principaux acteurs, mais alors il vaut mieux se contenter de donner des gardes qui les suivent et n'affaiblissent ni le spectacle ni l'action comme dans *Polyeucte* et dans *Héraclius*.[23]

> [Sometimes there arise moments when it is absolutely necessary to arrest as prisoners on our stages some of our main actors, but in those cases it is best to give them guards that follow them and weaken neither the spectacle nor the action, as in *Polyeucte* and *Héraclius*.]

Despite the precautionary tone Corneille adopts here, *Polyeucte* (1643), a martyr tragedy, in fact emphasizes the hero's imprisonment and his eventual execution, placing these events at the heart of the action since that experience is precisely what affords the hero his martyr status. The playwright's non-martyr tragedies, however, follow the model initiated by *Cinna*: the sovereign judge's decision moves to the centre of the plot, with the fate of all the characters hanging on it; the plot itself becomes a waiting game for royal decision-making.

As the tragic genre gains social prestige and political anchoring, the courtroom procedural loses its hold, and the *éclat* of Auguste's clemency hinges on the inability of the emperor's subjects, and Corneille's spectators, to grasp the basis for the emperor's judgment. Instead, they witness how clemency alters the sovereign's relationship to his subjects because it erases a dialectical exchange in favour of a hegemonic rule of the exception made by an exceptional figure. In other words, *Cinna* allows spectators entry into the *arcana imperii* of sovereign power, but only leads them in so far. The audience gets a close-up of the circumstances leading to the emperor's clemency, but because of the mystery and exceptionality inherent to such a verdict, *Cinna* ultimately accentuates the secrecy surrounding the sovereign's motives.

Fundamentally, *Cinna* questions where to draw the line between legality and illegitimacy, asking if a sovereign (or his prime minister) can rightfully operate in an extra-legal sphere. The tragedy displays the process by which crimes of state are erased as Auguste moves beyond all legal reference: "Le Passé devient juste et l'avenir permis" (v. 1612) [The Past becomes just and the future is permitted], we are told, once the heavens have allowed a sovereign to acquire the throne.[24] To be sure, in the case of Auguste, the Roman Empire ultimately benefits; but in displaying the inauguration of the regime of extraordinary decision-making, Corneille implicitly raises the spectre of the return of tyrants to Rome, thereby making Racine's *Britannicus* – the story of Nero's tyrannical turn – a true follow-up to *Cinna*. More than the portrayal of a decidedly generous action, *Cinna* constitutes a progression in Corneille's thinking on how to stage royal judgment on the seventeenth-century tragic stage while offering an in-depth reflection on the sovereign's relationship to the law.

3 The Spectre of Henchmen on the Tragic Stage

With *Cinna*, Corneille proves his command of the new tragic conception that Jean Mairet advocated for in the *Préface de la Silvanire* (1631) and that the critics of *Le Cid* had so forcefully accused him of flouting. Calls had grown loud since 1637 for tighter plots structured around a focus on anticipation – the strategy of suspense – and for less emphasis on the random effects of chance. In 1642 Corneille's *Cinna* reflects a better understanding of this view, which did not mean entirely abandoning the practices of tragicomedy, but involved centring the tragic plot around the fate of individuals instead of around a multiplicity of events. As Lyons describes, one of the aims of such changes was to "[keep] the dynamism of tragicomedy without straining the attention of the audience to the point at which it was difficult to foresee what might happen to the leading characters."[25] In the new tragic vein, the intrigue moves away from the domain of random encounters, frequent duels, sudden revelations, and inexplicable coincidences; simultaneously, the importance of characters' deliberations is heightened. Indeed, if Corneille's dramaturgy has differentiated itself from that of his contemporaries, it is in no small part due to his ability to stage a hero's internal divisions. By the 1640s Corneille was not alone in staging the deliberations of tragic heroes, but he became the playwright most recognized for successfully integrating such scenes into the dramatic plot, leading these divisions to be referred to, posthumously, as "*dilemmes cornéliens*."

Corneille's exceptional mastery of internal debate was recognized as early as *La Pratique du théâtre* (1657). Despite the shortcomings attributed to *Le Cid*, Rodrigue's *stances* brought Corneille prestige for his skill in provoking audience pleasure at listening to a hero deliberate over an impossible choice.[26] In the chapter "On Deliberations," after singling out Rodrigue, d'Aubignac moves on to praise *Cinna*, which he considers to be the perfect example of dramatic action conveyed through effective discourse:

> Vous y [dans ces scènes de délibération] voyez des esprits agités par des mouvements contraires, poussés de différentes passions, et emportés à des desseins extrêmes, dont le Spectateur ne saurait prévoir l'événement; les discours y portent le caractère Théâtral; ils sont impétueux et par les raisonnements et par les figures; *et c'est plutôt l'image d'une âme au milieu de ses Bourreaux, que d'un homme qui délibère au milieu de ses amis.*[27]

> [You see there (in these scenes of deliberation) spirits agitated by contrary movements, pushed by various passions, and taken with extreme intentions, of which the Spectator cannot predict the outcome; the speeches carry within them the Theatrical character; they are impetuous both in their reasoning and imagery; *and it is more the image of a soul among its henchmen than a man who deliberates amongst his friends.*]

D'Aubignac praises the deliberative moments of *Cinna* because they advance the plot without resorting to scenic effects. The dangers threatening the heroes are not displayed but instead evoked through eloquent speeches that replace action per se. Although in comparison to the Elizabethan tragic tradition, the long monologues in which Corneille's tormented characters express their ambivalence towards a decision may lead some readers to complain that "nothing happens" in neoclassical tragedy, *Cinna* encapsulates the new French tragic aesthetic espoused by the Richelieu circles. If in *Clitandre*, *Le Cid*, and *Horace*, the dramatic rhythm escalates at a frenetic pace, the dramatic action in *Cinna* consists of a series of non-actions. Emilie does not avenge her father as she had insisted she would; Cinna, despite his long harangues to the conspirators and his promises to Emilie, does not go through with the assassination; Maxime does not commit suicide despite the false announcement of his death, and though he hatches a plan to escape with Emilie, it falls apart.

And Auguste, in spite of his deliberations in Acts II and IV, does not abdicate the throne, nor does he violently punish the rebels. Rome looks quite the same in Act V as it did in Act I. The change that has taken place has happened within Auguste. His relationship to Rome and to his subjects is undeniably altered, but spectators and readers of the play are left to find their own explanation for what that change represents.

Instead of a display of physical action, especially at its climactic moment, Auguste becomes a supreme figure of judgment because of his non-action. In so doing, he incarnates the new monarchical-marvellous aesthetic of tragedy and redefines the meaning of heroism. In contrast to the royal judges of tragedies past, kings who were bent on punishment and who brutally, if blindly, enforced their authority at the close of a plot from which they had been absent for the most part, Auguste clears the stage of its *supplices* and its henchmen, turning these only into symbols of passion and figures of precious speech. Corneille's emperor refutes each one of the characteristics of royal judges of old by the play's close, thereby redefining the relationship between sovereign judgment and the guilty.

Cinna ou la clémence d'Auguste devotes extensive space to developing the adversarial perspectives of the sovereign and his subjects. As the full title of the play attests, the two storylines compete for preeminence within the tragedy's narrative. First, "Cinna," the drama of political conspirators, gives voice to the possibility of revolt when a sovereign infringes upon the legal order. Second, the story of "la clémence d'Auguste," considers how a sovereign should respond to personal threats and social upheaval. As in *Le Cid* and *Horace*, in *Cinna* those who loudly contest the king's judgment are heard at length but are eventually silenced. The latter differs from the two previous plays, however, in the deliberate pacing of the plot where Cinna and Emilie lay out the case against Auguste from the outset, as opposed to the fifth Act of *Horace*.[28] Then, over the course of *Cinna*'s Acts III and IV, the action slowly delegitimizes the conspirators' arguments and eventually places Auguste in the position of judging those who had judged him. The emperor co-opts the dramatic narrative and becomes the only character able to shape Rome's – and the play's – future by his response. At the tragedy's halfway point, Auguste's judgment becomes the central focus of the plot – will he or won't he punish the rebels? By the end of *Cinna*, the emperor has become the agent of action instead of its recipient. The decisive and unexpected *coup* intended for Auguste ultimately strikes his subjects in the form of clemency. At the tragedy's close, the sovereign has, literally, the final word.

4 The Strategy of Clemency from Corneille to Rotrou

We may be tempted to understand clemency on the French tragic stage as an expression of nostalgia for the ideal of a feudal judge, a longing for a proximate prince whose personalized justice was forgiving and paternal. In fact, as I have argued, the confluence of Richelieu's judicial politics and the new-found attention given within his artistic circles to theatrical sovereignty, explain clemency's emergence on the French stage as a viable political and theatrical royal action. For Corneille, clemency conveys a barely implicit violence. In *Cinna*, although the prince is seemingly an anti-executioner compared to his royal judge predecessors, clemency results in the sovereign operating in a new space of secrecy in which no one is certain regarding "ce qui [l']anime" (v. 1661) [what motivates him]. Cinna, Emilie, Maxime, as well as the spectators, are deprived of the ability to fully grasp and respond to Auguste's actions, leaving them only to wait for and wonder about what will come next.

The audience's interest in the judicial process, so evident from the topos it had become in early French tragedy and tragicomedy, is maintained by *Cinna*'s Act V, a trial of the conspirators, albeit held in the emperor's cabinet – the inner sanctum of the Roman Empire. As opposed to the unpleasant allusions to courtrooms, deemed too evocative of contemporary times, Cinna's trial scene is presented without the trappings of a court procedural, while still upholding the violence of the interrogation and the emphasis on Auguste's power to determine a verdict. And this is where the meaning of the verdict, the decision of clemency, is most revealing: *Cinna* traces the emperor's departure from the realm of consultation and intelligibility towards a new reign where the sovereign refers to no one but to himself. In this sphere, there is no dialogue between right and wrong; only the sovereign decision remains, and his decision is always deemed to be right.

Auguste's secretive stance, which denies exchange except on the emperor's terms, recalls Louis Marin's gloss of Gabriel Naudé's description of the coup d'état:

> Le coup d'état est [...] la révélation du secret d'état: il révèle le secret du prince par son action même, directement à ceux que ce secret concerne, les peuples, les sujets du prince ou tel ou tel d'entre eux, *mais qui sont les destinataires exclus de sa communication.* Comme l'écrit Naudé, "ils admirent les heureux effets de ces coups de maître, sans pour autant rien connaître de leurs causes et divers ressorts." (my emphasis)[29]

[The coup d'état is ... the revelation of a secret of state: it reveals the secret of the prince by its very action, directly to those whom that secret concerns, the people, the subjects of the prince or whomever among them, *all those who are the excluded recipients of his communication.* As Naudé writes, "they admire the happy effects of these masterful blows, without at the same time understanding their causes and various triggers."]

Auguste's withdrawal from the realm of precedent, legal debate, and communication ties the act of clemency to the exclusionary process – the communication of a non-communication – that Naudé (Corneille's contemporary) evokes. Called upon to judge the accused, the emperor's verdict is resolutely mysterious, unpredictable, and therefore infinitely susceptible to interpretation. Naudé does not equate the *coup* with a negative expression of power. For him, it is synonymous with mystery and surprise, its sources indecipherable to the people who can only admire the "happy effects" the prince has suddenly produced. In spite of clemency's intuitively agreeable moral nature, Auguste's judgment transgresses *vraisemblance* (resembling in this way Fernand's and Tulle's verdicts). Through his pardon, the emperor imposes a new, non-dialogical framework: what is there to judge in the verdict of clemency but the absence of something? That a sovereign should not only forgive, but also reward the betrayal of his closest allies pushes the limits of logic and legality. Indeed, Auguste's action contains within it a distinct element of lawlessness, and at the close of *Cinna* the exceptional becomes a technique of government, an "art d'être maître des cœurs" (v. 1764) [the art of being a master of hearts] as Auguste's wife, Livie, describes his pardon.

This portrayal of clemency as a monarchical sidestepping of law will reappear only a few years after *Cinna* in Jean Rotrou's *Venceslas* (1647) where we observe a similar alliance of transgression and royal pardon.[30] In that play, the king's clemency once again entails going against a pre-established moral and legal code, and asserting the sovereign's authority at the expense of legal precedent. Clemency in *Venceslas*, as in *Cinna*, insists on the sovereign's right to place personal and practical considerations above a respect for tradition and moral imperatives, thereby, in the case of Rotrou's play, justifying the forgiveness of fratricide in the name of preserving civil peace and safeguarding royal succession.

In this perspective, Rotrou is as invested in reflecting on the political moment in which his drama appears as Corneille. Both playwrights grapple with the contemporary shift towards a king as "living law" instead of simply a guardian of law.[31] It is in this same period, often identified as the French "baroque" period, stretching from 1610 to 1650, that Joël Cornette has documented a phenomenal rise in political treatises. These writings cease to reflect on theoretical notions of power, and move instead towards advancing more explicitly practical ideas on how to implement power and create order. Quoting from Richelieu's *Testament politique*, Cornette points to a new emphasis on the state's role in seducing, intimidating, and forcing subjects into recognizing the supremacy of royal authority:

> Si l'Etat s'incarne ainsi dans un espace – ou plutôt des espaces – à conquérir et à solidifier, des hommes à attirer, contrôler, fiscaliser, punir, des institutions à diminuer, détruire, ou mettre en place [l'etat est] aussi des paroles, des textes nouveaux greffés sur l'événement et adaptés à la spécificité d'une monarchie encore fragile [...] Leur seule unité [de ces textes] est leur fonction: il s'agit de justifier, de séduire, de faire peur, en érigeant s'il le faut "mille roues et mille potences" pour "imprimer à toutes personnes l'amour, la crainte et la révérence de sa Majesté" car "le dernier point de la Puissance des princes doit consister en la Possession du Cœur de leurs sujets."[32]

> [If the State is therefore incarnated in a space – or rather spaces – to conquer and solidify, made of men to attract, control, tax, punish, of institutions to diminish, destroy, or put in place, [the State] is also words, new texts grafted onto the event and adapted to the specifics of a still fragile monarchy: the goal is to justify, to seduce, to frighten, by erecting "a thousand wheels and a thousand gallows" to "impress onto everyone love, fear, and reverance for his Majesty" because "the last point of the Power of the princes must consist in the Possession of the hearts of Subjects."]

Corneille and Rotrou's sovereigns in *Cinna* and *Venceslas* resemble each other in the way they grapple with whether or not to resort to "a thousand wheels and a thousand gallows." They are unsure if they should "seduce" or punish their subjects. Both rulers are initially presented as fallible and hesitant in their exercise of judgment, but this space of uncertainty is followed by a celebrated final refusal to engage with notions of guilt and innocence: they reject the scaffolds. Crucially, however, whereas Corneille's dénouement by clemency inaugurated a triumph of sovereignty to be recorded by posterity ("O Siècles, ô Mémoire, / Conservez à jamais ma dernière victoire") (vv. 1697–8) [Oh Centuries, oh Memory, / conserve for eternity my last victory], in *Venceslas*, the elderly eponymous

Polish monarch abdicates. Nonetheless, for both playwrights, the royal verdict of clemency results in a new-found "possession of the hearts of the subjects." The tragedies similiarly offer a performance of the royal pardon's effectiveness in instilling reverence for a judicial decision that goes beyond the limits of law.

In *Venceslas*, the sovereign not only grapples with the transgression enacted through clemency, he ultimately condemns himself for it. His abdication – an explicit indictment of his pardon and all that it stands for – underscores the darkness and violence inherent in clemency. A summary of the plot will serve to illustrate that although Rotrou dubbed *Venceslas* a tragicomedy, a label given because of the king's marginal presence, the determining role of material objects like the curtain and the sword in the intrigue, and the case of mistaken identity – all well-established conventions of the genre – he offers a serious reflection on royal judgment onstage. Clearly influenced by Corneille, Rotrou tries his hand at the theatricality of clemency, but he departs from the ambiguous example of Auguste and the *deus ex machina* endings of tragicomedy, where the king's judgment has little political consequence, by emphasizing the unbearable weight of the royal verdict through Venceslas's abdication.

The play opens with the aging king of Poland, Venceslas, reproaching his first-born son, Ladislas, for not living the dignified life of an heir to the throne. Hot-headed, unreasonable, and dissolute, the prince reflects poorly on the king's authority, and Venceslas beseeches his son to act virtuously. In response, Ladislas suggests that the king's authority is in jeopardy, blames his father's old age, and asserts that Venceslas should rid himself of the weight of the crown by anointing him in his place. Furthermore, Ladislas's jealousy for his father's favourite courtier is another subject of contention. Indeed, the king's most valiant soldier, Duke Federic, also the closest friend of Ladislas's younger brother, Alexandre, possesses all the qualities Ladislas lacks. Federic, remaining composed and respectful, refuses to be goaded into anger by Ladislas's continuously disparaging insinuations. Alexandre, the virtuous brother, has come to the duke's defence numerous times against his older brother's threats, and Venceslas has promised to reward the duke with whatever prize he chooses for his service to the kingdom.

Ladislas's jealousy towards Federic stems from his passion for the beautiful Cassandre, Duchesse of Cunisberg, whom the prince has brazenly, but unsuccessfully, pursued, and whom he holds out hope of marrying. Ladislas believes Federic has not only out-manoeuvred him in the king's eyes, but in the duchess's heart as well. In fact, the duke secretly loves Princess Théodore, daughter to Venceslas and sister to Ladislas and Alexandre. Ever modest, the duke is afraid to aspire to a member of the royal family and has confessed his love to no one. To complicate matters, Duke Federic has pretended to love Cassandre as a favour to Alexandre, Ladislas's brother and true rival. When Ladislas offers his hand to the duchesse once more in Act II, he is met with brutal rejection and blames Federic. Meanwhile, Princess Théodore, who is secretly in love with the duke, is saddened to learn from Ladislas that Federic loves Cassandre. In response, she entreats the duchess to accept Ladislas's offer of marriage. Alexandre and Cassandre, however, desperate to unite, decide to marry secretly that night so no one can contest their love once she is his wife. In Act IV, Théodore awakens from a gruesome nightmare, only to encounter Ladislas hurt and bleeding. He has returned from Cassandre's palace convinced he has killed Federic. Venceslas, worried by the noise, arrives and demands to know why Ladislas is injured. To everyone's consternation, just as the elder son confesses his murder of the duke, Federic walks in. Cassandre follows him and, carrying Ladislas's knife as irrefutable proof, announces that the victim Ladislas killed in the dark was in fact his own brother, Alexandre.

Cassandre demands justice from Venceslas, imploring him to execute one son for the murder of the other. Venceslas imprisons Ladislas while he reflects on which course of action to take. He weighs his role as king and as father, lamenting the royal imperative to respect the law above all else. He decides to condemn Ladislas to death. Theodore begs her father to forgive Ladislas, playing on his paternal feeling; she also tells him that the kingdom's subjects support clemency towards the prince. Duke Federic adds his voice in support of clemency and asks that the reward he was promised come in the form of a stay of execution. Even Cassandre, touched by the others' pleas, approves the clemency. Venceslas rules that he cannot in good conscience pardon Ladislas and remain king. He decides to abdicate and give his crown to the son he has forgiven. Ladislas, a changed man, is suddenly overcome with emotion and repentance. He accepts the throne and embraces his defender, Federic, who pledges his allegiance to the new king. Venceslas gives Théodore's hand to the duke in marriage. The play ends with the possibility that, in time, Cassandre will accept the new king's hand, though first Alexandre must be laid to rest.

Despite the common assumption that in his tragedies and tragicomedies, Rotrou's kings are conceived according to a different dramatic formula from Corneille and Racine's sovereigns, we can see a conspicuously similar focus on the performance of royal judgment. Arguably, a more explicit lawlessness and disorder characterize Rotrou's kingdoms than those of his better-known counterparts. Indeed, Ellen McClure's comment that in *Le Véritable Saint Genest* (1645), "authority and legitimacy are without a clear anchor" could be extended to most of Rotrou's dramatic portrayals.[33] *Saint Genest* takes place under Dioclétian's reign when the emperor has divided Rome into three parts and given a part to his wife. For *Venceslas*, the playwright chooses Poland, a place of glorified exile, for troublesome French princes and princesses such as Henri de Valois who was elected king of Poland in 1573 and Louise Marie de Gonzague, the illustrious *frondeuse*. The not-so-distant land to the east becomes a laboratory where elective vote can be pitted against the French tenets of absolutist rule by divine right, biological succession, and Catholic supremacy.[34]

Rotrou's political drama is drawn to dire circumstances, not just threats to the stability of the throne, as we might see in Corneille or Racine, but to impending catastrophes of state, instances when the kingdom is on the brink of collapse. In *Venceslas*, as in other Rotrou plays, the monarch, despite his best efforts, cannot prevent chaos, and his authority is in jeopardy. Referring to Rotrou's best-known works, *Le Véritable Saint Genest*, *Venceslas*, and *Cosroès*, Catherine Treilhou-Balaudé notes that the kings in those tragedies offer contradictory portraits of royalty: "Le roi de théâtre selon le dernier Rotrou, tout en parlant à la manière d'un roi, donne à voir l'image d'une souveraineté affaiblie ou défaillante"[35] [The king in the later plays of Rotrou, while speaking as a king, is portrayed as a weakened or failing sovereignty]. This insight should not, however, be limited to Rotrou's last plays nor to his most famous ones since numerous sovereigns in his early works are either killed or commit suicide due to a fatal misjudgment on their part (Créon in *Antigone* (1639), Hercule in *Hercule Mourant* (1635), Justinien in *Bélisaire* (1644), and Antioche in *Crisante* (1637), as we will see below). Though Agamemnon survives at the close of *Iphigénie* (1640), the king's wish to "goûter un long repos" (v. 1914) [enjoy a long rest] upon his return to Argos after the Trojan War clearly underscores the futility of the sovereign's hopes for the future. Jean-Claude Vuillemin similarly remarks on the recurrent presence of surprisingly listless kings in the playwright's assortment of tragic actors: "chez Rotrou, face à l'adversité, le héros masculin s'avère généralement d'une passivité déconcertante"[36] [in Rotrou, faced with adversity, the male hero generally proves to be disconcertingly passive]. Thus, in the teleology of seventeenth-century tragedy's preoccupation with protecting the sovereign character, Rotrou does not fit easily within the trajectory I have drawn of an ever-more active and distinguished royal character. Why, if the image of sovereignty becomes increasingly narrow and preserved from demeaning portraits, do Rotrou's kings persist in their feebleness and passivity? How should we account for the resemblance of his kings – even after the quarrel of *Le Cid* and the success of *Cinna* – to Walter Benjamin's description of the melancholic, bored, and mournful sovereigns of the *Trauerspiel*?[37]

5 *Crisante*, Looking beyond Rotrou's Baroque

When explaining where to place Rotrou within the Corneille and Racine parallel, most scholars insist on his allegiance to the conventions of tragicomedy and his investment in the tradition of humanist tragedy where characters are so spectacularly unable to resist the onslaught of passion that overcomes them. Georges Forestier, for instance, separates Rotrou from Corneille and Racine because he deems that the canonical playwrights are unique in their opposition of reason and passion, while Rotrou belongs to an earlier conception of tragedy's display of an "esthétique de la fureur"[38] [aesthetic of furore]. Since Voltaire famously declared Rotrou to be Corneille's "father," and added that, ultimately, "the father was surpassed by the son," much of the critical interest in Rotrou has been limited to assessing how he differs from Corneille.[39] This focus on aesthetic cataloguing of Rotrou still overwhelmingly dominates critical readings of his plays. The two most complete studies on the author of *Venceslas*, Morel's *Jean Rotrou*, and Vuillemin's *Baroquisme et théâtralité*, never consider Rotrou's works within their political contexts, beyond the view that the plays' baroque style exemplifies early seventeenth-century theatre in contrast to what will replace it. As the following comment by Vuillemin attests, critics generally assume that the plays themselves have little to reveal because their value lies in their form:

> C'est un type d'esthétique théâtrale, moins préoccupé de psychologie que de beaux décors, et de vraisemblance que d'effets scéniques variés, qui caractérisera le mieux la quasi-totalité des textes dramatiques de Rotrou.[40]

> [It is a type of theatrical aesthetic, less preoccupied by psychology than by attractive surroundings, and less by *vraisemblance* than by various stage effects, which will best characterize the quasi-totality of Rotrou's dramatic texts.]

More recently the tide of critical analysis on Rotrou has turned. *Le Véritable Saint Genest*, a tragedy where religion and theatre are paired in depicting an actor/martyr at the moment of his spectacular conversion, has sparked renewed critical interest in the playwright.[41] Under Forestier's direction a new edition of Rotrou's *Œuvres complètes* has been recently completed.[42] Though Forestier and his collaborators typically adopt narrowly defined literary approaches (*études génétiques*), in the detailed introductions prefacing the plays, they situate Rotrou within a specifically early seventeenth-century cultural context. Notwithstanding this invigorating approach, most current studies of Rotrou's tragedies have limited themselves predominantly to *Saint Genest*.[43]

Critical reluctance to read Rotrou in a political or historical light – i.e., in the same way one reads Corneille or Racine – remains difficult to justify, especially given the complexity of the royal figures that span his tragic and tragicomedic corpus. Rotrou's staging of royal judgment, prison scenes, and judicial discourse have often been discounted as conventions of the early tragic genre, when, in fact, he offers complex reflections on the intersection of legal discourse and theatricality. Furthermore, the correspondences between his trial scenes and those of the better-known playwrights have been underappreciated. Although Rotrou's protagonists may be unable ultimately to reign in their passions – be they sexual or political – he grapples as extensively and intricately as Corneille and Racine, with the relationship between sovereignty, legality, and tragedy.

In analysing Rotrou's reflection on royal judgment, his early political tragedy, *Crisante* (1637), is a good counterpart to reflections on *Cinna* and *Venceslas* since Auguste is once again a sovereign-judge whose reign is troubled by the crime of a wayward subject.[44] In this earlier play, however, the tragedy presents a trial of the accused and, this time, a decision to execute him for the good of Rome. Written in a period of intense theatrical and political transformation of tragedy, the play was conceived just as Rotrou earned a position as one of five playwrights chosen by Richelieu, an honour that garnered him prestige and access to royal power.[45] It is thought that Rotrou's *Hercule Mourant* (1635), most likely written shortly before *Crisante*, had impressed the cardinal and drawn him to the playwright. Many consider it to be the inaugural play of the French tragic genre's renaissance. Rotrou stands at the forefront of the serious genre's re-emergence and transformation. *Crisante*, as a follow-up to the turn towards tragedy, should be read as a product of the playwright's mulling over of changes linked to Richelieu's efforts to redefine theatre.

Given this context, it may seem surprising that *Crisante* revolves around a king's reversal of fortune and sullen character, circumstances which prevent him from rising up against his sad fate. More striking, even, is the contrasting vitality of the queen. At the start of *Crisante*, the sovereign finds himself in a post-"state of emergency" moment.[46] Whereas for Benjamin, the prince in baroque theatre worriedly tries to prevent a crisis of state and laments its possibility, Rotrou's Corinthian king, Antioche, is a monarch recently dispossessed of his throne in the aftermath of Roman invasion. From his first arrival onstage to the last scene of the play, Antioche can only deplore the loss of his devastated kingdom and abducted queen, now a captive of the Roman army. Antioche speaks limited lines of dialogue and only makes brief appearances onstage; his marginality within the tragic plot is especially marked in comparison to the prominence of his wife, the title character.

Though Corneille in *Nicomède* (1651) and Racine in *Mithridate* (1672) respectively stage kings grappling with the threat of Roman invasion, in those cases Rome's arrival is imminent – the actual battlefields are situated at a vague distance beyond the limits of the stage – and those plays centre on heroic efforts to resist threatening imperial power. *Crisante*, by contrast, depicts the dire political, cultural, and even geographical consequences of the Roman invaders' presence. The evocations of conquest and defeat, combined with repeated memories of the sack, carnage, and rape of Corinth echo the images of a demolished Troy in the *Aeneid*; in Corinth, however, there is no hope for a rebirth as an independent state. If Corinth is to be rebuilt, it will be as an imperial outpost under Roman law and in a new Roman cultural space. Thus *Crisante* takes place in what Timothy Hampton has called the "monstrous territory" of the baroque where the stage becomes a space for conflicting definitions of the same location.[47]

Crisante portrays an intermediate moment when sovereignty passes from one governing body to another – an instance of extreme instability – when characters chart the place that law and legality must occupy so that order may reign. The intrigue tells of the painfully difficult establishment of Roman sovereignty, and accentuates the violence inherent to a lawless land. On one side, there is Antioche, the defeated king, unable to enforce his rule, and on the other side, there is the Roman Empire, dominant and powerful, seeking to establish its rule, but still encountering resistance. The play offers the perspectives of both sides: Antioche's lamentations of Roman devastation echo from a reversed standpoint, the opening lines of Act I uttered by the Roman general, Manilie, who boasts of trampling on monarchical sceptres in victory: "Que tout le monde tremble au bruit de nos exploits, / Et marchons triomphants sur les têtes des Rois" (vv. 20–1) [Let everyone tremble at the sound of our exploits/ And let us triumphantly march over the heads of Kings]. A few verses later, a nameless Roman soldier known as "Chef de guerre #1" [War Chief #1] provides yet another version of the same events, describing the utter defeat of the Corinthian armies: "Ils tombaient pêle-mêle, *étouffés* sous nos pas, / Et pour un de nos gens, cent d'eux suffisaient pas" (vv. 35–6, my emphasis) [They fell chaotically, *suffocated* beneath our steps, / And for every one of our men, a hundred of theirs were not enough]. These passages accentuate the gulf between the satisfaction of the victorious and the dismay of the defeated. The Roman aggressors are unstoppable: faster, stronger, better equipped. The image of the conquering Roman footsteps squashing Corinthian bodies piled up haphazardly ("pêle-mêle") heightens the sense that the invaders physically dominate their enemies and strategically out-manoeuvre them to a staggering degree.

Yet, as the repeated descriptions of unbounded Roman violence attest, the empire's arrival in Corinth does not equate with the onset of the rule of law. Rather, throughout the play we hear mournful regrets for the dying monarchy (now only a "reste" – a remnant) opposed to the Western power's chaotic expansion:

> Ce reste est le débris du superbe palais,
> Où régna si longtemps, la justice, et la paix.
> Et ce que fut Corinthe avant cette disgrâce,
> N'en garde que le nom, et n'est plus que sa place;
> Sa fumée a caché le ciel à nos regards,
> Elle fut un bûcher, ardent de toutes parts,
> Et demeure à nos yeux si nue,
> Et si déserte que même le vainqueur en déplore la perte.   (vv. 175–82)

> [These remains are the debris of a superb palace,
> Where once reigned justice and peace for so long.
> And of what Corinth was before this disgrace,
> Only remains the name and the place;
> Its smoke has hidden the sky from our eyes,
> She was a stake, burning from all parts,
> And remains so naked to our eyes,
> And so deserted that even the victor deplores her loss.]

In the wake of Roman invasion, the cultural jewel that was Corinth has gone up in smoke, leaving an overwhelming feeling of nostalgia and loss. The Corinthian city, recognized above all as a place where justice and peace had reigned, is now stripped of her virtues and bears only its name. In staging the immediate aftermath of battle when Antioche and his city of Corinth teeter on the verge of collapse, when the Roman armies have won but not completely established their rule, the play explores regime change, the process by which a new authority takes the place of an older one and seeks the recognition of its legitimacy in doing so. I believe the answer to what *Crisante* – the tragedy and the female protagonist at its centre – stands for is best understood at the intersection of contemporary political and dramaturgical considerations. As we explore Rotrou's play, we will see how Crisante becomes a symbol of the fallen Corinth, now entirely vulnerable and in disorder, but over which men fight to gain possession. Moreover, she also becomes a symbol for a new aesthetic order, a raped woman who asks that the violence against her be purged by a new rule of restraint and lawfulness. Crisante, in her search for authority, becomes an allegory for a new type of (legitimate) tragic spectacle.

Within the chaotic moment of transition depicted in *Crisante*, flight from power characterizes the monarchical and imperial authorities, for in the defeat of Corinth, Antioche's authority has not suffered alone. The absence that marks the Corinthian king, "Antioche, s'est fait par une heureuse fuite / Exempt de voir l'état où sa ville est réduite [...] / Sa fuite l'a soustrait au pouvoir de nos armées" (vv. 38–41) [Anthioche, by a lucky escape, /Has exempted himself from seeing the degree to which his city has been diminished ... / His escape has removed him from the power of our armies], also defines the Romans whose representatives have relinquished their power through delegation. The marginality of the sovereign, common in the structure of early French tragedy and tragicomedy, becomes integral to the political reflection in *Crisante*'s plot. The Romans in Corinth act in the name of the absent emperor Augustus: "Nous, qui sommes élus pour affermir ses lois, / Et qu'Auguste a jugé dignes de ces emplois, / Signalons en ces lieux notre adresse ordinaire, / Paraissons dignes fils d'une si digne mère [...]" (vv. 15–18) [We who have been chosen to affirm his laws, / And whom Auguste has deemed worthy of such a task, / Let us show in these parts our usual skill, / Let us appear worthy sons of such a worthy mother]. Despite the stated task of carrying out Auguste's law in the new territory, no sooner have the Romans invaded Corinth than the leader in charge must absent himself. As early as Act I, scene 1, the Roman general, Manilie, who officially rules Corinth on Auguste's behalf, appoints his lieutenant, Cassie, to rule over Corinth in his name while he leaves to continue Roman expansion: "Un voyage à Tégé, où ma charge m'appelle, / Me fait laisser l'armée en ta garde fidèle " (v. 74–5) [A trip to Tégé, where duty calls me / Forces me to leave the army under your watch]. The doubled delegation of power underscores the vacancy of law that results from it. The emperor's absence emphasizes the danger of a space not controlled by the sovereign's authority, and the theatre becomes a liminal space where society functions beyond the control of positive law.

Manilie remains absent from the stage until Act V when he returns to render a decisive judgment, a set-up typical of early tragedy and tragicomedy, as we have seen, but in this case his absence serves a political purpose as well as a dramatic one. As for Auguste, he will never appear. Though referred to repeatedly, he occupies the role of a distant authority who must be answered to as the true Roman sovereign, but who is cut off from the reality on the ground in Corinth. Thus, the sovereign himself – the person, Auguste – disappears entirely from the stage in this play, leaving only the notion of a sovereign will that must be carried out. In short, the royal decision is present without the dramatic character meant to enforce it.

In the emperor's and the general's absence, Cassie becomes Corinth's de facto ruler but this allocation of power is clearly perilous, as the man charged with imposing law confuses his individual body with the sovereign body entrusted to him. Finding himself in charge, he jubilantly exclaims: "Favorable départ! Douce commission! / Qui laisse un libre cœur à mon affection" (vv. 79–80) [Favourable departure! And sweet duty! / That leaves a heart free for its affections], and, "Je puis user des droits d'un souverain pouvoir" (v. 84) [I may now use the rights of a sovereign power]. His enthusiasm towards the liberty he has to "use the rights," in other words, to bend the law to suit his desires, emphasizes the instability of Roman authority in the still unsettled land of Corinth.

Still, precisely when the Corinthian kingdom's continuity is doomed and the rule of law suspended, a female character emerges as the symbol of the kingdom's defence. Queen Crisante's beauty not only threatens to topple the Roman Empire in Corinth, but also provokes indifference to Rome's destruction in the very person vested with Roman authority, a sentiment so clearly expressed by Cassie's fatalistic declaration of submission to the queen: "Que j'offense l'Etat, et que Rome périsse; / Je suivrai mon dessein, Crisante a des attraits / Plus forts que tous respect, que tous intérêts" (vv. 162–4) [Whether I offend the State and Rome perishes; / I will follow my design, Crisante has a beauty / Stronger than all respect and all interests]. Thus, from the play's opening act, Rome and Crisante are paired as powerful queens. Manilie's account of the success of the Roman armies, "Tout succède à nos vœux, et Rome est toujours Rome" (v. 6) [Everything accedes to our wishes, and Rome is still Rome] confirms in his eyes Rome's all-powerful identity. Speaking of the empire he adds, "Et le plus fier orgueil de la terre, et de l'onde, / Contemple avec respect cette Reine du Monde" (vv. 10–11) [And the proudest pride of the earth and the seas / Contemplates with respect this Queen of the World]. Yet, the general's attention moves directly from speaking of Rome as a "Queen of the World," to insisting on the power of Crisante:

> Ses yeux, ces feux d'amour, ces deux foudres des cœurs,
> Lors qu'on triomphait d'eux, triomphaient des vainqueurs,
> Crisante en se rendant nous força de nous rendre,
> Et ce ne lui fut qu'un, qu'être prise, et que prendre.   (vv. 47–50)

> [Her eyes, those flames of love, those two lightning bolts of hearts,
> While we triumphed over them, triumphed over their victors,
> Crisante in surrenduring to us, forced us to surrender,
> And it was but one gesture to be taken and to take.]

To be sure, the language of Crisante's defeat of Roman hearts draws from the lexicon of chivalric gallantry; however, in this case the "fires" and "flames" of the queen's eyes serve to replicate the Romans' literal devastation of Corinth. The detailed violence of the Roman army – "Des rivières de sang ont arrosé la terre, / Comme foudres, nos bras tombaient sur les vaincus, / Et fendaient à la fois les corps, et les écus" (vv. 30–2) [The rivers of blood watered the earth, / Like lightning, our arms fell over the vanquished, / And broke both their arms and their shields] – is suddenly countered by the power the beautiful Roman captive exerts. In answer to the bloodshed in Corinth and the irrelevance of the defeated king, Crisante launches an assault against the Romans.

Crisante's body, specifically, becomes a last hold-out against the empire – a status of which she is all too aware: "Il me reste un seul bien, dont [Cassie] veut triompher, / Et le traître me baise, afin de m'étouffer" (vv. 231–2) [There remains for me only one good of which [Cassie] wishes to triumph, / And the traitor kisses me so as to suffocate me]. The last word, "suffocate" resonates with the earlier description of the Corinthian soldiers suffocating beneath the weight of the Roman army's heels. Now Crisante, in another parallel between the kingdom and herself, defends her body as the last Corinthian "good," which the Romans have not yet plundered. As long as Corinth in the person of its queen resists Roman violence, then the kingdom's invasion is not consummated. Crisante's "empire" (v. 260) over the Romans threatens their own empire.

The relentless energy Rotrou's queen displays, so contrary to the Corinthian king's plaintive melancholy in the face of the Roman invasion, seems to refuse, or refute, her husband's (baroque) disorder. It is as though the vigorous and forceful heroine amidst the Corinthian ruins belongs not just to another mindset from that of Antioche, but to a different aesthetic altogether. In his discussion of the *Trauerspiel*, Benjamin devotes little attention to female figures, a surprising omission from the French literary perspective where so many of the tragedies most associated with the baroque aesthetic include strong women, such as Tristan L'Hermite's *Marianne* (1637) and Corneille's *Rodogune, Princesse des Parthes* (1645). But both of those heroines are characterized by their embrace of rebellion and their impassioned calls for civil disorder at the tragedies' dénouements. In contrast, Crisante eclipses the feeble king when he is unable to rule and is defined by her pursuit of the rule of law. Much like the tragic genre in this period, Crisante is a figure pulled in two directions, demanding that the men around her institute limits and punish the violence run wild in the Corinthian no-man's land.

In writing his first Roman tragedy, Rotrou separates his play from early tragedy and tragicomedy by staging an explicit search for an absent sovereign judge. Counter to the *deus ex machina* arrivals of royal judges who suddenly appear at the plot's dénouement to close the tragedy, *Crisante*'s intrigue pinpoints the problem of the absent sovereign from beginning to end. The play takes seriously the question of judgment by delegation – how to ensure law is upheld when no clear sovereign body is present to enforce it. The Act IV arrival of Manilie – not Auguste – to punish the crime and criminal is not just a way of tidying up loose ends but the result of a central concern about delegated legal authority and the theatrical manifestation of sovereignty – key issues for the tragic genre, as we have seen over the course of this study.

While Crisante stands for limits and order, the men around her fall prey to unchecked passions. Cassie's rape of the queen is specifically framed as the conduct of a ruler acting without restraint while Crisante's confidante pleads with the Roman lieutenant (*lieu-tenant* – i.e., place holder), begging him to implement law for himself: "Régnant sachez

aussi vous prescrire des lois, / Et pouvant tout dompter, domptez-vous
une fois" (vv. 412–13) [As you reign you must also know how to prescribe
laws for yourself / And having the power to overcome, overcome yourself for once]. Cassie rejects her pleas, and unleashing his carnal desire,
flouts all legal or emotional restraint:

> Crisante sera mienne, ou libre, ou dans les fers,
> S'en défendant, ou non, inhumaine, ou propice,
> Par force, ou par amour, de droit ou d'injustice.   (vv. 438–40)

> [Crisante will be mine, either free or in irons,
> Defending herself from me or not, inhuman, or receptive,
> In strength, or in love, in law or in injustice.]

The Corinthian confidante denounces Roman rule as "brutale fureur"
(v. 469) [brutal furore] and "barbare" (v. 475) [barbaric], terms often associated with the shocking spectacles of early French tragedy. Crisante's
subsequent rape stands as a sign of Roman shame, and her assaulted
body becomes a testament to the absence of justice. She resolves to live
until justice reigns:

> Vivons, et devant lui, publions notre honte,
> Vivons jusqu'au moment qu'un traître doit périr,
> Et vivons, pour tuer, avant que de mourir.   (vv. 744–6)

> [We shall live, and before him, publish our dishonour,
> We shall live until the last moment when a traitor must perish,
> And we shall live, to kill, before dying.]

Throughout the remainder of the plot, Crisante will vituperate against
Roman lawlessness, proving the guilt of her attacker by her relentless
presence. She laments the absence of a sovereign leaving no one to
take up her call for condemnation. She turns first to her wretched husband, Antioche, but he suspects her of colluding with the Romans. Then
she turns to the Romans, but finds that their authority figure has left
Corinth, "Manilie absent ne m'en put garantir" (v. 894) [The absent Manilie could not shield me from it].

The forceful representation of the resolute queen in Rotrou's tragedy prompts the same question that Mary Jacobson asked of Freud's
Gradiva: "Is There a Woman in This Text?"[48] For whom or for what does

Crisante speak? She has a voice, one that demands restraint from her captor, revenge from her husband, and justice from the Romans, but does that constitute a clarion call for female authority? Is Rotrou advocating through her for deference towards a feminine authority and for recognition of the queen's role as the king's other half?

I believe the answer to that questions is no. The playwright conceives of this queen metaphorically. Crisante stands for Corinth at a time when pro-monarchical juridical texts begin to insist on the French king's indissoluble union with the state, or the "République." Although under the ancien régime the monarch's symbolic alliance with the kingdom through the exchange of the royal ring had been part of the French coronation ceremony for many centuries, in the wake of the chaos of the sixteenth-century's civil wars and the spectre of two regicides, jurists began to more explicitly recuperate the notion of a union between the king and the state in legal texts. The king's royal body is said to wed the kingdom in what, for instance, the *procureur général* of the Parlement of Toulouse, Pierre de Belloy, calls a "mariage civil, moral et politique" [a civil, moral, and political mariage], or what the *procureur du roi au Trésor*, Léonard Regnard, refers to as a "mariage mystiquement politique, saint et sacré"[49] [a mariage mystically political, saintly and sacred]. As the seventeenth century forges an ever clearer image of the king's idealized and mystical body joined to, and fused with, the abstract political body of the state, the language used to describe such a union is often quite explicitly sexual: "Le prince entre en possession et jouissance de l'Etat, se donne à l'Etat absolument, indéfiniment et sans exception ni réserve quelconque [...] Le roy et l'Etat par ce moyen ne sont qu'un et un pour toujours"[50] [The prince enters into possession and satisfaction of the State, gives himself absolutely to the State, indefinitely and without exception, nor hesitation ... The king and the State by this means are but one and one forever]. As a result of her husband's metaphorical union with the state, the living queen's status is marked by ambivalence and exclusion: she must submit to the interests of the Crown whom jurists designate as the "épouse mystique et privilégiée"[51] [the mystical and privileged spouse].

In this context, Crisante personifies the "mystical spouse": she is the *res-publica* who oscillates between the king's and the emperor's hands, searching for a legitimate authority to punish the offence done to her. Given the devastation of Corinth, its soldiers and subjects remain oddly silent. While their absence might be attributed to the tragic genre's narrow portrayal of characters of only the highest nobility, we nonetheless repeatedly hear from common Roman soldiers. If the Corinthians in this play do not have a voice, it is because the resilient queen subsumes their laments.

6 A Search for Sovereignty

Crisante, however, is more than just an embodiment of a political concept: she is also a strong theatrical character whose role participates in the renewal of the French tragic genre. Crisante represents a figure of order against Antioche's baroque figure of chaos and the Roman absence of law. She belongs to a rare category of queens in French tragedy because she is at once virtuous and enmeshed in the kingdom's political affairs. She differs from female characters whose names have become synonymous with terror and monstrosity, such as Corneille's Médée, Cléopâtre (in *Rodogune*), and Marcelle (in *Théodore vierge et martyr*), or Racine's Roxane (*Bajazet*), Agrippine (in *Britannicus*), and Athalie. A variation on the character of the menacing queen is the usurper-wife such as Arsinoé in *Nicomède* or Syra in Rotrou's *Cosroès*. In such cases, the king is present but controlled by the queen who governs him and his throne. The female figures of this variety are politically guilty since their influence oversteps the boundaries between the familial and the public domain. Crisante, however, does not seek to rule Corinth, nor does she plot against her husband's best interests. But she also bares no resemblance to the queens as secondary characters, the women defined as wives rather than queens; unlike them, she is not powerless to affect the events of the plot nor is she a figure of mourning such as Jocaste in *La Thébaïde*, Clytemnestre in *Iphigénie*, Rodelinde in *Pertharite*, and Cornélie in *La Mort de Pompée*.

Crisante's active resistance to her rape and then her determination for its revenge constitute the plot's defining struggle, and ultimately ratifies the shift in Corinth's political rule. The centrality of her rape evokes the story of the more famous Lucrèce, but whereas in that case revenge leads to the overthrow of the Tarquinian tyranny (i.e., the abolition of monarchy) and the advent of the Roman republic, Crisante's rape by a Roman results in the demand that the imperial invader institute law.[52] Her struggle to avenge her body becomes a quest to install law in the midst of the nation's disorder. Significantly the queen's body stands for order, for the search for a male authority figure – a Roman sovereign judge – who will heed her call to clear Corinth of the brutality and injustice she has suffered. This determination for a trial of her assailant, and her resolution to kill herself once his Roman head has been handed to her by the Romans themselves, constitutes a search for a cathartic enactment of justice. In a metatheatrical structure, she searches for the sovereign who will finally show himself, acknowledge the crime, and then see to the execution of the perpetrator.

In her introduction to her edition of *Crisante*, Anne Duroux suggests that Rotrou based his plot on a passage from Plutarch's *Les Vertueux faits des femmes*. According to this reading, Crisante's character was inspired by the account of a noblewoman – not a queen – who was raped by a Roman captain after the invasion of a remote Asiatic province. In Plutarch, the Roman captain decided to return the woman, Chimara, to her husband out of greed for the large reward offered for her release. When the soldier prepared to take his leave of the noblewoman, she signalled to her suite and they decapitated the Roman captain. In the presence of her husband, Chimora threw the Roman's head at his feet and, before killing herself, asserted that only one living man had had the pleasure of her affections.[53] As told by Plutarch, the story includes no judgment of the Roman rapist, no confrontation between the Asian woman and the invading authorities, and no discussion of "Roman values." In rewriting the story, Rotrou alters the plot in four important ways: 1) he moves the action from a remote Asian province to Corinth – the crossroads of the ancient world and the second major Greek city after Athens; 2) he turns Chimora's tribal chief husband into the Corinthian monarch (also emphasizing that Antioche's decline is so profound that he cannot even afford to pay a ransom for Crisante); 3) he includes a trial scene of Crisante's offender; 4) although the Romans invaded Corinth under the Republic, Rotrou situates the Roman invasion under the Empire through repeated allusions to the absent Augustus. In light of these amendments, Duroux concludes that Rotrou's historical context is anecdotal, that "les enjeux historiques de la pièce deviennent bien minces et l'histoire ne sert plus que de toile de fond à l'action" [the historical stakes of this play become quite slim, and history only serves as background to the action].[54]

My view is that when situated within the early seventeenth-century context of political-aesthetic efforts to revise portrayals of sovereign judges in the tragic genre, *Crisante*'s search for authority in the face of surrounding chaos has a great deal to reveal. From this perspective, the move to Corinth from a remote Asian province is historically meaningful. Corinth, commercial and governmental capital of Peloponnesia, was a flourishing port city before the Romans famously burnt it to ashes under the Republic in 46 BCE. Its location on the Isthmus River was

economically and militarily desirable, garnering military talk of "strategically penetrating" the city through its waterways.[55] Furthermore, the
infamous Roman theft of Corinthian art and goods evoked language of
rape and defilement in chronicles of the period. Yet, as a Roman colony
under Julius Caesar, the city underwent extensive rebuilding and was
repopulated with Roman freedmen.[56] Rotrou chose Corinth because of
the city's renowned annihilation and eventual return to prosperity, a possible analogy to the status of the tragic genre in France. Second, Rotrou's
modification of Antioche from a tribal chief to a king not only emphasizes the change in regime that occurs – the transfer of power which
ends the monarchical dynasty in Corinth – but also enables reflection
on the process of instituting a new regime linked to order and restraint,
something akin to the implementation of codification, *bienséance*, and
regularity.

The alteration of the chronology from Republican to Augustan Rome
should prompt reflection, especially because *Crisante* stages fictional
characters. The sole historical character – present only in name – is
Auguste, whose rule stood for a Roman golden age. Auguste's physical
absence in Corinth poses the question of how far the emperor's body
can extend. In spotlighting his remoteness, a theatrical and political difficulty within the tragedy, *Crisante* asks how a sovereign can make his
authority felt in spite of his physical absence. How can the emperor rule
over a distant land? How can his symbolic body encompass new territory?
And how can that symbolic body be rendered present onstage for the
spectators?

7 Rebuilding and Reuniting: Making the
Absent Sovereign Present

In portraying Crisante's rape and the end of an independent Corinth,
Rotrou depicts the difficult inauguration of a new legal order, challenging to establish even in an all-powerful Empire. The play goes to great
lengths to stress the anarchic violence of Roman misrule in Corinth.
Replicating Cassie's rape of the queen but at a lower echelon, Crisante's
confidante, Marcie, is given up for rape to two Roman soldiers. However,
in a sign of fatal Roman lawlessness, just as the soldiers are about to
accomplish their brutal act, they turn their violence against each other
(vv. 792–4). A few scenes later, we hear from a Roman *chef de guerre* that
the soldiers' idleness in Corinth has caused them to, once again, turn
their weapons on one another.[57] Roman military valour – so crucial to

Roman identity – leads to dangerous chaos in a space devoid of a distinct authority. When harnessed for military conquest in the name of the emperor, Roman brutality brings honour and prestige, but in the absence of an authority to regulate the soldiers' actions, that ferocity quickly turns destructive. As the Romans drive out the Corinthian monarchy, the values defining Rome (honour, *Romanitas*, and *virtu*) prove to be unsteady. The play's remarkable refusal to idealize the emperor's power stresses the indispensable need for careful management of the kingdom in his name.

Cassie's failed governance of Corinth in the absence of Manilie and Auguste attests to the fragility of the imperial system since the lieutenant's despicable act threatens the authority of the militarily dominant nation. It also emphasizes the limits of the sovereign's will without his physical presence to assert it. After Crisante's rape, Cassie slips into a remorseful melancholia, oscillating between a crazed repentance which he calls a "brutale fureur" (v. 749) [brutal furore], "furieux transport" (v. 782) [furious transport], and a shameful recognition of the consequences of his actions: "O trop lâche fureur! Indigne acte d'un homme, / Mais d'un fils de Cassie, et d'un enfant de Rome" (vv. 763–4) [Oh cowardly furore! Shameful action of a man, / But so much more so of a son of Cassie, and of a child of Rome]. In his hallucinatory madness, the Roman soldier imagines Crisante overpowering and killing him, ultimately achieving a Corinthian victory against Rome (vv. 974–9).

As Cassie's Roman friend, Cléodore, tells him, in betraying Roman values Cassie has put in danger Roman identity and threatened the foundations of the Roman Empire:

> Depuis que dessous nous tout l'Univers respire,
> Par quoi présumez-vous que fleurissent nos lois?
> Et qui rend les Romains, maîtres de tant de Rois?   (vv. 133–5)
> [...]
> La vertu seulement est l'appui des états,
> Nos devoirs, nos respects, et notre révérence,
> Des autres, et de nous forment la différence,
> Leurs crimes seulement affligent leurs maisons,
> Et nous sommes heureux comme nous sommes bons.   (vv. 139–43)

> [Ever since beneath us all of the Universe breathes,
> How do you think that our laws flourish?
> And what makes the Romans, masters of so many Kings?

[…]
Virtue alone is the support of states,
Our duties, our respect, and our reverance,
Of others and of ourselves mark the difference,
Their crimes only hurt their homes,
But we are only as happy as we are good.]

Cléodore's speech attests to the Romans' loss of their "difference." Crisante's rape is a sign that the Romans are no longer Roman. If they cease to obey the laws of virtue, they sully the person of Auguste, and their future will be jeopardized as the anarchy in Corinth proves. We are told that because of the rape, César's glory is "noircie" (v. 1131) [blackened]. Thus, even a political system at its apogee – Augustan Rome – remains fragile; the unifying values ("our duties, our respects, our reverance") are always at risk of being erased and forgotten.

If Cassie's actions are thoroughly un-Roman and degrade the idea of Rome, the Roman general Manilie is also at fault. His misconception that sovereignty is linked solely to military exploits proves to be fundamentally flawed. In Act IV, when Manilie finally reappears onstage, unaware of the reigning chaos in Corinth, he thinks only of new conquests:

Un repos glorieux bornera nos conquêtes,
Et pour toutes nos mains Rome a des palmes prêtes;
Pour servir un César, paraissons des Césars,
Sur les trônes des Rois plantons nos étendards.   (vv. 1067–70)

[A glorious rest will meet our conquests,
And for all our hands Rome has palm leaves ready;
To serve a Caesar, let us resemble Caesars,
On the thrones of Kings let us plant our banners.]

Blinded by his confidence in Roman superiority, Manilie is no wiser than his *chef de guerre* who vaunts Rome's effortless domination over its enemies, as he says, "Paraître et triompher n'est plus qu'une action" (v. 1078) [To appear and triumph is but one action]. These Romans mistakenly believe that grandeur and a virtuous rule are instituted simply on the basis of "appearing." The play demonstrates the contrary: Auguste never appears but will ultimately institute his law, and Roman triumph over Corinth comes long after the Roman banners have been planted.

Upon hearing of Crisante's rape, Manilie admits to his own guilt.[58] The Corinthian queen asks Manilie to make present the absent sovereign by instituting his justice: "Telle je viens à vous ainsi qu'aux pieds d'Auguste, / Ce roi de l'Univers aussi puissant que juste" (vv. 1115–16) [I come to you as if I were at Auguste's feet, / This king of the Universe as powerful as he is just]. Ultimately Roman glory is seen to rely not on brute force and bloody spectacles but on careful, controlled, and virtuous displays of justice. The judge must act "as if" he were the emperor and victims must pray at the judge's feet "as if" they were Auguste's. In fact, this displacement of the sovereign underscores how he is not a person, not an actor within the play, but instead represents a concept, an idea of justice and virtue which his delegates must enact. Recognizing the disorder he has wrought, the rapist Cassie falls on his sword as a means of purging Roman violence and establishing a dignified Roman order in Corinth. The militarily subjugated Corinthians become willing subjects of the Roman Empire only when they can trust in the consistent exercise of Auguste's rule.

8 Endings

In analysing the relationship between literature and law under the ancien régime, Christian Biet identifies the second half of the seventeenth century and the beginning of the eighteenth as a time when fiction, and in particular the comedic genre, was drawn to depicting individuals motivated by self-interest who veer outside the law and circumvent authority. Such wayward characters challenge, and even undo, the reigning legal order, but are ultimately undone by a figure of authority; they are humiliated and punished, a spectacle which serves to re-establish more firmly the power already in place.[59]

We see a similar dynamic in the tragedies of the mid-seventeenth century we have considered alongside each other in this chapter – *Crisante*, *Cinna*, and *Venceslas*. In all three, wayward subjects transgress the dominant legal order and are confronted by a sovereign whose judgment over them ultimately makes the state stronger than before the crime. Cassie's rape, Cinna's conspiracy, and even Ladislas's murder all give rise to a transformative judgment which situates sovereignty above individual passions and interests. However, while the dynamic of crime and punishment Biet describes for comedy is relatively straightforward, the tragic verdicts depicted by Corneille and Rotrou require bidding farewell to an earlier reign. Rather than re-establish more firmly the existing authority, the royal judgments end the system that was in place at the start of the play. *Crisante* sees the end of the Corinthian monarchy; *Cinna* ends the Republic; and *Venceslas* closes with a king's abdication. The characters announcing the verdicts in the last moments of these tragedies' theatrical day all seek to transcend the chaos that crime has wrought, but they all realize that to succeed, the legal order must be altered. Rather than re-establish a reign, the articulation of a verdict in Rotrou and Corneille similarly underscores the power of royal judgment to transform government and the person representing the state.

Before Corneille devised the Auguste who appears in *Cinna* and Rotrou conceived of his Venceslas – two models of the sovereigns as judge and accuser, *Crisante* offered an early model of the political and personal transformations brought about by a decisive verdict. Yet *Crisante* retains the form of the public trial, the courtroom decision, not the private royal cabinet. The sovereign himself remains at an unknowable distance, closer to the sovereign of tragicomedy. Manilie, like the comical judge Dandin in Racine's *Les Plaideurs*, rules in the name of an absent monarch whose law he is assigned to enforce. In trying one of his own soldiers and punishing his lieutenant's lawlessness, the Roman general Manilie acknowledges the personal toll the judgment costs him:

Sa perte m'est sensible, et je dois toutefois
Abandonner son crime à la rigueur des lois;
Je crains, et je dois presser un châtiment si juste,
Je plains en Manilie, et j'ordonne en Auguste;
Il importe à l'état que cette impunité,
Ne soit pas reprochée à mon autorité.   (vv. 1185–90)

[His loss touches me, but I must however
Abandon his crime to the rigour of law;
I fear, but I must press for such a just punishment,
I feel for him as Manilie, but I command as Auguste;
It is important for the State that this impunity,
Not be reproached to my authority.]

Here, the language of the divided self, or "two bodies" is not the king's personal and public selves, but an awareness of his position as a delegate who must perform "as Auguste." Although Rotrou evokes the sadness Manilie feels for the punishment of Cassie, the general realizes he is but a stand-in for a greater power. Drawing on the emotional weight of a dramatic theatrical judgment, Corneille and Rotrou in his later works will move the trial scene within the inner sanctum of the sovereign's closed quarters. They will eliminate the delegate's performance and insist on the dramatically engrossing divisions *within* the sovereign, as expressed in *Venceslas* when the eponymous elderly king abdicates rather than find his son guilty: "O justice inhumaine, et devoirs ennemis, / Pour conserver mon sceptre, il faut perdre mon fils! [...]/ Je ne puis rien pour lui, le sang cède a la loi, / Et je ne lui puis être, et bon père et bon roi]" (vv. 1649–54) [Oh inhuman justice, and enemy duty, / To conserve my sceptre, I must lose my son! ... / I can do nothing for him, blood submits to law, / And I cannot be both a father and a good king]. Similarly, Auguste in *Cinna* silences his personal sense of vengeance and embraces the power that comes from siding with the state.

In Rotrou's earlier play, Crisante's struggle for Cassie's punishment is not, in the end, a defeat of the imperial invader, nor does it signal a Corinthian victory. Her act is not revenge *over* Rome, but revenge *for* Rome, with the Corinthian queen forcing the Romans to at last prove their Roman character. In this 1637 tragedy, Rotrou's aim is not to make Auguste come alive, but to reflect on how to convey authority onstage. When the verdict is pronounced, Crisante instantaneously recognizes Roman sovereignty in words that prefigure *Cinna*'s closing prophecy:

Ainsi dessous vos lois tout le monde respire,
Ainsi malgré le temps respire votre Empire,
Ainsi le grand Auguste ait un jour des autels
Et partage le Ciel avec les immortels.   (vv. 1135–8)

Therefore under your laws everyone breathes,
Therefore despite the passage of Time your Empire breathes,
Therefore the great Auguste one day shall have altars,
And will share the Heavens with the immortals.]

The queen allies a recognition of Auguste's authority with a sense of being able to breathe again. Reiterating the earlier boasts of the Romans, and in contrast to the suffocating (*étouffés*) Corinthian casualties piled up across the kingdom at the start of the play, a sense of recovered breath marks the advent of the empire's legal legitimacy. The verdict has been pronounced for Auguste, but not by him, and the tragedy ends with the strength of Rome reaffirmed. The sovereign himself is only a spectre, an indistinct source of power that never takes shape on the stage. Auguste wields great influence at this distance and maintains the aura of the sovereign to whom all must answer, in contrast to the all-too-human Corinthian monarch whose flaws the audience sees far too clearly.

After Manilie's judgment, Crisante asks for Cassie's head. "Je demande sa tête, / D'elle, je tirerai la satisfaction / de prouver ma vengeance, et sa punition" (vv. 1253–5) [I ask for his head, / From it I will obtain the satisfaction / Of proving my vengeance, and his punishment]. Act IV closes with Manilie's command that Cassie's head should serve as a symbolic warning to all Romans of what will become of them if they transgress Roman law; with that, the Romans leave the stage to extend their rule elsewhere.[60] Crisante leaves the realm of the newly instituted Roman authority, with Cassie's head in her hands, and returns to the (baroque) space of King Antioche.

The shift back to the world of the Corinthian king entails a return to the domain of the melancholic prince pronouncing sad *stances* about the fragile nature of glory and the vicissitudes of fate. The forlorn Antioche, is "seul dans une chambre tapissée de deuil appuyé sur un lit" (stage directions, V.1) [alone in a room upholstered in mourning, leaning on a bed]; he speaks of his desire for rest and asks his "tiresome servants" (v. 1314) who interrupt his gloomy meditations to leave him alone. He is a defeated and irrelevant king, a vestige of an earlier era, who will have neither successor nor succession – the antithesis to Auguste's immortal reign. In the tragedy's final scene, Antioche climbs onto his bed and pulls the bed curtains around him so his servants will not observe him as he prepares to kill himself. The use of the curtain as a prop visually registers the end of his reign and the obscurity to which he is now relegated. It also signals the end of the theatre of Antioche, the baroque spectacle of a feeble king. But before he can kill himself, Crisante forces her way into his quarters, flings Cassie's head at his feet, says she is not afraid to die, and stabs herself. Realizing his mistaken judgment of her, Antioche returns behind the curtains and kills himself. The last image of the play presents the fatally wounded Antioche lying over the body of his dead queen.[61] Though his final words betray a resistance to Roman power, they are also a pronouncement of Roman sovereignty: "Qu'Auguste maintenant triomphe de ces lieux" (v. 1476) [May Auguste now triumph in this place]. The death of the Corinthian royal family officially marks the end of the monarchical regime in Corinth, but, above all, it clears the stage for a new presence in this "place." Roman order will eliminate the traits associated with Antioche's rule – "furore, force [and] violence." Crisante, lying dead beneath her king, attests to the final erasure of the queen as a living publication of Roman indignity. Auguste triumphs in Corinth without ever needing to set foot in the kingdom.

With *Crisante*, Rotrou demonstrates that even for a great empire like Rome, the legal order is vulnerable and must be actively upheld if the absent sovereign is to be made present. Rotrou takes the tragi-comedic convention of the arrival of an absent king to bring closure to the intrigue and turns it into the basis for Crisante's quest for justice. Caught between two reigns – one of excess and irregularity, and another that claims to bring order and rule – she searches for the scene of judgment that will punish the crime, resolve her fate, and clear the stage of chaotic violence. In the end, the sovereign himself never arrives, but the ideal he represents is so strong that his delegates enact his law.

Throughout *Crisante*, Rotrou debates the place of violence, lawlessness, and female power on the political stage and on the stage of the newly conceived French tragic genre. Corneille and Rotrou will return to each of these considerations in *Cinna* and *Venceslas* to varying degrees, but the issue of lawlessness will remain central to their dramaturgy as the playwrights continue to reflect on theatrical royal judgment and the staging of sovereignty. In the later plays, the sovereign is very much a character, with many facets to his role, and the intrigue accentuates the suspense of his ultimate judgment. Instead of Rotrou's physically absent Auguste, at the close of *Cinna* Corneille presents an unknowable Auguste, one who is present onstage but who has retreated into a realm of legal and emotional distance from his subjects. As for King Venceslas, he has gone in the opposite direction and become too knowable: he is a father with as much closeness and love for his son as any spectator might recognize in his own household. That closeness, however, costs the Polish monarch his throne. Thus, when the verdicts of clemency arrive in *Cinna* and *Venceslas*, spectators are left feeling uneasy about the sovereign's ability to disregard positive law. While both of these plays end with the promise of great reigns ahead, the spectre of crimes left unpunished and of law subverted remains.

In the next chapter we will examine how Racine pursues the topos Rotrou and Corneille have advanced of an elusive sovereign-judge. In *Mithridate* and *Phèdre* Racine similarly draws on the theatricality of the judge's disappearance and appearance onstage. In both tragedies the father/king unexpectedly returns from the dead, and a central issue of the plot is the kingdom's lawlessness in the monarch's absence, Racine, à la *Venceslas*, focuses on crimes committed within the inner family circle. In contrast to Auguste, the distant and unknowable sovereign of

mid-century tragedy, Racine portrays his royal judges as active investigators of crime, personally implicated in uncovering the guilty and personally responsible for their punishment. Yet, as we will see, the royal
judge's initial absence leaves him incapable of judging matters accurately and the tragedy exposes the profound violence bound up in the
king's judgment.

Chapter Six

Racine and Royal Fathers of Injustice – *Mithridate* and *Phèdre*

Qui m'a trahi? Pourquoi ne suis-je pas vengé?[1]

Jean Racine, Phèdre

Voyons, examinons. Mais par où commencer?
Qui m'en éclaircira? Quels témoins? Quel indice?[2]

Jean Racine, Mithridate

1 The Burden of the Father's Judgment

Racine's first tragedy, *La Thébaïde ou les frères ennemis* (1664) turns on a legal question surrounding royal judgment: to what extent must a deceased king's testament be obeyed? The Theban sovereign, Œdipe, decreed before his death that his sons would share the throne, alternating each year as king. At the start of the play, Etéocle who has spent the first year on the throne refuses to relinquish it to his brother, Polynice. He holds the view that he agreed to abide by his father's will when he was a mere subject, but now that he has become a sovereign, his judgment should reign supreme and he should not abandon his position:

> Le devoir d'un Sujet n'est pas celui d'un Roi.
> D'abord que sur sa tête il reçoit la Couronne,
> Un Roi sort à l'instant de sa propre personne,
> L'intérêt du public doit devenir le sien,
> Il doit tout à l'Etat, et ne se doit plus rien. (vv. 118–22)

[The duty of a Subject is not the same as that of a King.
As soon as on his head he receives the Crown,
A King instantly ceases to be himself,
The public interest must become his own,
He owes the State everything, and owes himself nothing.]

Through the articulation of political *sententiae*, Etéocle describes an immediate ("instantly") transformation in his person as soon as he places the crown upon his head. Becoming king means undergoing a change that eclipses all concerns except for what is owed to the state. Kings are not like other people. Hence, Etéocle propounds, the judgment of a former sovereign is irrelevant, and the current king alone is fit to decide what is good for Thèbes.

Racine's first foray into the tragic realm appeared less than four years after Corneille wrote *Trois Discours sur le poème dramatique* (1660), a practical poetics detailing his understanding of tragedy; at about the same time, the elder playwright had also staged his version of Sophocles's tragedy – *Œdipe* (1659). Despite Racine's novice status, with his first tragic effort he enters the ongoing conversation between the leading playwright of the seventeenth century, Corneille, Rotrou, who had written *Antigone* (1639), and the man deemed to be the greatest dramaturgical authority of all time, Aristotle, who hailed *Oedipus Rex* as the pinnacle of the tragic genre. In inserting himself amid such illustrious authors, Racine enters the debate – political and theatrical – over the portrayal of sovereignty onstage and, in so doing, must confront the complex question of how to best stage royal decision-making.

In what will become a hallmark of Racinian dramaturgy, the playwright contends with the portrayal of sovereignty by drawing on the theatricality of a king's absence and presence onstage. In Euripides and Seneca's *The Phoenician Women*, the source of Racine's *La Thébaïde*, Oedipus is not yet dead when the brothers' rivalry for the throne begins. In the ancient plays the Theban king has already ceded power to his sons, after the discovery of his fatal incestuous crime, but the fraternal struggle does not stem directly from the elderly king's testament, a legal form, as it does in Racine. The French playwright markedly amends the ancient plot by turning the brothers into twins and by presenting the father/king's royal decree as the impetus for the plot's tragic struggle. Thus, from Racine's earliest play, the weight of the absent father/king's authority over the younger generation and the guilt linked to trespassing his will – a dynamic that comes to define his dramaturgy – is set in place.

Scholars have often remarked that the father/sovereigns in Racine represent a burden to their sons who cannot escape the weight of the paternal generation. Roland Barthes describes Racinian fathers as the source of the tragic crime the sons perpetuate: "C'est le père qui institue la faute, mais que ne l'assume pas"[3] [The father institutes the crime, but does not acknowledge it]. The critic expands on the impossibility for the child to shed the paternal memory:

> Qui est cet autre dont le héros ne peut se séparer? [...] C'est le père. Il n'y a pas de tragédie où il ne soit réellement ou virtuellement présent [...] Son être, c'est son antériorité: ce qui vient après lui est issu de lui, engagé inéluctablement dans une problématique de la fidélité.[4]

> [Who is this other from whom the hero cannot separate ... It is the father. There is no tragedy where he is not either literally or virtually present ... His being is his anteriority: what comes after him stems from him, inescapably engaged in a problematics of loyalty.]

Racine's tragic characters struggle to define themselves against the testament, be it literal or figurative, left behind by the father. The examples, actions, and, above all, the decisions of the preceding generation envelop the heroes onstage who cannot break free from their "coming after" (*un reste*) status; the memory of the father's volition haunts their decisions, and their own actions are inevitably judged according to their faithfulness to the paternal will.

This dynamic appears most vividly in Racine's *Andromaque* (1667) where the notion of coming after defines every character of the plot. Pyrrhus, son of Achilles, and Astyanax, son of Hector, cannot escape the legacy of their fathers who govern their interactions with others and determine their identity. Oreste and Hermione, also the descendants of legendary actors in the Trojan war, appear to be only a pale reflection of their parents' generation. As Andromaque emphasizes, speaking of her son: "Qu'il ait de ses aïeux un souvenir modeste, / Il et du sang d'Hector mais il en est le reste. / Et pour ce reste enfin j'ai moi-même en un jour/ Sacrifié mon sang, ma haine, et mon amour" (vv. 1125–8) [Let him not glory in his ancestors: / He's Hector's blood, but all that remains of it; / Because of that I sacrifice today / At once my life, my hatred, and my love].[5] The tragic sacrifice that spectators witness onstage derives from the memory of the absent father whose legacy overshadows the identity of the younger generation.

Barthes's framing of the father/son opposition is helpful because he does not suggest that the younger generation is doomed to fail in its efforts to live up to the father-sovereign simply because it is less heroic or lacks power. Instead, Barthes pinpoints a paradigm of Racine's dramaturgy, the "problematics of loyalty," the conflict of adherence to or rupture with the will of the father. The younger generation's ambivalent attitude towards the father's legacy should not be read solely as the product of Racine's biography (i.e., his status as an orphan and his complicated relationship with Jansenism) or in psychoanalytical terms, as critics have often done; it stems, I believe, from the long-standing debates surrounding the portrayal of royal judgment on the seventeenth-century stage.[6] Racine recasts the prevalent political-theatrical dynamic of royal judgment in tragedy by strengthening the familial component in the king's decision, asking whether the child will follow the judgment of his father/king and perpetuate his will, or whether he will turn away from that judgment and break with the paternal decree.

To be sure, this turn towards the familial is not new. Racine puts into practice Aristotle's recommendations in *The Poetics* that tragic incidents "between those who are near or dear to one another," as for example a brother killing his brother or a son murdering his father, are ideal tragic conditions since they are sure to strike the audience as terrible and pitiful.[7] Corneille had staged family imbroglios, notably in *Rodogune, Princesse des Parthes* (1645) and *Nicomède* (1651), but Racine diverges from these and Aristotle's examples, which emphasize heroes acting in ignorance of the identity of their adversaries, in favour of trial scenes where a father/king knowingly judges his son. He presents the character from the younger generation either implicitly or explicitly as the accused whom the father/king/judge must evaluate to determine the degree of guilt. This dynamic seems to draw most significantly from the vein of Rotrou's *Venceslas* (1647) where a father must be a judge to his son who has killed his other son. King Venceslas suffers at the thought of condemning his firstborn: "Plus condamné que vous mon cœur vous y suivra [à l'échafaud]. / Je mourrai plus que vous du coup qui vous tuera" (vv. 1601–2) [More condemned than you, my heart will follow you (to the scaffolds). / I will die more than you from the blow that will kill you]. Racine understands well the pathos of a scene where a father must rule against his own children in spite of the love he feels for them, and will stage such a dynamic in *Iphigénie* (1674).

More often, however, Racine leaves paternal tenderness and sympathy aside until the last moments of the play. The playwright, writing in the second half of the seventeenth century, is interested in the battle for power between the two generations and imagines an angry father/judge who wishes to dominate and punish with *éclat* his children whom he so hastily believes to be guilty. In terms of the dynamic of authority and submission between the father figure and the son, Racine's father/judge resembles more closely Corneille's Auguste, in *Cinna*, where the emperor is only an adoptive father or a symbolic father to his subjects, but possesses absolute authority to determine the fate of the accused. Until the play's close the father/judge is bent on the execution of his son. In the trial scene in Act V within Auguste's private quarters, Cinna must answer to the charges of the sovereign-judge whom he has betrayed, aware that his life lies entirely in the emperor's hands. Such an asphyxiating scene of judgment prefigures Racine's portrayals of tense tête-à-têtes between an all-powerful father/judge and his son in the playwright's most developed tragedies of royal judgment, *Mithridate* and *Phèdre*. Racine moves from tragedies that evoke the memory or spectre of the father, as in *La Thébaïde* (1664), *Andromaque* (1667), as well as *Britannicus* (1669), *Bérénice* (1670), and *Bajazet* (1672) where the fathers have either died or are absent, towards an ever more threatening onstage presence of the royal father/judge, culminating in *Mithridate* (1672), *Iphigénie* (1674), and *Phèdre* (1677). In these plays, a father/sovereign blinded by anger, pride, and jealousy must decide whether to take his child's life.[8]

Before turning to consider the portrait of these menacing father/judges, and how they relate not only to Racine's tragic aesthetic, but also to the evolution of royal judgment, we will briefly discuss the only one of Racine's plays where the father or his memory are not factors in the decision-making of the sovereign onstage. This perspective will enable us to understand Racine's subsequent focus on the thematic of absence and presence of the father, which will define his later plays.

2 A King That Fits the Bill

Only in the playwright's second tragedy, *Alexandre le Grand* (1665), is the sovereign judge not also a father. The play is commonly described as the most gallant of Racine's tragedies because of the prominence of the affairs of the heart within the intrigue at the expense of political and military discussions. This most chivalrous of works does, however, include a closing scene where Alexandre dons the role of judge and embraces clemency over punishment. He thus garners the admiring submission of his enemies. Ironically, then, the tragedy deemed to be farthest from

Corneille's tragic aesthetic because of its excessive gallantry reproduces the elder playwright's most lauded dénouement, and in an echo to the subject matter of *Cinna*, the author of *Alexandre* tells his readers that, "le véritable sujet de la pièce n'[est] autre chose que la générosité de ce Conquérant"[9] [the true subject of the play is nothing other than the generosity of this Conqueror]. Yet, far from resulting in the same critical success Corneille had encountered with his portrayal of clemency, Racine's detractors accentuated *Alexandre*'s lack of dignity and feeble grandeur, emphasizing that the act of clemency alone does not endow the sovereign with the requisite *éclat* of his position.

Most famously and most scathingly, the critic Saint-Evremond insists on the contrast between the idea of Alexandre that spectators and students of history are led to anticipate, and the derisory Alexandre who walks Racine's stage:

> Ce n'est pas qu'Ephestion n'en donne une belle idée, que Taxile, que Porus même ne parlent avantageusement de sa grandeur: mais quand il paraît lui-même, il n'a pas la force de la soutenir, si ce n'est que par modestie, il veuille paraître un simple homme chez les Indiens, dans le juste repentir d'avoir voulu passer pour un Dieu parmi les Perses.[10]

> [It isn't that Ephestion does not give a good idea of him, that Taxile or Porus, even, do not speak advantageously of his grandeur: but when he appears in person, he does not have the strength to uphold it, unless it is that, out of modesty, he wants to appear to be a simple man with the Indians, out of a feeling of repentance for having wanted to be seen as a God among the Persians.]

Although more than thirty years separate the criticism directed at Don Fernand's lack of dignity in *Le Cid* and Saint-Evremond's disapproval of Alexandre, the terms with which the critics depict the royal character's failure to live up to spectators' expectations are similar. The anticipated "grandeur" of the character and of his position is not corroborated by the simplicity of the man who appears onstage. In the critic's damming evaluation, Racine failed to endow the hero onstage with enough substance, what he calls the "strength to sustain" the grandeur historically attributed to him. The discrepancy between the idea and the appearance leads the critic's commentary to devolve into a humorous appraisal of the demeaned character. While Saint-Evremond differs from critics such as La Mesnardière or d'Aubignac in his attachment to depicting theatrical characters according to their legendary traits and the image passed down from ancient authors – and not according to French tastes – he nonetheless pinpoints the same problem the *doctes* of the 1630s and 1640s saw in presenting an uninspiring sovereign:

A parler sérieusement, je ne connais ici d'Alexandre que le seul nom, son génie, son humeur, ses qualités ne me paraissent en aucun endroit: je cherche dans un Héros impétueux des mouvements extraordinaires qui me passionnent, et trouve un Prince si peu animé, qu'il me laisse tout le sang-froid ou je puis être.[11]

[To speak seriously, I only recognize in Alexander the name; his genius, his character, his qualities appear nowhere: I search for an impetuous Hero with extraordinary movements that will fascinate me, and only find a barely animated Prince, that leaves me with all my calm composure.]

According to the critics, the greatest conqueror of antiquity, a model Louis XIV seeks to resemble and to whom he is compared, should not leave audiences cold. He should be more than an average man and exude an extraordinary presence, not the mediocre heroism Saint-Evremond detects in Racine's character.

Despite a similar vocabulary of "grandeur" and "extraordinary movements" between early poetic directives regarding royal characters and Saint-Evremond's reactions to *Alexandre*, the latter's remarks allow us to gauge the shift in theatrical criticism in the 1660s. Saint-Evremond underscores the new attention given to presenting a local colour of sovereignty on the tragic stage. Rather than stress the inherent dignity a great ruler must possess and link all monarchical portrayals back to the image of the French king, he stresses the variations of sovereignty according to political context – not all royal portraits can be drawn from the same palette:

Il faut dépeindre un Roi de l'Asie autrement qu'un Consul Romain; l'un parlera comme un Monarque absolu, qui dispose de ses sujets comme des ses esclaves; l'autre comme un Magistrat qui anime seulement les lois, et fait respecter leur autorité à un peuple libre [...] Il faut dépeindre différemment des personnes de la même condition et du même temps, quand l'histoire nous en donne de différents caractères.[12]

[It is necessary to depict an Asian king differently than a Roman Consul; the first will speak like an absolute Monarch, who treats his subjects like his slaves; the second, like a Magistrate, who will only animate the laws, and make the free people respect their authority ... It is necessary to depict differently people of the same condition and of the same time, when history gives us their different characters.]

Different monarchs require different traits; their relationships to their subjects and their varying cultural perspectives on law and legality must be taken into account when devising their portrayals. The cultural setting, as, for example, Asia versus Rome, will require sovereigns to judge in contrasting ways – whim versus respect for the law, as the critic illustrates. Beyond the "man of authority" Corneille evoked as a broad category under which to place any character in a position of sovereignty, Saint-Evremond insists on the specificity of history and culture in portraying a theatrical king.

Racine's kings were regularly the subject of critiques regarding their perceived Frenchness; they were often deemed to be too romantic, too close to the young marquis of the seventeenth century. In turn, Racine will defend himself by insisting on his adherence to history and to the sources from which he draws. In *Alexandre le Grand*, his response stresses the generosity and superiority displayed by his character through his renowned act of clemency.[13] Nevertheless, after *Alexandre le Grand*, Racine returns to the father/sovereign/judge dynamic he had initially tried out with *La Thébaïde*. After *Alexandre*, Racine privileges an "extraordinary" but elusive father/judge, defined by his dignity but also by his absence from the stage, as a way of responding to attacks on his all-too-human royal characters. In this vein, the paternal figure, the source of power and admiration, may or may not appear onstage to punish his guilty heir. His memory and the recollection of his exploits creates a dynamic in which the onstage hero is introduced from the outset as a lesser being than his illustrious predecessor. Again, we see this most vividly with the examples of Pyrrhus in relation to Achille, and Hermione in relation to Hélène, in *Andromaque*, the tragedy that follows *Alexandre*. These characters possess some of the traits associated with their legendary parents, but they intentionally represent minor, paler, and degraded versions of their celebrated ancestors' distinction. Racine adopts the strategy throughout his dramatic corpus of setting low expectations for the grandeur of his characters by presenting them as coping with the guilt of not living up to their glorious forefathers. In this way, the characters onstage escape the critical pressure of conforming to a predetermined portrait, and Racine's hand is freer to depict them as flawed and not awe-inspiring. He varies this approach slightly in the case of Néron in *Britannicus* when the playwright answers critics who found the tyrant not to resemble his classical portraits by describing the Néron of his tragedy as "not yet" the monster history knows him to have been, but as undergoing a transformation towards monstrosity within the plot.[14]

3 The Royal Judge Returns

Having emphasized the importance of the absent father/judge in Racine as a model the son must compare himself to, I now wish to focus on his two later tragedies where the dramatic plot takes a sudden twist as the father, whom everyone had believed to be dead, returns. Structurally similar, *Mithridate* and *Phèdre* present sovereigns who make a spectacular entrance at the midpoint of the plot, followed closely by their announcement of a crucial judgment condemning their sons and successors. The transition from one generation to the next, which had begun to take place in the opening acts, now hangs in the balance, since in both of these tragedies the roles of father, judge, and king are merged into one person.

Mithridate* and *Phèdre* open with the younger generation reacting to the absence, and then the announced death, of the father sovereign. As the sons set in motion the succession to the next generation, their actions become linked to trespassing the father's will. In *Mithridate*, the loyal son Xipharès admits his love to Monime, the king's young fiancée. In *Phèdre*, Thésée's successor, Hippolyte, confesses his love to Aricie whom Thésée has forbidden to marry. Aricie, a character of Racine's invention, is the "reste" (v. 51) [the remains or a left-over], the last surviving descendant of the Athenian royal family whose male members Thésée has killed and whose throne he has taken.[15] Hence, while regretting the father's death, the sons prepare to assert their own rule. Yet, the two tragedies revolve around a striking *coup de théâtre*, for, just as the sons begin to make decisions as the new sovereign in place, the elder king returns and reclaims his position on the throne. The spaces occupied by the younger and the older generation blur. As the domains of the father and son collide, rivalry and violence become the defining factors in their relationship as they lay claim to the same space – the unique space of the throne, which cannot be divided or shared, as Racine first depicted in *La Thébaïde*.

In *Mithridate* and *Phèdre*, the sons, who are virtuous despite small transgressive actions, immediately submit to the father's authority upon his return, but the father/sovereign/judge regards his successor with suspicion and believes he has been betrayed by him. In *Mithridate*, Xipharès immediately steps back into the role of faithful son and relinquishes any claim to Monime, the woman he loves but who had been destined to be his father's wife: "Quand mon père paraît, je ne sais qu'obéir" (v. 366) [When my father appears, I only know how to obey]; as for Hippolyte, he repeatedly begs his father to let him leave the kingdom of Trézène. He prefers to depart rather than offend him by revealing the incestuous crime the queen, Phèdre, has committed in her husband's absence. Hippolyte's submission to paternal authority is so profound he loses his own voice and is reduced to silence.

While both Xipharès and Hippolyte seek to show deference to their fathers, the kings are too prompt to assume the worst about their progeny. Specifically, Mithridate and Thésée are persuaded that their sons have committed an inexcusable crime in taking for themselves what belonged to the father/king. The conflict of overlapping royal bodies presented in both plays not only affects the family's honour and continuation, it jeopardizes the kingdom's future and stability, which depends on a successful passing on of royal power. Barthes's lapidary insight into the dynamic of guilt in Racine: "L'absence du père constitue le désordre; le retour du père institue la faute" [the father's absence constitutes disorder; his return institutes the crime], underlines the role of guilt so crucial to Racine's tragic plots and to these two plays in particular in which the father is so thoroughly convinced of the son's guilt.[16]

In contrast to the sudden arrivals of the royal judge in tragicomedy to set things straight at the close of the plot, the father/judges' arrival in *Mithridate* and *Phèdre* occurs as a central turning point of the play. The king's arrival does not resolve the plot; on the contrary, it sets the tragic motor into motion by provoking the confrontation between the king and the prince who would have been king. Contrasting the funerary and matrimonial ceremonies of ancien régime France, Abby Zanger explains that the royal funeral was defined by a concept of linearity: "The funeral is [...] a ritual that marks an end and anticipates a beginning, merging two moments together to preserve the integrity of one state. It is a process of substitution that reduces multiplicity to singularity."[17] In these tragedies of the father/judge's return, we observe a thwarted "process of substitution" in which two royal bodies and two royal volitions lay claim to the same space in a disruption of order. In these plays, the crisis becomes one of literal and figurative space; one of the royal bodies has to disappear, and a resolution can only be achieved if (in *Mithridate*'s case) the son proves his loyalty, and the father recognizes his innocence and then dies, or (in *Phèdre*'s case) if the father/judge rules that his son is guilty, eliminates him, and re-establishes his supremacy as sovereign. Either way, for Racine, the return of the father results in the trial of the son, a stain on the father, and a disruption in the natural course of succession.

4 Scenes of Cross-Examination

Mithridate begins with the announcement of the king's death. A new day dawns on Nymphée, where the action takes place. From the start, Mithridate's two sons are set in opposition: one loyal, the other a traitor, both vying to replace their father. Xipharès distinguishes himself as the only heir faithful to his father's politics and memory, while the other brother, Pharnace, has decided to side with Rome, Mithridate's eternal enemy.

Significantly, Pharnace is the older brother of the two. According to the ancien régime law of primogeniture, the empty throne should, in fact, not go to Xipharès but to the eldest son. In his analysis of the play, Richard Goodkin rightly remarks on the oddity of this omission in Racine.

> In reality, *Mithridate* is neither about primogeniture or ultimogeniture, but rather about choice: the choice of an heir, the choice of a leader, the choice of a spouse. Mithridate makes it perfectly clear that far from considering Xipharès his natural heir, he has *chosen* him as an heir.[18]

The emphasis Goodkin places on Mithridate's "choice" is crucial, especially when viewed through the lens of the royal decision. Racine does not present Mithridate's succession as a predetermined event, one in which a set law designates the next king. Instead, the tragedy hinges on the king recognizing his true heir, the one who is a younger version of him. Regarding the older bother we are told "[Pharnace] est dès longtemps tout Romain dans le cœur" (v. 25) [Pharnace for a long time now is entirely Roman in his heart], while Xipharès states his hatred of Rome and reiterates his obedience towards "Un père dont je fus dévoué depuis l'enfance" (v. 100) [A father to whom I have been devoted since childhood]. Mithridate, in the closing scenes of the play will recognize Xipharès as "un autre moi-même" (v. 1067) [another me], but until the king ceases to see his son as a culprit, he risks executing the person most likely to preserve his reign. The father/king/judge therefore acts against his best interest. If Mithridate had died on the Roman battlefield as was first believed, Xipharès would have carried on his father's memory. Instead, the tragedy is fuelled by Mithridate's suspicions of his faithful son's guilt, and the play becomes a waiting game to see if the Asian king will make a tragic judgment, blind to the innocence of his son.

In contrast to Corneille's most famous royal judges, such as Don Fernand, Tulle, and Auguste, who possess full knowledge of the crimes upon which they must pronounce, Racine's sovereigns lack a crucial understanding of what has transpired in their absence. Before they rule on the accused, Mithridate and Thésée pose a string of questions that go unanswered, and they rely on faulty witnesses to give them the information they lack. In Mithridate's first encounter with his sons upon his return, he reproaches them for being "here": "Votre devoir ici n'a point dû vous conduire" (v. 424) [Your duty should never have brought you here]. Their presence in the space of the stage indicates their guilt, and he immediately views himself as their judge: "Mais vous avez pour juge un Père qui vous aime. / Vous avez cru des bruits que j'ai semés moi-même. / Je vous crois innocents puisque vous le voulez" (vv. 427–9) [But you have as a judge a father who loves you / You have believed the rumours I created myself. / I believe you innocent because you wish it]. While he reassures Xipharès and Pharnace that he will let his affection for them guide his judgment, the father/judge in fact turns to an eyewitness and trusted advisor, asking for details about his sons' behaviour in his absence, opening an investigation into their crimes. Detective-like, he questions his confidant:

> Mais tous deux en ces lieux que pouvaient-ils attendre?
> L'un et l'autre à la Reine ont-ils osé prétendre?
> Avec qui semble-t-elle en secret s'accorder?
> Moi-même de quel œil dois-je ici l'aborder?
> Parle. Quelque désir qui m'entraîne auprès d'elle,
> Il me faut de leurs cœurs rendre un compte fidèle.
> Qu'est-ce qui s'est passé? Qu'as-tu vu? Que sais-tu?
> Depuis quel temps, pourquoi, comment t'es-tu rendu?   (vv. 475–82)

> [But both of them here, what were they expecting?
> Did one or the other dare aspire to the queen?
> With whom did she seem in secret to agree?
> How should I view her when I greet her myself?
> Speak. Whatever desire leads me towards her,
> You must give me a faithful account of their hearts.

What happened? What did you see? What do you know?
Since when, why, and how have you been here?]

Mithridate's torrent of questions stems from his desperate urge to read
into the hearts of his sons by using objective evidence, such as their con-
versations and their actions, to evaluate their behaviour. He grasps at
details, clues, and evidence – any proof that will shed light on what occurred in his absence. Far from the all-seeing ancien régime ideal of sovereignty, the king struggles with the disturbing awareness that he does
not know what to believe. Much like Oedipus's quest for a sure witness
to reveal the truth behind the death of the Theban king who preceded
him, Mithridate searches intently for answers and yet is incapable of dis-
cerning the innocent from the guilty. His questioning underscores the
chasm between his professed will to uncover the truth and his blindness
in correctly differentiating between his sons. The king's judgment becomes the central problem of the play, not its resolution.

Blindness similarly characterizes the sovereign/father/judge in *Phè-*
dre when Thésée relies on the authority of circumstantial evidence and
the testimony of a faulty witness to condemn his son. Œnone places
before the king Hippolyte's sword, hoping to fool him into believing the
prince could have drawn it in his rape of Phèdre. The confidant's plan to
incriminate Thésée's son works only too well as the king's recognition of
the object equates with the recognition of Hippolyte's culpability – "J'ai
reconnu le fer, instrument de sa rage /Ce fer dont je l'armai pour un
plus noble usage" (vv. 1009–10) [I know the sword he drew to appease
his lust: / The sword I armed him with for nobler use]. He is a father/
judge too prompt to believe the worst about his son and to blame him
for the disorder he finds in the kingdom.

Just as Mithridate fervently searches for answers upon his return,
Thésée is characterized by a passionate desire to penetrate the mystery
around him:

Qui m'a trahi? Pourquoi ne suis-je pas vengé?
La Grèce a qui mon bras fut tant de fois utile,
A-t-elle au Criminel accordé quelque asile?
Vous ne répondez point. Mon fils, mon propre Fils
Est-il d'intelligence avec mes ennemis?   (vv. 980–4)

[Who is the traitor? Why am I not avenged?
Can Greece, that owes so much to my strong arm,

Be sheltering the one who has betrayed me?
You do not answer. Can my son, my own
Son be conspiring with my enemies?]

His quest to "connaître à la fois le crime et le coupable" (v. 986) [Know at once the crime and the culprit] leads him too quickly to conclude that his son must be implicated or he would not have allowed a crime to occur. The father/judge/sovereign who was the victim of an offence becomes culpable in turn for punishing the wrong person. Mithridate and Thésée's verdicts constitute the tragic knot, proving that their faulty judgments can be more dangerous even than Phèdre's desire for Hippolyte or Pharnace's betrayal.

Thésée's immediate condemnation of his son contrasts with the earnestness with which Hippolyte had demonstrated his desire to obey his father from the start of the play. In Act I, scene 1, Hippolyte is portrayed as aching to prove his filial devotion (vv. 93–113) and distinguish himself as his father's heir. Literally following in Thésée's footsteps, the audience learns that he is fleeing Trézène not only to find his father, an act symbolic enough in and of itself, but also to obey him. He refers to the father's will as an "eternal obstacle" (v. 104) and out of respect for Thésée's wishes, he is running away from his forbidden love for Aricie. The son seeks to emulate the father by obeying and following him. It must be emphasized that this insistence on Hippolyte's allegiance to Thésée is specifically a Racinian addition. In neither Euripides's nor Seneca's versions of the play does Hippolyte contemplate leaving the kingdom to find his father. Racine also invents the renouncement of Aricie, an act of self-sacrifice for Thésée, which works to underline Hippolyte's devotion to the paternal will.

In *Phèdre*, the father's and son's bodies are consistently juxtaposed, a dynamic which leads to crime. The fundamental opposition between the king and prince is portrayed first through the eyes of the king's wife. Racine's original title for the play, *Phèdre et Hippolyte*, accentuates Thésée's absence and his replacement by his son. Phèdre's guilt lies in her attraction to Hippolyte, and this attraction is formulated in terms of physical appeal. Comparing the king to the prince, she gives no weight to Thésée's body as a unique royal body and therefore one that should have no equal. When Phèdre recounts first laying eyes on her husband's son, she says she was overcome by a feeling of desire expressed in her own bodily reaction: "Un trouble s'éleva dans mon âme éperdue. / Mes yeux ne voyaient plus, je ne pouvais plus parler. / Je sentis tout mon corps et transir et brûler" (vv. 274–6) [A tumult rose in my bewildered soul; / My eyes forgot to see, I could not speak; / I felt my body burn and freeze at once]. While the prince's body provokes an uncontrollable physical reaction in the king's wife, the king's body is eclipsed by Hippolyte who is substituted for Thésée in the queen's fantasy.

Phèdre's attraction to the prince leads her to erase the singularity of Thésée's royal body as she dangerously blends father and son together. In a distortion of the sacred principle of eternal monarchical renewal that governed French succession, "The king is dead, long live the king," her desire does away with the linearity separating the father and the son. The queen describes a reversal in which the king becomes a reflection of the prince: "O comble de misère! Mes yeux le retrouvaient dans les traits de son père" (v. 290) [O crowning woe! I found him mirrored in his father's face]. Her adoring gaze is displaced from the king to his heir as the great Thésée becomes only a reflection of Hippolyte. Phèdre eliminates chronology as she reimagines history by placing Hippolyte in the Minotaur's labyrinth instead of Thésée (vv. 641–50). The father's exploits, actions that identify him and set him apart from others, are negated by the insertion of Hippolyte in his place. As such, Thésée's claims to superiority and glory are abolished as Hippolyte can effortlessly double as his father in the queen's mind. Instead of circumscribed spaces for the father's and the son's body, as presented in the French royal funerary ceremony, for example, the older and younger generation dangerously overlap. The joining of the two is not a cementing of unity between royal bodies, but a dilution of the king's individuality and superiority.

Whereas Phèdre's guilt lies in the intensity and detail with which she intertwines the father and son, Thésée proves to be guilty of separating himself too strongly from Hippolyte. Instead of privileging his role as father over his role as judge, and considering his son as part of himself – his successor – he deliberately distances himself from Hippolyte, adhering too strictly to the role of judge/punisher until it is too late. Learning that the king has called on Neptune to be the executioner of his son, Phèdre calls Thésée a "père insensé" (v. 1315) [maddened father] and attempts to ignite his paternal affection by reminding him that Hippolyte is "[his] race, [his] blood" (v. 1117).[19] After Œnone's accusations, however, Thésée ceases to refer to Hippolyte by name or to see a connection between himself and his son. His vocabulary is tainted with anger as he defines the prince as a culprit, alternatively labelling Hippolyte "traitor," "perfidious," "profane," "adulterer," "monster," and "left-over of the brigands" – a mishmash of society's worst crimes. Thésée deems him to be a danger to society and no better than the legendary monsters he has defeated in the past. Jacques Scherer has noted the extent of the king of Athens's blindness, so all-consuming of the royal character: "Son aveuglement rare dans l'histoire de la tragédie est nécessaire pour expliquer l'horreur de son crime. Thésée, seul de tous les pères de Racine, est directement responsable de la mort de son fils"[20] [His blindness, rare in the history of tragedy, is necessary to explain the horror of his crime. Thésée, alone among Racinian fathers, is directly responsible for the death of his son]. Aricie also expresses incredulity at the king's inability to recognize his son's innocence and to judge him accurately. She asks Thésée: "Avez-vous de son Cœur si peu de connaissance? / Discernezvous si mal le crime de l'innocence?" (vv. 1429–30) [Have you so little knowledge of his Heart? / Can you not tell baseness from innocence?]. The fundamental proof of Hippolyte's innocence, she argues, is his heart. Rather than trust fallible circumstantial evidence, Thésée should rely on the truth of who Hippolyte is. She asks the father to abandon his position as a judge, and instead to embrace his role as a loving father in assessing Hippolyte's actions.

We see how deeply Racine fleshes out the character of the royal judge in *Mithridate* and *Phèdre*, especially in contrast to the royal judge typology that preceded these sovereigns. Taking to heart Corneille's precept in the "Examen de *Clitandre*" (1660), that kings who are "only" judges should be eliminated from tragedy for they lack the needed dignity of a sovereign character, Racine entirely intertwines the role of the judge with the role of the father and king. In fact, he goes so far as to build the tragic plots in *Mithridate* and *Phèdre* around the unwillingness of the sovereign/fathers to put aside their function as judge so that they may interact with their families without the menace of their judgment.[21] Every exchange these kings have with their queen or sons interrogates their motives, searches for proof of their culpability. Racine creates a royal judge entirely blinded by his human weaknesses – pride, suspicion, and jealousy.

The judge's ill-judgment because of his personal involvement in the case fuels the tragic intrigue. In *Mithridate*, even Monime's submissive promise to obey the king out of duty is viewed by the king as an admission that her heart belongs to someone else. He considers her tears to be irrefutable evidence of her guilt and menacingly concludes: "Je vous entends ici mieux que vous ne pensez" (v. 587) [I understand you better than you think]. In a later monologue, after his son has sworn allegiance to him, Mithridate mutters: "Non ne l'en [Xipharès] croyons point, et sans trop nous presser, / Voyons, examinons. Mais par où commencer? / Qui m'en éclaircira? Quels témoins? Quel indice?" (vv. 1021–3) [Let's not believe him, and without rushing, / Let us see, let us examine. But where to begin? / Who will enlighten me? What witnesses? What clue?]. In behaviour similar to Thésée's, Mithridate cuts off feelings of filial love and sentimentality, and simply refuses to take Xipharès at his word based on his proven loyalty. He believes truth to be attainable only through adhering to the role of a judge who conducts an investigation of "clues" and "witnesses."

Unlike the desperate Hérode in Hardy and Tristan's *La Marianne*, however, neither Mithridate nor Thésée are monstrous tyrants defined by their folly. Neither king holds a sham trial in which all the witnesses are threatened in advance of punishment if they testify in favour of the accused queen. Racine's kings believe they are relying on objective evidence. Thésée has Hippolyte's sword and Phèdre's tears: "Je crois des témoins certains, irréprochables /J'ai vu, j'ai vu couler des larmes véritables" (vv.1441–2) [But I have sure witnesses that I can trust: / Their tears, true tears, I've seen with my own eyes]. Mithridate, meanwhile, doggedly searches for proof. Far from Hérode's lunatic rants about torture and adultery, the king of Pont turns to dissimulation and trickery to get honest testimony; he proves himself to be a good calculator of human responses, despite his blindness to the nature of his children and the crimes committed.

Ultimately, in *Mithidrate* Act IV, scene 5, the king reaches an apex of frustration at not being capable of reading into the hearts of his children. He gives in to his anger, simply condemning for the sake of condemning:

Ma colère revient, et je me reconnais.
Immolons en partant trois Ingrats à la fois. (vv. 1385–6)
[...]
Je le dois, je le puis, ils n'ont plus de support.
Les plus séditieux sont déjà loin du bord.
Sans distinguer entre eux qui je hais, ou qui j'aime,
Allons, et commençons par Xipharès lui-même. (vv. 1389–92)

[My anger returns, and I recognize myself.
Before I depart, let's kill three ingrates at once ...
I must, I can, and they have no more support.
The most seditious are already far from the border.
Without distinguishing whom I hate and whom I love,
Let's go and begin with Xipharès.]

The difference between the innocent and the guilty, the faithful and the disloyal, the ones the king loves and the ones he hates, disappears. He loses all ability to see clearly and gives himself over entirely to the role of a judge who must punish. In leaving behind his human self – the side capable of affection and devotion – he jeopardizes his kingdom and almost commits a fatal crime.

5 Verdicts of Recognition

In *Mithridate*, if the announcement of the father's death at the beginning of the play had spelled the possibility for new beginnings, the death of Xipharès would have meant the end of all hope for the kingdom, since the Roman invaders would have found no other opponent in their way. Instead, Racine opts to stage a recognition of affection and resemblance between father and son. This realization allows the play to turn away from a sad tragic ending to one closer to the genre of tragicomedy with the anticipation of the wedding of the young lovers at the king/father's behest.

Just as Monime is about to commit suicide in response to Xipharès's announced death, the king's confidant, Arbate, arrives in time to stop her and tell her of Mithridate's "conversion."[22] He describes Mithridate's actions in a vocabulary of death and finality, marking a succession from father to son as Mithridate is on the battlefield "las et couvert de sang et de poussière" (v. 1595) [tired and covered in blood and dust]. The dust of the battlefield prefigures the dust the king's physical body will soon become, while the spilling of his blood emphasizes his relationship to Xipharès by rendering visible in Mithridate's death the link that ties the king to his successor. As the father's life verges on extinction, he suddenly realizes his son will embody his remains and give him new life. With the king at his last breath, the prince comes forward from among the dead heralding a resuscitation of the king. This sudden coming forward of the "dauphin" as the king is being put to rest echoes the contemporary ceremony of the king's coronation where the chapel doors of Reims Cathedral burst open to reveal the king's heir as he comes forward to receive the crown during the *sacre*.[23] Racine's tragedy builds on the theatricality of that moment, but in showing how close the line came to extinction, he emphasizes the difficulty of royal succession, the dangers inherent in the passage of power from father to son.

Xipharès's awe-inspiring arrival on the battlefield is described as spectacular, a quasi-hallucinatory vision, as all the men at war seem to stop what they are doing to turn their gazes on this shadowy form making its way among the dead towards his father: "Et le Vainqueur vers nous s'avançant de plus près, /A mes yeux éperdus a montré Xipharès" (vv. 1621–2) and "A travers mille morts, ardent, victorieux, / S'était fait vers son Père un chemin glorieux" (vv. 1629–30) [And the Victor towards us advanced closer and closer, / To my distraught eyes showed Xipharès ... Among thousands of the dead, ardent, victorious, / He made towards his Father a glorious path]. From then on, father and son are united, and the father ceases to see his son as a rival, a guilty party whom he must punish. In no longer regarding Xipharès as separate from himself, the king and prince blend together to erase their physical differences – they combine "le sang du père, O Ciel, et les larmes du fils" (v. 1650) [the blood of the Father, O heavens! And the tears of the son!]. The division between the two royal bodies, which had been so firm when the father clung to his role of judge, disappears as their unity is sealed in a mutual embrace.

In the final scene of the play, the king accepts his son and relinquishes his punisher-self – "J'ai vengé l'Univers autant que je l'ai pu" (v. 1657) [I avenged the Universe as much as I could]. The abandonment of his prosecutor role allows Monime and Xipharès to form a loving circle around the elderly father; past anxiety, danger, and threats of violence dissipate. In a scene that might as well belong at the close of Diderot's *drame bourgeois*, the family gathers around the father to mourn his passing in an outpouring of filial devotion and domestic unity. Importantly, Mithridate does not give his sword or crown to Xipharès as a sign of forgiveness: he gives Monime – future wife and mother. Sylvaine Guyot has convincingly shown how pathos and sentimentality characterize the king at the closing moments of Racine's tragedy. Guyot emphasizes the role Monime plays in bringing about the affective transformation of the elderly sovereign and sees the young woman as facilitating the "intrusion des marges affectives et féminines dans le centre héroïque et patriarcal"[24] [intrusion of emotional and feminine margins into the heroic and patriarchal centre]. In my view, the change Mithridate undergoes, which indeed provokes a new emotional basis for his relationship to his son, stems from a reversal of tragedy's set scenes of closing royal judgment. In this case, the determining factor of reconciliation comes when the sovereign relinquishes the role of judge – steps away from the conventional closing verdict – and instead embraces his paternal relationship to his son. The young and beautiful Monime, who came so close to death, becomes the bride whom the patriarch gives away in marriage as a promise of a future for the family, which suddenly becomes the most important unit. The king's attachment to his son, based on feelings of the heart, replaces his attachment to "empire and crown" and enables his family to thrive.[25]

Racine presents a Mithridate who abandons his urge to condemn and, therefore, becomes an uncontested figure of authority. His last request to Xipharès is for him to retire and not seek vengeance. Specifically, he asks that his son not punish Pharnace and leave the work of judgment to the Romans: "Fiez-vous aux Romains du soin de son supplice" (v. 1696) [Trust the Romans to take care of his punishment]. At the close of his life, the king abandons the role of judge for himself and for his son, leaving the execution of justice to providence, or the Romans.[26] The threat of judgment erased, son and father can now be united.

The celebrated image of the "King of the Pont," associated in the minds of French spectators with epic heroism and legendary grandeur, but under attack from the moment Mithridate entered the stage, is re-established through the pathos of the tragedy's closing scene of paternal agnition. In recognizing the innocence of his son and letting the most human and natural of traits – a father's love for his son – direct his understanding, Mithridate inaugurates a new model of princely behaviour based on the primacy of the family unit. In 1673, a contemporary of Racine, Donneau de Visé, sensed the exemplariness of Mithridate's behaviour before his death:

> Quoique ce prince fut barbare, [Racine] l'a rendu en mourant un des meilleurs princes du monde. Il se dépouille en faveur d'un de ses enfants, de l'amour et de la vengeance, qui sont les plus violentes passions ou les hommes soient sujets, et ce grand roi meurt avec tant de respect pour les dieux qu'on pourrait le donner pour exemple à nos princes les plus chrétiens.[27]

> [Although this prince was barbaric, (Racine) made him in his death one of the best princes of the world. He deprives himself in favour of one of his children of love and vengeance, which are the two most violent passions from which men suffer, and this great king dies with so much respect for the gods that we might give him as an example to our most Christian princes.]

He relinquishes the role of enforcer and punisher in favour of the role of unifier and provider – "Venez, et recevez l'âme de Mithridate" (v. 1708) [Come, and receive Mithridate's soul]. In this closing scene where the king's soul is transferred to his son through the new-found dynamic of generous giving from the older generation to the younger one, the tragedy ends with a sense of calm. Although the young couple promises to search for support in their revenge of his death, Mithridate's peaceful passing, in contrast to the tempestuous violence that characterized his lifetime, heightens the sense of quiet closure proposed by the play's dénouement.

6 A Royal Execution

In contrast to the conciliatory family portrait offered in *Mithridate*, *Phèdre* graphically describes the erasure of the son through his father's command. Théramène's *récit*, perhaps the most famous verses of French neoclassical theatre, depicts in astonishing detail the disfigurement, destruction, and ultimate erasure of the prince in terms that evoke the execution of the guilty in early seventeenth-century "Tragedies of the Scaffolds." Misguided and blind to the truth, Thésée wrongly believes he has lost control of his son. He acts to reclaim his authority by separating himself too radically from him. As Théramène's account unfolds, Hippolyte's body becomes more and more unrecognizable, but as his body is destroyed, his loyalty to his father becomes increasingly evident. Hippolyte's willingness to face the sea monster becomes certain proof that he is Thésée's heir. A positive moral judgment of Hippolyte is slipped into Théramène's description, "Hippolyte lui seul digne fils d'un héros" (v. 1527) [Hippolyte alone, worthy son of a hero]. We learn that when confronted by the monster, the prince faced him alone while his guards took refuge in a nearby temple. At the end of the encounter, once Hippolyte has been stripped of his clothes and skin, all that is left of him is his blood – the immutable link to his father. We hear of his gradual dismemberment, reminiscent of the frightening accounts of the "Tragedies of the Scaffolds": "Dans les rênes lui-même il tombe embarrassé [...] / J'ai vu, Seigneur, j'ai vu votre malheureux Fils, / Traîné pas les chevaux que sa main a nourri" (vv. 1547–50) [He fell at last, entangled in the reins ... / Dragged by horses that his hand had fed until his body was one whole wound]. This wound, symbol of the disappearance of the formerly threatening physical body of the son, once deemed to be so culpable by the father/judge, shows Hippolyte for who he really was at his core: an heir of royal blood and the last of his line.

Théramène's description ends with a final emphasis on Hippolyte's passage from living body to corpse, as if recounting in slow motion the process of execution until the prince's punishment is complete: "A ce mot, ce héros expiré / N'a laissé dans mes bras qu'un corps défiguré, / Triste objet, où des Dieux triomphe la colère, / Et que méconnaîtrait l'œil même de son père" (vv. 1567–70) [And then this hero passed away. / Leaving only in my arms a disfigured corpse, / A sad object, upon which the anger of the gods triumphs, / And that even his father would not recognize]. Théramène's description emphasizes the tragic irony of the unrecognizable form Hippolyte has taken because Thésée was unable to recognize his son's innocence when he was alive. The change of Hippolyte from human being to object "upon which" the will of the gods – through the will of the father – is demonstrated, underlines how the father's inability to be the judge of his son's character has turned his son's body into an inanimate entity, a simple sign of the brutality of royal power. The deceased body demonstrates how the king's verdict so completely erases life. Hippolyte as son, prince, and individual ceases to exist, and becomes only a "sad object," his corpse a testament to the king's misjudgment.

The vivid descriptions of the son's blood strewn over his father's land further highlight the carnage of Hippolyte's body, depicting a crime scene where today investigators would comb through the wreckage to recover whatever evidence could be used to convict a culprit of such a massacre:

> J'y cours soupirant et sa garde me suit.
> De son généreux sang la trace nous conduit.
> Les rochers en sont teints. Les ronces dégoutantes
> Portent de ses cheveux les dépouilles sanglantes.   (vv. 1555–8)

> [I and his guards hastened to him in tears.
> The traces of his blood showed us the way.
> The rocks were stained with it, the cruel thorns,
> Dripped with the bleeding remnants of his hair.]

In *Mithridate*, the son's tears united with the dying father's blood, giving the elderly king new life through his heir. In *Phèdre*, the tears of a witness to Hippolyte's execution mix with the dying prince's blood, producing only a scene of horror and regret, as the father/king/judge remains absent and the unity of the royal family unfulfilled. Hippolyte's dripping blood on the rocks of Trézène and the "trace" it leaves on the earth coincides with the disappearing trace of the family's lineage now that Hippolyte is dead.

7 Reconciliatory Judgments

The tragic irony of the father/judge who so desperately seeks answers to his questions, but whose condemnation is so misguided, forms the *pérépétie* of *Mithridate* and *Phèdre* rather than the plays' dénouements. In *Mithridate*, the king's judgment occurs at the close of Act III, scene 6, when the eponymous king condemns his son: "Ah Fils ingrat! Tu vas répondre pour tous. / Tu périras [...] / Perfide, je te veux porter des coups certains" (vv. 1118–21) [Oh ungrateful son! You will answer for all/ You will perish .../ Perfidious, I will give you sure blows]. The Asian king reiterates his condemnation in Act IV, scene 4, as his judgment becomes more and more ominous of the seemingly inevitable tragic ending to come.

In *Phèdre*, Thésée pronounces his *arrêt* against Hippolyte in Act IV, scene 3:

Misérable, tu cours à ta perte infaillible.
Neptune par le Fleuve aux Dieux mêmes terrible
M'a donné sa parole, et va l'exécuter.   (vv. 1157–9)

[Damned soul, your death is certain.
Neptune swore to grant my wish upon that river dreaded
Even by the gods: he'll keep his word.]

....

Mais à te condamner tu m'as trop engagé.
Jamais Père en effet fut-il plus outragé?
Justes Dieux, qui voyez la douleur qui m'accable,
Ai-je pu mettre au jour un Enfant si coupable?   (vv. 1163–6)

[But you yourself compelled me to condemn you:
Was ever any father injured so?
Just gods, who see the grief that crushes me,
Can I have fathered such an evil child?]

The rapidity with which the royal decisions are made in these plays echoes the royal judgments of tragicomedy, except that in *Mithridate* and *Phèdre* the verdicts intertwine personal and political vendettas, since both kings believe their sons have seduced the queen, leading to distinctly political consequences for the state. The vocabulary of fatherhood ("Fils ingrat" and "Jamais Père") underscores the blended role of the king as a father/judge who cannot separate the alleged crime from a personal affront. The fathers' verdicts come down as inescapable judgments of guilt, seemingly destined to end in a tragic execution.

Despite the gravity of these verdicts, however, in staging the royal judgment earlier within the tragic structure, not at the dénouement, the royal decision is eventually eclipsed by its aftermath. Though Racine's royal judges are tragically mistaken in their condemnations, there remains a final act to undo the decision in the case of *Mithridate*, or, in the case of *Phèdre*, for the characters onstage and the spectators watching them, to literally, move beyond the judgment scene towards a scene of reconciliation. In both cases, the tragedy's spotlight moves away from the pronouncement of a misguided royal verdict and turns instead to the post-judgment world of the kingdom.

Paradoxically, Racine's erroneous royal judge, Thésée, retains his dignity because the culmination of his role is not, in the end, to judge, but to invite the audience to shed tears over his mistaken verdict. As Thésée begins to doubt his decision, Phèdre arrives with poison in her veins to confess her crime, pointing to Œnone and to the gods as her accomplices and the source of her guilt. There is no need, therefore, for Thésée to act as a judge and punish once again since the queen and Œnone have taken the judgment upon themselves and committed suicide, leaving Thésée to pick up the pieces and exert his paternal and monarchical roles. As a closing image, Racine offers Thésée's belated but determined wish to "expiate" his "error" by uniting in tears with Aricie over Hippolyte's dead body.[28] Thésée's acceptance of Aricie signals a new era in Trézène, and the accent is placed on forgetting and looking ahead. At its ending, the play eerily reverses *Mithridate*. In *Phèdre*, it is the father who calls for the preservation of his son's spirit and the appeasement of his "remains." As opposed to the Euripidean and Senecan versions where the mistaken father laments his error at length, Racine's Thésée shakes off his guilt and responsibility for his son's death with astonishing rapidity. Read in light of *Mithridate*, we observe a similar willingness to reunite the family, to create a new future for the royal line, as Thésée adopts Aricie for the sake of Hippolyte's memory, "Que malgré les complots d'une injuste Famille / Son amante aujourd'hui me tienne lieu de Fille" (vv. 1653–4) [Let his beloved, despite her brothers' crime, / Be a daughter to me from this day]. Thésée, last of his line, vows to join himself to Aricie, last of her line. Instead of Xipharès's and Monime's marriage, here Aricie replaces ("tenir lieu de") Hippolyte. We must recognize, however, that if Aricie is to signal a restored legitimacy, she will need heirs of her own and will need to bear children. Instead of a touching domestic portrait, Racine offers a darker and more perplexing version of familial unity.

In heeding Thésée's resolute call to move beyond the devastating consequences of his judgment, a correlation emerges between the swiftness of the condemnation and the speed of its erasure. Racine does not make Thésée's intentions regarding Aricie clear. Does his adoption of her suggest he will look benevolently, as a father, on her future suitors? Or does it indicate that replacing Hippolyte with Aricie, a daughter for a son, also entails Thésée taking Hippolyte's place, a father for a lover? Thésée's reputation as an incorrigible ladies' man (explicitly alluded to at the start of the play (vv. 17–25) hints at the possibility that the future of the kingdom and the family depends on the union of the two. Or does the adoption mean that, perhaps, against ancien régime tradition, in taking the place of Hippolyte, Aricie will become the heir to Trézène's throne? The only certainty is that Thésée sees Aricie through new eyes. No longer the guilty remnant of a criminal family, she now fills an empty space, "me tienne lieu de fille" (v. 1654) [takes the place of a daughter]. In a tragedy so solidly built on familial guilt and the condemnation of offspring by the gods, the play's ending insists on a new willingness by the king to reconceive of the family line through adoption and integration in an act of forgetting family origins and crimes – he explicitly adopts Aricie "malgré les complots d'une injuste famille" (v. 1653) [despite the plotting of an unjust family]. The time of royal judgment has shifted into a deletion of past mistakes and guilty actions in favour of new alliances.

On the one hand, Racine proposes a new dramaturgy of royal judgment by placing the moment of condemnation at the dramatic centre of the play. In so doing, he devotes extensive stage time to the portrayal of the devastating effects of royal verdicts. On the other hand, the playwright ends the tragedy on the king's reparation of the past and embrace of the future. Thésée rapidly sheds his role of persecutor/ judge for the role of paternal unifier and guardian, a testament to the resilience of the king and kingdom, even after the worst of catastrophes. As Racine prepares to abandon the public theatrical stage for a position as Louis XIV's official historiographer, he demonstrates a keen awareness of the imperative of not dwelling on tragic royal decisions. *Phèdre* invites the characters onstage, and spectators viewing them, to move on with the king in a promotion of monarchical continuity, no matter the cost. We know that by the time Racine wrote *Phèdre*, Louis XIV had already suffered the loss of five of his children, with more to come, and we might be tempted to read the emphasis on continuity as a call for strength, even after the death of French heirs. I believe, though, that we should consider royal judgment in *Phèdre* and *Mithridate* as proposing a new type within the typology of the tragic royal judge. Leaving behind the search for clues, evidence, and proof that failed both fictional kings who acted more as judges than as fathers, these tragedies ultimately embrace a sovereign who judges from the heart, more father than judge. In adopting Aricie, the definition of fatherhood expands and the relationship becomes one based on a shared love and respect for the good of the royal family, rather than on objective and fallible proof of hereditary ties. The structural shift Racine presents within these tragedies, the focus on the world *after* royal judgments, deflects attention from the verdicts themselves to heighten attention to the unique power of the king/father to counteract tragedy through the primacy of paternal emotion.

Opening the door to the eighteenth century's *drame bourgeois* and *comédies larmoyantes,* Racine's royal judge turns away from the model proposed by his elder rival, Corneille, where the sovereign judge punishes or rewards according to how the state benefits. Racine images a more sentimental figure, a king defined by his human and emotional side. Yet, in so doing, the specificity and grandeur of royal dignity is diluted and must be replaced with strong affective responses. In the realm of tragedy, playwrights such as Voltaire or Crébillon Père will draw from Racine's spectacular return of the fathers from the dead as part of a new tragic aesthetic that privileges emotion, including through special effects and horror, as in Voltaire's *Sémiramis* (1748) where the father's ghost walks the stage, or as in Crébillon's *Atrée et Thyeste* (1707) where a goblet full of the blood of the king's son is presented in vengeance for him to drink. The later playwrights, however, will struggle to elicit a genuine emotional response from the audience towards these sovereigns.

Mithridate and *Phèdre* constitute a key step in a progressive reduction of the "judge" facet of the king. Racine belongs to a long line of playwrights who strive to breathe new life into a royal character whose symbolic power as living law proves so difficult to translate to the stage and whose hold on the imagination of spectators seems increasingly tenuous. The changes Racine and later tragedians make to the royal judge type are linked to the inherent artificiality of the stage. They increasingly turn towards the special effects the stage can offer, such as in the case of the two plays considered here, the suspense of a royal disappearance and the dramatics of a royal return from the dead.

Early in the century, Richelieu's faith in the stage as an ideal space for modelling the relationship between royal authority and royal subjects led him to encourage playwrights to find ways of showcasing royalty in the most positive light. Yet, as the search for new fictions of royal judgment revealed, the theatre is inevitably dogged (or energized) by the possibility that the illusion will collapse, suddenly seem ridiculous, or contradict official royal narrative; there is always the possibility that audiences will suddenly become aware that what they are seeing is not the marble magnificence of a royal palace but veneer painted in a trompe-l'oeil pattern; they become aware that the "man of authority" is not a king with a divinely invested power to uphold justice, but a blind old man who verges on the comical in his inability to interpret evidence. The appearance onstage of an actor pretending to be a king, pretending to enact royal decisions, and trying to embody royal dignity is never far from provoking the dark thought that the king himself is only playing at the role of king: if the pretend-king's dignity is always in danger of a sudden deflation, the tragic stage asks, why is the real king's dignity not also a product of pure artifice?

In an ongoing attempt to buttress the audience's belief in the theatrical king's power and dignity, Racine turns towards a sentimental father/king rather than a judge/king. Building on earlier tragic structures, he adopts the *coup de théâtre* with the kings' sudden return, but places these jolts to the intrigue early in the plot to emphasize the threat and surprise that accompany the royal character. The special effects of later tragedies attest to the lessons learned from Racine and to the continued search for new means to endow the royal character with a dignity and presence superior to those of other characters, even as the king's political weight flounders outside of the theatre. Even at the height of neoclassical theatre's glory, we see how playwrights experimented with and searched for answers to the challenges of how to most effectively guard against the royal character's loss of grandeur and descent into ridicule.

Racine's model of the paternal royal judge heralds the touching and virtuous fathers of the *drame bourgeois*, characters explicitly situated at the border between comedy and tragedy, and who are defined by their embrace of sentiment in providing morally upright lessons to their family. The sovereign judge also finds successors in the surge of legally minded eighteenth-century comedies Christan Biet has memorably examined.[29] Perhaps, above all, Beaumarchais's Comte d'Alma Viva in *Le Mariage de Figaro* (1784) is Thésée's most direct heir. Between his adulterous pursuits, his inability to know whom he should and should not trust, and his fruitless efforts to dominate the members of his household through the menace of his judgment, he stands as the archetype of misguided sovereign judgment in the eighteenth-century. The tragic topoi of royal judgment, such as the Comte's threats to exile Chérubin, Figaro's trial, and the play's *in extremis* scenes of agnition, become one with farcical portrayals of incompetent and corrupt justice. The dangers Thésée's erroneous judgment causes to his kingdom are replayed on a domestic level within the Comte's troubled household. Beaumarchais's prerevolutionary depiction of the tragico-comedic abuses of the judgments of the "man of authority" underscores the perseverance of the king as judge model, and makes explict its always subversive potential.

Conclusion

This study has traced the evolution of French tragedy and the evolution of the poetic discussions that inevitably accompanied the genre's transformation over the course of the seventeenth century. In following poetic debates regarding what constitutes an admirable royal action onstage, a persistent yet overlooked character of tragedy emerges as an essential dramatic representation of sovereignty – the king as judge. Beginning with the vein of the "Tragedy of the Scaffolds" in the first quarter of the century, the king onstage is assigned the role of judge, a character who holds a trial, articulates a verdict, and punishes the guilty in often brutal ways. As the century advances, this tragic type undergoes profound change even as the royal character in a tragic work is increasingly thought to relate to, and speak for, the contemporary French monarch. Playwrights take part in vehement debates over how to protect the royal image on the theatrical stage; they search for new ways of presenting the old type of the king as judge, drawing on a variety of creative strategies to turn him into a model of sovereignty more compatible with the politics of royal grandeur associated with absolutist discourses.

Passing Judgment has considered canonical and non-canonical works of French tragedy side-by-side, revealing their common use of the royal judge type to perform specific structural functions, such as bringing about the dénouement and tying up the play's loose ends. In keeping the critical gaze consistently focused on the presence, role, and subject of the king as judge, the motivations behind the changing norms and conventions of tragedy come into focus, as well as the theatrical responses playwrights provided to the poetic precepts laid forth by the *doctes* regarding royal portrayals. As critics advanced ever more narrow and often conflicting definitions of how a king onstage should behave,

Corneille, Rotrou, and Racine needed to rethink the dramatic structure of their plots and the parameters they should allot to the theatrical king.

Viewing French tragedy through the prism of the king as judge has allowed us to juxtapose multiple scenes of royal judgment and thereby gain a better understanding of the perilous waters playwrights had to navigate between creating coherent intrigues and protecting the dignity of royal theatrical characters. We see how in the wake of the controversy surrounding Corneille's *Le Cid*, examples of what the royal judge should not do became pronounced and a code of conduct for tragic royal behaviour emerged. Suddenly, it was no longer enough for the king simply to judge; he needed to do more; he needed to contribute centrally to the intrigue. The ongoing efforts by playwrights to find a workable formula for depicting the supposedly unique dignity of the monarch, especially as a character supposed to incarnate law, reveal to us that there was never a perfect solution, a unified framework for presenting the sovereign onstage even at the height of tragedy's success and proximity to royal power.

In taking the long view of how a tragic type evolves, we come to see more clearly the continuous struggles playwrights faced in satisfying the politics within the poetics. By confronting the specifics of dramatic theory regarding acceptable royal portrayals alongside the character of the king as judge, this analysis invites readers to behold the inadequacy of the dramatic theory advanced, and the extent to which playwrights do not do what they say they have done or planned to do. The panorama that emerges from such an exploration is far from a homogenous or monolithic dramatic corpus which can neatly be placed under the category of French neoclassical tragedy.

Discussions on the aims of literature and its consequences have usually pitted those who credit fiction with being able to subvert power, on the one hand, against those who believe it merely reinforces it, on the other. Yet, both sides seem to share a key premise: that literature is capable of simply and unequivocally replicating social power, that it is possible to create literary works that align perfectly and completely with the values and interests of the dominant class. In *Passing Judgment* I have sought to read neoclassical theatre's relationship to the period's absolutist project as neither subversive nor hegemonic. The playwrights studied here should be understood outside of a narrow dialectic that either sees them as intentionally undercutting royal narratives or as seamlessly supporting them. Focus on the royal judge demonstrates that a perfect alignment between literature and power is itself a fantasy.

Corneille, Rotrou, and Racine wanted to create embodiments of the seventeenth-century's dominant values regarding kingship; in contrast to Alexandre Hardy whose earlier mindset did not demand such an acknowledgment of contemporary monarchical values, the three playwrights tried to offer portrayals of the king which would correspond to the monarchical ideals of their day. And yet they could not do it; they moved from one attempt to another, with each new play patching up the problems in the previous work while springing new leaks that arose precisely from the attempt to deal with the problems that had been identified in the last piece. They bent every bit of their enormous talent and intelligence to create art that might voice the reigning ideology, and yet they never fully succeeded.

Partly, the failure was a matter of artistic temperament – Corneille's attraction to tragicomedic themes and structures or Rotrou's fascination with chaos, and Racine's overly pessimistic yet sentimental leanings. But more importantly, I have suggested that the playwrights failed because the task itself was impossible. Any governing ideology is so shot through with contradictions, and the attempt to embody absolutist narratives in artistic form is so undercut by the resistance of the theatrical forms and materials, that the task is inherently impossible. That is not to say that the plays are themselves failures. Their place within the canon, in the case of Corneille and Racine, and the dramatic complexity and creativity of Rotrou, demonstrate the tremendous literary value of these plays. Nonetheless, the artistic success of the tragedies is intimately linked to their failures as expressions of monarchical ideology.

Notes

Preface

1 By the term "ornamental," I reference the debate Georges Forestier
and Hélène Merlin-Kajman have led over the meaning of Corneille's
characterization of politics in his plays as "broderie" [ornamentation].
In a letter written to the Abbé de Pure, the playwright states: "[Je] crois
qu'après cela, il n'y a guère de question d'importance à remuer et que ce
qui reste n'est que la broderie qu'y peuvent ajouter la rhétorique, la morale,
et la politique" [I think that beyond that, there is no other question of
importance to take up and that all that remains is the ornamentation that
rhetoric, morality, and politics can add]. Corneille, *Œuvres complètes*, ed.
Georges Couton) 3:7. I will use Couton's Pléiade edition in three volumes
throughout. All translations of French texts are my own except where
noted. For the roots of the discussion on "ornamentation," see Forestier's
Essai de génétique théâtrale and Merlin-Kajman's, *L'Absolutisme dans les lettres ou
la théorie des deux corps*, esp. "Corneille et la politique," 21–48.
2 La Mesnardière, *Poétique*, 120. See Blocker, *Instituer un "art,"* 122–46, for a
biography and details of La Mesnardière's career in Richelieu's favour.
3 Bray, *La formation de la doctrine classique en France*, 80. See La Mesnardière,
Poétique, 84–5, and Scudéry, L'*Apologie du théâtre*, 3–4. See Blocker, *Instituer un
art*, ch. 3, "Agir par la scène: Richelieu et le théâtre," 203–78, and Jouhaud,
Les Pouvoirs de la littérature, for discussion of the cardinal's explicit support
of theatre as a "mode of action" whose goal would be to mould subjects into
submission to the Crown's aims.
4 La Mesnardière, *Poétique*, 176 and 113, respectively.
5 Aubignac, "De la vraisemblance," in *La Pratique du théâtre*, 126. I have
chosen to respect d'Aubignac's capitalization in my English translations.
Although *La Pratique* was only published in 1657, d'Aubignac most likely

composed the work in the 1640s. I will return to a discussion of this quote in chapter 1. Later in the century, the poetic demands will be heightened further as monarchical narratives insist that even the king in disguise should be recognized as king: "Et quand V.M. pour mettre nos yeux à l'épreuve, et pour faire essai de ce qu'elle est, serait cachée dans la foule de ses Gardes, nos yeux ne laisseraient pas d'aller droit à elle: et toute la pompe, toute la magnificience qui se montrerait ailleurs, ne détournerait point ailleurs notre vénération et notre culte" [And if Your Majesty to test our eyes, and to test what your majesty consists of, should hide itself in a crowd of Guards, our eyes should still go straight to it: and all the pomp and all the magnificence that would be on display elsewhere, would not distract us from our veneration and our worship]. Le Moyne, *De l'art de Régner* (1663), cited in McClure, *Sunspots and the Sun King*, 57.

6 Corneille, *Œdipe*, in *Œuvres complètes*, vol. 3, vv. 1348–50.

7 Schmitt *Political Theology*. For a discussion of the political weaknesses of Schmitt's views on sovereign decision-making, see Agamben, *State of Exception*; see also, Kahn, *The Future of Illusion: Political Theology and Early Modern Texts* and the special issue of the journal *Representations* 106.1 (spring, 2009) dedicated to political theology, including Schmitt's philosophy of sovereignty in contrast to Kantorowicz's discussion of the king's two bodies, especially in relation to early modern fiction.

Introduction

1 La Mesnardière, *La Poétique*, 36–7. "A king will be grave, guard his authority jealously, blend the rigour of a Master with the tenderness of a Father, and he will severely punish the lack of respect shown towards him."

2 Forestier's chapters, "Acte de décès: Une tragédie devenue tragi-comédie" and "Six années de débat (1628–1634): De la modernité anticlassique au classicisme moderne" in *La Tragédie française* stand as the authoritative study of the "renversement complet de tendance" (12) [the complete reversal of the tendency], which transformed tragedy's status in the 1630s.

3 On the rise of tragicomedy, see Guichemerre, *La Tragi-comédie*, and Baby, *La Tragi-comédie de Corneille à Quinault*, 13–100, which offers a detailed analysis of the debates surrounding the poetics of tragedy and tragicomedy.

4 See Dotoli, *Temps des Préfaces*, which groups together all the works instrumental in this debate over the codification of tragedy and its position on the literary value-spectrum.

5 For a detailed discussion of the rules and conventions of the tragic genre, including the impossibility of claiming ignorance of them despite a lack of consensus on their application, see Lyons, *Kingdom of Disorder*.

6 The political significance of tragedy's formal changes has been well documented by Blocker, *Instituer un "art*," and Ibbett, *The Style of the State in French Theater, 1630–1660*.

7 For the specifics on the Académie Française's political-aesthetic role, see Blocker, *Instituter un "art*," and *La Querelle du Cid (1637–1638), edition critique intégrale*, ed. Civardi; on religiously grounded opposition to and limitations of theatrical representations, see Thirouin, *L'Aveuglement salutaire*.

8 Genette, "Vraisemblance et motivation," 74.

9 Biet, "La plume et la loi," 187. This volume is dedicated to the practice of juridical writing under the ancien régime as a mode of action. It provides a precious critical bibliography on the written production of positive law in this period. Marc Fumaroli has shown how the French wars of religion saw the social and professional elevation of magistrates and lawyers trained in legal rhetoric. Influenced by humanist readings of Cicero in particular, they saw themselves as magistrate-orators and magistrate-authors, eager to "revendiquer la grandeur qui s'attache à l'exercice de la parole dans la cité" [claim the grandeur that is attached to the exercise of speech in public life]. *L'Age de l'éloquence*, 586. See also Chatelain, "Héros Togatus."

10 Hutson, *The Invention of Suspicion*. See also *Rhetoric and Law in Early Modern Europe*, ed. Hutson and Kahn.

11 See Frisch, "French Tragedy and the Civil Wars." For a contrasting reading that sees Corneille as inviting a closeness, a sense of shared feeling and objectives in a "theater of friendship," see Ibbett, "Mon ami, ce héros."

12 Frisch, "French Tragedy and the Civil Wars," 311.

13 Foucault, *Discipline and Punish*, 48–9.

14 For a discussion of the role of the public's judgment and social critique advanced through literary form, see Merlin-Kajman, *Public et littérature en France au XVIIe siècle*, 115–239.

15 "La littérature, parce qu'elle est spectacle, dévoile, joue, évoque les fondements abstraits des notions qu'elle exprime concrètement, exemplifie les contradictions internes au droit, met en scène les contradictions du droit avec les pratiques sociales, souligne que les fictions juridiques sont aussi, littéralement, des fictions et qu'elles ont une source historique et non transcendantale, et surtout confronte les certitudes ou les règles juridiques en dehors du terrain juridique" [Literature, because it is spectacle, unveils, plays with, alludes to, the abstract foundations of the notions it explains concretely, exemplifying the internal contradictions present in law, staging the contradictions between law and social practices, underscoring that juridical fictions are, also, literally, fictions, and that they have a historical and non-transcendental source, and, especially, confronting juridical rules

and certainties outside of the legal domain]. Biet, "La plume et la loi," 187. See also Biet's *Droit et littérature sous l'Ancien Régime.*

16 Marin, *Le Portrait du roi*; see also, Ferrier-Caverivière, *L'Image de Louis XIV dans la littérature de 1660 à 1715,* and Assaf, *La Mort du roi.*

17 See Guyot, *Racine et le corps tragique,* and, regarding Corneille, Guyot, "En contrechamp: le héros sous le regard des personnages" in *Héros ou personnages?* 95–109.

18 This is the argument Guyot makes in "'Un silence d'étonnement et d'admiration.'"

19 Guyot articulates the contrasts between the two spheres: "Ce non-silence paradoxal [...] signale d'emblée que la scène théâtrale ne saurait être tout à fait identifiée à la scène politique, puisque se dit sur la première ce qui s'impose comme non-dit, ou non-dicible, sur la seconde" (ibid., 215) [This paradoxical non-silence ... signals from the start that the theatrical stage cannot be entirely equated with the political stage, since everything that must be said on the former is what is always already understood or unspeakable on the latter].

20 This was a period of sustained reflection by Corneille on the art of tragedy. In addition to drafting the "Examens" of his plays, he also wrote three essays, veritable meditations on the tragic genre, the *Trois discours sur le poème dramatique* (1660). See Georges Couton, "Notice" in Corneille, *Œuvres complètes,* vol. 3, on Corneille's edition of his complete works, and also Corneille, *Trois discours sur le poème dramatique,* ed. Escola and Louvat.

21 Corneille, "Examen de *Clitandre,*" in *Œuvres complètes,* 1:103.

22 Roland Mousnier describes the legal notion of an ever-present monarch: "Mais pour les affaires de justice ou de police qui sont de routine et peuvent être réglées d'après les précédents, le roi est absent. Mais il est censé y être. Cette fiction est nécessaire, car, autrement, l'arrêt du Conseil n'aurait pas de force contraignante. Le Conseil seul n'a pas d'existence. A plus forte raison n'a-t-il pas de délégation du pouvoir. Le roi est censé prendre la décision. L'arrêt du Conseil porte donc la formule: 'le roi en son Conseil'" (*La Vénalité des offices sous Henri IV et Louis XIII,* 1:135) [But in matters of justice or policing which are routine and can be determined according to precedent, the king is absent. But he is supposedly there. This fiction is necessary since, otherwise, the *Conseil*'s decision would have no compulsory value. The *Conseil* by itself has no meaning. A fortiori, it cannot delegate power. The king is supposed to make the decision. The *Conseil*'s decision is always accompanied by the formula: "The king in his Council"].

23 See, for example, Père Le Moyne, *De l'art de régner,* cited in McClure, *Sunspots,* 58: "Il est certain que comme le Tyran ne croit être que pour lui,

le vrai Prince aussi ne croit être que pour son Peuple. Le Droit des Gens sur lequel est fondée l'institution des Princes, le veut ainsi: et la nature de la Justice, qui est leur propre caractère, le demande ... Et Saint Ambroise nous apprend, que n'étant pas née pour soi-même, et ayant sa fin hors de soi, toute sa gloire est de s'abandonner, et de résigner tous ses intérêts au Public: de mettre son bien, et d'établir son repos dans l'ordre, dans le calme, dans l'harmonie de la Société civile." [It is certain that just as the Tyrant believes he exists only for himself, the true Prince believes he exists only for his People. The *Droit des Gens* on which is founded the institution of Princes wants it to be thus: and the nature of justice, which is his own character, demands it ... And Saint Ambrose teaches us, that not having been born for oneself, and having one's end beyond oneself, all the prince's glory is to abandon himself, and to resign all his interests to the Public: to put all his means, and to establish his rest in the order, the calm, and the harmony of civil Society.]

24 The notion of *dignité*, often evoked in royal theatrical portrayals, is an amalgamation of political and moral considerations. It is both an "office" that a person may hold, as in "*la dignité royale*" or "*la dignité magistrale*," and a character trait. For a detailed discussion of the concept of the royal *dignité* as "office/function," a juridically constructed fiction meant to solve the problem of the physical impermanence of the king's body by instituting the doubling of that body through the creation of an immortal body that is permanent, continuous, and stable, see Kantorowicz, *The King's Two Bodies*.

25 Furetière, *Le Dictionnaire universel*, "Dignité."

26 Corneille, "Examen de *Clitandre*," in *Œuvres completes*, 1:102. My emphasis.

27 Ibid., 1:103.

28 In *L'Absolutisme dans les lettres*, 16, Merlin-Kajman describes what she sees as the wholly antiquated role of the royal judge, only a memory for a post-*Le Cid* Corneille: "A côté de la figure du roi dont la volonté souveraine constitue la source de la loi, Corneille se souvient du 'roi de justice,' simple conservateur des lois ou du droit. Sans doute est-ce au niveau de ce 'juge' que la théorie des 'deux corps' a le plus laissé ses traces. Car il est évident que comme 'juge,' le roi se trouve dépersonnalisé" [Alongside the figure of the king whose sovereign volition constitutes the source of the law, Corneille remembers the "king of justice," simple keeper of laws or of justice. It is perhaps at the level of this "judge" that the "two body" theory has been most decisive. For it is evident that as a "judge" the king becomes depersonalized].

For Merlin-Kajman, the royal judge's role as "keeper of justice" in early tragedy is decisively displaced onto other characters and onto the space of theatre, which becomes a form of social tribunal: "Véritable tiers symbolique, [le roi de justice] dessine une fonction médiatrice de la représentation dont il est alors le représentant, fonction qui ne se trouve pas forcément perdue quand le roi n'apparaît plus dans ce rôle. Il faudra se demander dans quelle mesure ce n'est pas la représentation théâtrale elle-même qui peut alors tenir cette place" (16) [Veritable symbolic third party, (the king of justice) outlines the mediating function of representation of which he is then the representative, a function that does not necessarily disappear when the king no longer appears in that role. It is necessary to ask to what degree it may be that the theatrical representation itself occupies that position].

29 Ibid., 14.

30 Ibid., 18. A similar argument has been made in the rhetorical realm by Gilles Declercq, responding to Aron Kibedi-Varga who identifies French tragic discourse as resorting most often to the judicial genre of rhetoric. Declercq argues that within a given plot numerous characters occupy the role of judge at different times and that none acts as a supreme arbiter over all the others: "Les personnages occupent tour à tour selon leurs interlocuteurs, la fonction d'accusateur et d'accusé [...] Cette labilité des rôles résulte de la complexité de l'intrigue et de la dynamique dramatique qui engendrent un enchevêtrement de procès contradictoires" [Characters occupy in turn, depending on their interlocutors, the function of accuser and accused ... This fluidity of roles results from the complexity of the intrigue and the dramatic dynamic which create an entanglement of contradictory trials]. Declercq, "L'identification des genres oratoires en tragédie française du 17e siècle," 232.

31 Corneille, "Examen de *Clitandre*," in *Œuvres complètes*, 1:103.

32 With few exceptions, this was the case at least until the eighteenth century when Voltaire and others, influenced by the English stage, began to take a keen interest in staging national heroes. See Lahouati and Mironneau, *Figures de l'histoire de France*, and Frisch, "French Tragedy and the Civil Wars" for examples of sixteenth-century tragedies that depict French history.

33 Scudéry, *Observations sur* Le Cid, 401. Mondory was the renowned actor and owner of the Parisian Théâtre du Marais.

1 The Critique of *Le Cid*: Richelieu, Royal Judgment, and the Rules

1 Corneille, "Sonnet. Epitaphe de Louis XIII" in *Œuvres complètes*, vol. 1, verse 2, l. 1704. (Sonnet attributed to Corneille by Georges Couton (see pp. 1700–7 for discussion of reasons for attribution). "Ambition, pride, audacity, avarice/ Seized his power, gave us laws / And while he was the most just of kings, / His reign was, however, one of injustice."

2 Mousnier, *Les Institutions de France*, 20, describes the reasons for choosing that sobriquet. For a detailed history of the validity of Louis XIII's nickname which insists on the king's punitive approach to justice, in particular as a response to the lawlessness he perceived within the French kingdom, see Moote *Louis XIII, The Just*. On Louis's fraught relationship to justice, see also Marvick, *Louis XIII*.

3 For a detailed account of efforts to theorize a satisfactory model of royal authority in the wake of the wars as "neither an entirely mystical and mythical enterprise nor a wholly cynical and rational expression of reason of state," see McClure, *Sunspots and the Sun King*, 1.

4 See Jouanna, "Vers la sacralisation du pouvoir absolu," in *Le Pouvoir absolu*, and Le Roux, *Le Roi, la cour, l'état de la Renaissance à l'absolutisme*, esp. ch. 14, "Roi du miracle," 267–90.

5 Bodin, *Les Six livres de la République* (1576), Livre I, ch. 8, 511. For discussion of Bodin's theories, including the king's status as "untied" to law, and the difference between times of "ordinary" versus "extraordinary" justice, when he can break with precedent, see Jouanna, *Le Pouvoir absolu*.

6 Cosandey, *La Reine de France*, 265.

7 In this *lit de justice* Sarah Hanley identifies a move towards a "biogenetic stripe" and sees it as inaugurating a "rude break with French constitutional tradition." *The* Lit de Justice *of the Kings of France*, 251.

8 See Le Bret, *Traité de la souveraineté du Roy*, livre 1, chap. 9: "Qu'il n'appartient qu'au Roi de faire des Loix dans le Roïaume, de les changer, et les interpreter." See also Loyseau, *Les Œuvres de Maistre Charles Loyseau* [1608]: "Car il n'y a point de plus propre effet de la souveraineté, que de faire de sa propre autorité des lois qui obligent tous les sujets en général, et chacun en particulier, tout ainsi que le Prince a pouvoir et commandement sur eux tous sans exception" (14) [For there is no more proper effect of sovereignty than to make his own authority of laws that constrain all of his subjects generally, and each one individually, since the Prince has power and command over them without exception]. See Descimon for a study of Loyseau's dogmatic theories regarding monarchical legal power in contrast to his practice in the *office seigneuriale*, "Les Paradoxes d'un juge seigneurial."

For a summary of the growing opposition between the *officiers,* who held their positions on a hereditary basis, and the *commissaires,* who were appointed for specific and contingent legal commissions, as a product of the increasing efforts by the monarchy to shift legal authority away from more independent-minded entities like the *Parlements,* see Gordon, *Citizens without Sovereignty*, esp., 9–42 ("Absolutism and the Ideal Type of

Sociability"). For local examples that speak to the larger issue of the battle for authority and a notion of legality separate from the monarch, see Biek, *Absolutism and Society*, and Kettering, *Judicial Politics and Urban*.

9 See Le Goff, *Saint Louis*, 645. Passages echoing this description are widespread. They always stress Saint Louis's proximity to those he judged: "Combien grande fut sa justice, cela apparut manifestement non seulement par des exemples mais on pouvait le toucher du doigt. Il s'asseyait en effet presque continuellement par terre sur un tapis pour entendre les causes judiciaires, surtout celles des pauvres et des orphelins et il leur faisait rendre complètement justice" (645) [How great was his justice, that was manifested not only by examples but one could touch him with one's finger. Indeed, he sat almost continually on the ground, on a carpet, to listen to judicial requests, especially those of the poor and orphaned, and he delivered justice onto them completely]. See also Richard, *Saint Louis, roi d'une France féodale*.

10 See Apostolidès, *Le Roi-Machine*, for a reading of the gradual incursion of bureaucracy and the state apparatus into royal displays, politics, and relations.

11 Mousnier, *Des Offices*, 135.

12 See Fernandez-Lacôte, *Les Procès du Cardinal de Richelieu*, ch. 3, "Institutions," 141–81.

13 De Thou, *Histoire universelle*, lib. LXXV, vol. 3, 567, first published in Latin as *Historia sui temporis* (Paris: Pierre de la Rovière, 1620). To understand this quote in the context of de Thou's frustration with royal politics and his background as a member of the *noblesse de robe*, see De Smet, *Thuanus: the making of Jacques-Auguste de Thou*. On how the Parlement sought to limit royal decrees and how de Thou worked to appeal the official condemnation of his *Histoire universelle* see Tesissier-Ensminger, "Histoire de re-dire le droit."

14 For details, see Fernandez-Lacôte, *Les Procès du Cardinal de Richelieu*, as the authoritative study on the subject of Louis XIII's legal transformations and Richelieu's recourse to public trials. Beyond an account of the narratives and archival materials that remain of the political executions of the more famous and lesser-known members of the nobility, she examines the "extraordinary" procedures that were implemented to short-circuit regular legal practices. This includes an in-depth study of the Chambre de l'Arsenal, a specially constituted bench of hand-picked *commissaires* loyal to Richelieu and his "raison d'état" philosophy. The Chambre de l'Arsenal was constituted as an institutional means of bypassing and diminishing the authority of the members of the Parlements. Fernandez-Lacôte provides

a definitive bibliography on the subject of political trials under Louis XIII. See also Kitchens III, "Judicial Commissaires and the Parlement of Paris." See also Bercé and Fasano Guarini, *Complots et conjurations dans l'Europe moderne*; and Chiffoleau, "Le Crime de majesté, la politique et l'extraordinaire."

15 "La distinction entre intrigue de cabinet et conspiration de grande envergure ne doit donc pas être regardée comme un anachronisme; c'est au contraire l'attitude du pouvoir politique qui provoque l'étonnement des acteurs et des observateurs de la cour. Le procès d'Etat est bien devenu, au cours des années du ministère de Richelieu, une des armes du pouvoir – il s'est trouvé amplifié, consolidé et s'est révélé d'une efficacité redoutable comme instrument de mise en ordre de l'histoire en train de se faire" [The distinction between cabinet intrigue and large-scale conspiracy must not be seen as anachronistic; on the contrary, it is the attitude of the political powers that provokes the surprise of the actors and observers of the court. The state trial became, during the years of the Richelieu ministry, a weapon of power – it was amplified, consolidated, and revealed itself to be of formidable efficiency as an instrument for ordering history in action]. Fernandez-Lacôte, *Les Procès du Cardinal Richelieu*, 395. Similarly, Jouanna speaks of a "judiciarisation du politique" [judicialization of the political] in "Conclusions," 665.

16 On trials held in the name of *lèse-majesté*, see Delatour, "'Les armes en main et les larmes aux yeux': Le procès de Cinq-Mars et de Thou." For discussion of monarchical legal reprisals, see Soman, *Sorcellerie et justice criminelle*, and Ranum, *Richelieu and the Councillors of Louis*, as well as, Moote, *The Revolt of the Judges*, esp: Part I, "Prelude to the Fronde."

17 On the intricacies of the nobility's efforts to retain influence over the French legal system, see Jouanna, *Le Devoir de révolte*. On the nobility's complex relationship to the Crown, one where favours went both ways, see Constant, *La Noblesse en liberté, XVI–XVIIe siècles*. On aristocratic ambition in reaction to the rise of court life, see Dewald, *Aristocratic Experience*.

18 Jacques d'Apchon de Saint-Germain, dit le père Chantelouve, "Lettre," quoted in Fernandez-Lacôte, *Les Procès du Cardinal de Richelieu*, 256.

19 On these questions and for additional bibliographical references on the quarrel, see Merlin-Kajman, *Public et littérature en France au XVIIe siècle*.

20 On the institutionalization of the tragic genre leading up to and in the wake of the quarrel, see Blocker, *Instituter un "art."* For all the documents pertaining to the quarrel, as well as a detailed introduction to its sources and consequences, see Civardi, *La querelle du Cid (1637–1638). Edition critique intégrale*. All quotes from the polemic will be taken from this edition.

21 For a detailed study of the notion of impropriety/*bienséance* in *Le Cid*,
see Lyons, *Kingdom of Disorder*, esp. 122–7; and for feminist readings and
defences of Chimène, see Carlin, *Women Reading Corneille.*

22 For an important exception to the critical indifference to Don Fernand's
decision, see Braider, "Cet hymen différé: The Figuration of Authority in
Corneille's *Le Cid*," in *Indiscernible Counterparts*, 53–99, in which he considers
how Corneille sought to soften the play's ending by having Fernand suggest
that *in time* Chimène might marry Rodrigue, but then the play was taken
to task for lacking a definite ending, a disturbing "*différance*" of the royal
decision. Braider, however, sees Don Fernand as a necessary figure of power
and political order while, at the very least, I aim to show that Corneille's
king was an ambiguous sovereign figure, lacking in unity, deemed faulty,
and a work-in-progress for the playwright's conception of royal characters.

23 Chapelain, *Les Sentiments*, 930. Civardi's edition offers the two versions of the
Sentiments. The first was read aloud before the members of the Académie
Française and, as its title indicates, was portrayed as a direct response to
Scudéry's *Observations*. The second version, from which I will quote because
of its status as the definitive text, was the final published version which
sought to present itself as new poetic doctrine. On the manuscript of this
second version we find Richelieu's comments and edits of Chapelain, which
add to the impression that it is a code of imperatives playwrights needed to
follow; see Civardi's editorial comments, 917–29.

24 Chapelain, *Les Sentiments*, 930. The first version was even more explicit in
its judicial language here: "Ils perdent tout le droit qu'ils y ont aussitôt
qu'ils l'exposent à la lumière [...] qu'autant qu'ils en ont besoin pour les ·
réformer lorsqu'ils y reconnaîtront des fautes" (930) [They (authors) lose
every right they have to it as soon as they expose it to the light or at most
they conserve what they need to reform it when they recognize its mistakes].

25 Chapelain, *Les Sentiments*, 934–5.

26 Ibid., 933.

27 See Merlin-Kajman, *Public et littérature au XVIIe siècle*, 218–22, makes this point,
but does not tie the Académie's portrayal of itself as a judge to the broader
cultural-political debates over acceptable representations of royal judgment.

28 Scudéry, *Observations sur* Le Cid, 401.

29 Ibid., 402.

30 Ibid., 401: "Il fait agir ce sage Prince, comme un enfant qui serait bien
enjoué" [He makes this wise Prince behave like a playful child].

31 "The fourth point is consistency: for though the subject of the imitation,
who suggested the type, be inconsistent, still he must be consistently
inconsistent." Aristotle, *Theory of Poetry and Fine Art*, ch. 15, 55.

32 Scudéry, *Observations sur* Le Cid, 376.

33 Chapelain, *Les Sentiments*, 289.

34 Aubignac, *La Pratique du théâtre*, 123.

35 Ibid.

36 Ibid., 126.

37 See Blocker, *Instituer un "art,"* ch. 2, 109–84, for a study of d'Aubignac's career and relationship to the cardinal, and Baby's introduction, pp. 11–31, in her edition of his *La Pratique du théâtre* for a complete biography of d'Aubignac, including his efforts to gain Richelieu's favour.

38 D'Aubignac, "Commentaires sur Corneille," 112.

39 Corneille, "Examen du *Cid*," 1:702.

40 Ibid., 1:703.

41 Ibid.

42 D'Aubignac, *La Pratique du théâtre*, 465.

43 Scudéry, *Observations sur* Le Cid, 401.

44 See Blocker, *Instituer un "art,"* esp. ch. 3, "L'Art et l'action: les théâtres de Richelieu," 185–279, and Civardi editorial comments, 25–54.

45 For a detailed analysis of the careers of these authors and how the publication of their poetics constituted a political "operation" by which they sought to ingratiate themselves to their common patron, Cardinal Richelieu, see Blocker, *Instituter un "art,"* esp. ch 3, "Publier les règles de l'art, Scudéry, Sarasin, La Mesnardière, d'Aubignac," 109–84.

46 Chapelain, *Les Sentiments*, 948.

47 Aristotle, *Theory of Poetry and Fine Art*, ch. 16, 57.

48 On these changes, see Forestier, "Imitation parfaite et vraisemblance absolue."

49 Chapelain, *Les Sentiments*, 948.

50 Ibid.

51 Ibid., 938.

52 Ibid., 961.

53 Scudéry, *Observations sur* Le Cid, 401.

54 Ibid., 400.

55 Chapelain, *Les Sentiments*, 1020. In an earlier instance of this forceful desire to protect the royal person, Chapelain had lamented the "insupportable audace avec laquelle [Don Gomès] parle du Roi son Maître" (969) [the insuperable audacity with which [Dom Gomès] speaks to the king his Master].

56 Chapelain, *Les Sentiments*, 987.

57 Speaking of the king and the princess in *Médée*, Corneille writes: "ces deux mourants importunent plus par leurs cris et par leurs gémissements qu'ils ne font pitié par leur Malheur. La raison est qu'ils semblent l'avoir mérité par l'injustice qu'ils ont faite à Médée, qui attire si bien de son côté toute la

faveur de l'Auditoire qu'on excuse sa vengeance, après l'indigne traitement qu'elle a reçu de Créon et de son mari" [These two dying figures are so loathsome with their cries and moans that their misfortune does not cause pity for them. The reason for this is that they seem to have deserved this because of their injustice towards Médée who draws all of the audience's favour on her side so that we excuse her vengeance after the undignified treatment she received from Créon and her husband]. Corneille, "Examen de *Médée*," 1:540.

58 Corneille, "Examen de *Clitandre*," 1:103.

59 Ibid., 1:95.

60 Corneille, "Examen de *Mélite*," 1:95.

61 Corneille, "Préface de *Clitandre*," 1:95.

62 He goes on in the preface to say that he operated in complete freedom, "je me donne ici quelque sorte de liberté de choquer les Anciens, d'autant qu'ils ne sont plus en état de me répondre" (1:95) [I give myself here a sort of freedom to shock the Ancients, all the more so since they are in no position to answer me]. See also the "Excuse à Ariste" in which he famously proclaims his independence and individual genius, drawing the ire of his contemporaries.

63 Baby, *La Tragi-comédie de Corneille à Quinault*, 201.

64 Lyons, *Tragedy of Origins*, 101.

65 La Mesnardière, *La Poétique*, 120.

66 Baby, *La tragi-comédie de Corneille à Quinault*, ch. 2, "Un Genre codé, les types de la tragi-comédie," 103–23. For further discussion of royal typology outside of the tragic genre, see Morel, *Agréables mensonges*, "Rois de comédie et de tragicomédies dans le théâtre de Rotrou," 179–88. See Ekstein on the difficulty of endowing the authority figure with tragic dignity.

67 Baby, *La Tragi-comédie de Corneille à Quinault*, 201.

68 My view is therefore at odds with Paul Scott's who argues that Corneille purposefully made Don Fernand a weak leader so that the French could identify him with their own king, Louis XIII, and France's tenuous political situation at the time of the play's staging. See Scott, "'Ma force est trop petite,'" 292–304.

69 Chapelain, Les Sentiments, 992.

70 Ibid.

71 Ibid.

72 Chapelain, "Discours de la poésie représentative" (version 2), 304.

73 Chapelain, *Les Sentiments*, 992.

74 See Forestier, *Essai de génétique théâtrale*.

75 Ibid., 15.

2 Failed Judgments, Thwarted Justice: Alexandre
Hardy's *Scédase ou l'hospitalité violée*

1 D'Aubignac, *La Pratique du théâtre*, Livre II, ch. 7, 84–5.
2 For studies tracing the evolution of French theatre from Renaissance drama
   to the classical stage, see Murray, "Richelieu's Theater." See also Reiss,
   Toward Dramatic Illusion. For surveys of plays from the early century, see
   Lanson, *Esquisse d'une histoire de la tragédie française.*
3 Rousset, *Circé et le paon*, devotes a seminal chapter in his analysis of
   the baroque to the "Théâtre de la cruauté." More recently Biet, in his
   introduction to *Théâtre de la cruauté*, reprises the term to characterize this
   early vein of French tragedy.
4 Biet, *Théâtre de la cruauté*, XXXI.
5 Rousset, *Circé et le paon*, 6.
6 Biet, *Théâtre de la cruauté*, XXXI. See the introduction to this volume for a
   discussion of the scaffolds genre, as well as an analysis of the overlapping
   semantics of "*échaffauds*" (scaffolds) in the judicial, theatrical, and religious
   spheres, XXIV–XLIII. Rousset makes a similar analysis: "Plus que le théâtre
   de la mort et de son tragique, c'est le théâtre macabre où la mort devient
   supplice et le supplice spectacle" [More than a theatre of death and its
   tragedy, it is within the macabre theatre that death becomes torture and
   torture spectacle]. Rousset, *Circé et le paon*, 89.
7 The latter play is available in Biet, *Théâtre de la cruauté*, 10–38; the former is
   available in Hardy, *Théâtre du XVIIe siècle*, vol. 1.
8 Two recent volumes of the journal *Littératures Classiques* have been devoted
   to a discussion and analysis of onstage crime. See *Réécritures du crime; l'acte
   sanglant sur la scène (XVIe–XVIIIe)* in *Littératures Classiques* 67 (spring, 2009),
   and *Le théâtre, la violence et les arts en Europe (XVIe–XVIIe)* in *Littératures
   Classiques* 73 (autumn, 2010).
9 For a study of the history and evolution of this rhetorical device in French
   tragedy, see Howe and Waller, *En Marge du Classisicisme*, 27–63.
10 Biet, "Le Spectacle du sang," 32.
11 I have chosen to characterize early French tragedy as "pre-classical" since
   that term has the benefit of differentiating it from the regular, rule-driven
   genre that follows it, although I recognize that this entails assigning a
   label to the early works based on a comparison with what followed them
   historically, generating a certain anachronistic identification. I will therefore
   place the term "pre-classical" in quotations.
12 Biet, "Le Spectacle du sang, 32.
13 Foucault, *Discipline and Punish*, 48–9.

14 The staging of Alexandre Hardy's plays is notoriously difficult to date because of the lack of reliable sources. For more on the playwright's biography, see Deierkauf-Holsboer, *Vie d'Alexandre Hardy*, and Howe, "Alexandre Hardy and the French theater in 1615."

15 See, for instance, *Le Tragique*, ed. Ribard and Viala, and Delmas, *La Tragédie de l'Age Classique 1553–1770*. Jacques Scherer calls Hardy "le seul écrivain de théâtre important pendant une vingtaine d'années entre le renoncement de Montchrestien et l'esprit nouveau qu'apporteront Théophile et Racan" [the only playwright of importance over the course of twenty years between Montchrestien's abandonment and the new spirit Théophile and Racan will bring]. Hardy, *Théâtre du XVIIe siècle*, 1:1166. Giovanni Dotoli sums him up as, "Ronsardien, contraire aux règles, violent, baroque, Hardy est le maître de l'intrigue et de la scène à faire, mais son style est trop archaïque [...] Toutefois de Tristan à Scudéry, de Mairet à Corneille, de Rotrou à Mareschal, tous les dramaturges des années 1630 lui doivent le sens du théâtre" [Ronsardian, against the rules, violent, baroque, Hardy is the master of intrigue and the set-piece, but his style is too archaic ... However from Tristan to Scudéry, from Mairet to Corneille, from Rotrou to Maseschal, all the playwrights of the 1630s owe him their sense of theatre] in *Temps de Préfaces*, 327.

16 On Hardy, his patrons, and his position as writer for the Hôtel de Bourgogne troupe, see Deierkauf-Holsboer, *Vie de Hardy*, and Rigal, *Alexandre Hardy et le théâtre français*.

17 Corneille, *Œuvres complètes*, "Discours de la tragédie et des moyens de la traiter, selon le vraisemblable ou le nécessaire," 3:145.

18 Aristotle, *Theory of Poetry and Fine* Art, ch. 13, 45.

19 La Mesnardière, *La Poétique*, cited in Cave, *Recognitions*, 87.

20 Aristotle writes: "The change of fortune should be not from bad to good, but, reversely, from good to bad." *Theory of Poetry and Fine* Art, ch. 13, 47.

21 See definition in the *Dictionnaire de l'Académie Française* (1694). HUISSIER. s. m. Officier qui ouvre & ferme la porte du cabinet, de la chambre du Roy, & chez les Princes. *Huissier du cabinet. huissier de la chambre.* Il se dit aussi de ceux qui ont cette Charge dans les Compagnies souveraines, & autres grandes assemblées. *Premier huissier du Parlement. huissier de la Chambre des Comptes &c. Huissier Audiencier* [Officer who opens and closes the door of the king's cabinet and bedroom, and those of the Princes ... It is also said of those who have this Charge in the sovereign Companies and other large assemblies. First *Huissier* of Parlement. *Huissier* of the Treasury Chamber and *Huisser* Usher]. http://artflsrv02.uchicago.edu/cgi-bin/dicos/pubdicо11ook.pl?strippedhw=huissier.

22 Benjamin, *On the Origin of German Tragic Drama*, 125–6.

23 Chapelain, "Sentiments de l'Académie Française sur la tragi-comédie *du Cid*," 289.

24 Ibid.

25 Chapelain describes Don Fernand's dénouement as "un merveilleux qui tient du monstre et qui donne de l'indignation et de l'horreur aux spectateurs plutôt que de l'instruction et du profit" [a marvel that approaches the monstrous and provokes indignation and horror in the spectators instead of instruction and profit]. Ibid., 289.

26 Forestier, *La Tragédie française*, 152–3.

27 Lyons, *Phantom of Chance*, 53.

28 Ibid.

29 Ibid., 39.

30 Chapelain, "Sentiments de l'Académie française sur la tragi-comédie du *Cid*," 201.

31 Molière, *L'Impromptu de Versailles*, in *Œuvres complètes*, 698.

32 Rousset, *Circé et le paon*, 91.

33 Ibid., 92.

34 See *Britannica Online Encyclopedia*, "Agésilaus II" and "Battle of Luctria," consulted 21 January 2016.

35 Fernandez, "Représenter un procès politique au XVIIe siècle, 430.

36 Biet, Bouteille, Chevallier, and Jobez, "L'écriture du crime dans le théâtre de la cruauté," 237.

37 D'Aubignac, *La Pratique du théâtre*, 126. "Quand un Roi parle sur la Scène, il faut qu'il parle en Roi et c'est la circonstance de sa dignité contre laquelle il ne peut rien faire qui soit vraisemblable, s'il n'y avait quelque raison qui le dispensât de cette première circonstance, comme s'il était déguisé" [When a king speaks onstage, he must speak as a king and it is the circumstance of his dignity against which he can do nothing that would be believable, unless there was some reason that would dispense him from acting according to that first circumstance, such as being disguised].

38 Frisch, *The Invention of the Eyewitness*.

39 D'Aubignac, "Du dénouement ou de la catastrophe et issue du poème dramatique," *La Pratique du théâtre*, 203. D'Aubignac departs here from a well-worn tragic convention. Even as late as 1631, the playwright Jean Mairet defines tragedy according to its ending which causes a "disgust for life," as stated in the preface to *La Silvanire*: "De manière que le commencement de la tragédie est toujours gai, et la fin en est toujours triste; tout au rebours de la comédie, dont le commencement est volontiers triste, pour ce qu'il est ambigu, mais la fin en est infailliblement belle et joyeuse; l'une cause

un dégoût de la vie à cause des infortunes dont elle est remplie; et l'autre
nous persuade de l'aimer par le contraire" [In such a way that the start of
a tragedy is always happy, and its end is always sad; the complete opposite
of comedy, where the start is often sad, because ambiguous, but the end is
infallibly beautiful and joyous; one causes disgust with life because of the
misfortunes with which it is filled; and the other persuades us to love it for
the opposite reason]. Mairet, "Préface, en forme de discours poétique," 482.

40 D'Aubignac, *La Pratique du théâtre*, 203.
41 Ibid., 219.
42 Ibid., 211. Italics are in the original.
43 Ibid., 218.
44 Hardy, *La Force du sang*, "Notice," in Hardy, *Théâtre du XVIIe siècle*, 1:1183.
45 Lyons, "Material Fatality."

3 The Ceremony Unravels: Tragedy's Comedic Turn

1 Racine, *Œuvres complètes – Prose*, 2:343. "We are all rivals in the passion to
contribute something to the glory of such a great prince: each one of us
draws on the talents that nature has given us."
2 La Mesnardière, *La Poétique*, 36–7.
3 See Lanson, *Esquisse d'une histoire de la tragédie française*; Bray, *La Formation de
la doctrine classique en France*; and Marin, especially *Les Pouvoirs de l'image* and
Le Portrait du Roi. More recently, Christopher Braider speaks of Corneille
as having the ambition to "create his own literary memorial" and as having
"invented French literary grandeur, casting himself in the role of its epoch-
making creator." See *The Matter of Mind*, 124.
4 On the so-called ceremonialists known for their deeply erudite
descriptions of the particulars of royal rituals without, however, much
addressing how the various publics present understood these, see
Giesey, *The Royal Funeral Ceremony in Renaissance France*, and *Rulership in
France*; Jackson, *Vive le Roi!* and Hanley, *The* Lit de Justice *of the Kings of
France*.
5 Boureau, *Le Simple corps du roi*: "La théorie des deux corps n'engendre
aucune sacralisation réelle du corps royal, précisément parce qu'elle n'est
qu'une fiction – une formation discursive qui permet de penser, d'exprimer,
d'augmenter, sans donner à croire, ni même à voir [...] La fiction fonde le
pouvoir dans et par le langage, non plus dans le réel empirique ou spirituel
(la croyance)" (19) [The two-body theory engenders no actual sacralization
of the royal body, precisely because it is only a fiction – a discursive
formation that enables one to conceive of, express, augment, without

producing belief nor even visualization ... The fiction founds power in and through language, not in an empirical or spiritual reality].

6 Katherine Ibbett has exposed the patriotic investment of such perspectives, see *Style of the State*. See also Canova-Green, *La Politique-Spectacle au grand siècle*.

7 Lyons, *Kingdom of Disorder*.

8 See, respectively, Biet, *Racine ou la passion des larmes*, and Chaouche, *L'art du comédien*.

9 Merlin-Kajman, *L'Absolutisme dans les lettres*, and Sylvaine Guyot's attention to the figuration of bodies in Racinian texts and stage both stand as prime examples of the attention given to the diversity of representations in seventeenth-century tragedy and to its possible resistance against social norms. See Guyot, *Racine et le corps tragique*, 19: "Le corps tragique est donc le produit combiné d'un legs culturel, d'un effet de structure, d'un investissement idéologique et d'une prise de position esthétique" [The tragic body is therefore the combined product of a cultural legacy, the effect of a structure, an ideological investment and an aesthetic stance].

10 Foucault, "Il faut défendre la société," 155.

11 Ibid., 157.

12 Scherer, *Racine et/ou la cérémonie*, and Maulnier, *Racine*, ch. 6, 121–42. Biet, *Théâtre de la cruauté*, XXX, describes how the early French tragic genre offered a spectacle of ineluctable punishment followed by a perfectly ordered celebration of sovereignty:

> Dans le cas de l'échafaud des hautes œuvres, la scène est un espace-temps singulier où la mort devient une cérémonie juridique, sociale, justifiée et légitime, mais aussi un rituel destiné à d'une part représenter la punition de la loi, d'autre part à célébrer le passage du condamné contrit à l'espérance d'un salut via l'expiation et la réintégration.
>
> [In the case of the scaffolds of great works, the stage is a unique spatial time where death becomes a juridical and social ceremony, justified and legitimate, but also a ritual designed, on the one hand, to represent the punishment of the law and on the other to celebrate the passage of the condemned who can only show contrition in the hope of salvation through expiation and reintegration.]

13 La Mesnardière, *La poétique*, 205.

14 Burke, *The Fabrication of Louis XIV*. See Jouhaud, *Sauver le Grand-Siècle?* esp. ch. 2 "Voir" and ch. 3 "Commémorations."

15 Corneille's *Œdipe* is the author's first play after a six-year silence following the failure of *Perthardite* (1653), and one year before he edits his complete

works, including critical analyses of each play written up until then. Voltaire, who publishes his own *Œdipe* in 1718 and who is never one to mince words, will agree with Corneille on the impossibility of staging the ancient plot as is. He speaks of the "sécheresse" [dryness] of Sophocles's tragedy and states that *Oedipus Rex* along with *Philoctète*, *Electra*, and *Iphigénie*, "sont [les sujets] les plus ingrats et les plus impraticables; ce sont des sujets d'une ou deux scènes tout au plus, et non pas d'une tragédie" [are the most thankless and unworkable subjects; they are the subjects of one or two scenes at most, but not of an entire tragedy] in "Lettre IV Contenant la critique de l'*Œdipe* de Corneille in *Œdipe*," 198.

16 Corneille, "Examen d'*Œdipe*," *Œuvres complètes*, 3:20.

17 Corneille, "Notice d'*Œdipe*," *Œuvres complètes*, 3:1366–73.

18 Corneille, "Examen d'*Œdipe*," 3:20.

19 See Escola and Louvat, "Le statut de l'épisode dans la tragédie classique," which describes the inclusion of these characters as part of a blend of tragedy and an extended *épisode* of tragicomedy.

20 D'Aubignac, "Des Sujets," *La Pratique du théâtre*, 119–20.

21 D'Aubignac, "Troisième dissertation," *La Pratique du théâtre*, 112.

22 Ibid.

23 Ibid.

24 D'Aubignac, "Lettre sur *Œdipe*," 108.

25 "Je dis qu'un Roi, un héritier de la Couronne, un Gouverneur de Province, et généralement un homme d'autorité, peut paraître sur le Théâtre en trois façons: comme Roi, comme homme, et comme Juge, quelquefois avec deux de ces qualités, quelquefois toutes les trois ensemble" [I say that a king, an heir to the throne, a governor of a province, and generally a man of authority, can appear on the stage in three ways: as a king, as a man, and as a judge, and sometimes with two of these qualities, sometimes with all three at once]. Corneille, "Examen de *Clitandre*," *Œuvres complètes*, 1:103.

26 Racine, *Iphigénie*, *Œuves complètes –Théâtre-poésie*, vol. 1, vv. 1740–1.

27 Voltaire, "Avertissement de *Sémiramis*," 486.

28 La Mesnardière, *La poétique*, 205.

29 See discussion in ch. 2 above and Fernandez-Lacôte, *Les Procès du Cardinal de Richelieu*.

30 Bakhtin, *The Dialogic Imagination*, 19.

31 "In the high genres all authority and privilege, all lofty significance and grandeur, abandon the zone of familiar contact for the distanced plan (clothing, etiquette, the style of a hero's speech, and the style of speech about him). It is in this orientation toward completeness that the classicism of all non-novel genres is expressed." Ibid., 20.

32 Ibid., 23.

33 De Thou, *Histoire universelle*, lib. LXXV, 3:567. See ch. 1 for a discussion of this portrayal.

34 Tristan's *La Mariane* (1637) substantially quiets allusions to torture despite continued mention of punishment and imprisonment, such as when Hérode orders the "grand prévôt" [prison officer]: "Allez diligemment vous saisir de ce traître, /Que tout chargé de fers il me vienne trouver. / Mais ne lui donnez pas le temps de se sauver, / Qu'en divers cachots à même heure on dévale / Ceux qui seront suspects d'être de sa cabale. / Vite, et que les Bourreaux ne les épargnent point" (vv. 950–5) [Go diligently to arrest this traitor, / That burdened with irons he come before me. / But do not give him time to escape, / We will fill various prison cells with / Those whom we suspect of being part of his conspiracy. / Quick, and do not let the executioners spare them].

35 "[L'homme d'autorité] ne paraît que comme juge quand il est introduit sans aucun intérêt pour son Etat" [The man of authority only appears as a judge when he is introduced without any interest in his State]. Corneille, "Examen de *Clitandre*," *Œuvres complètes*, 1:102.

36 Mousnier's *Les Institutions de la France*, esp., "Le Gouvernement par grand conseil," and "Les Cours et jurisdictions de justice et de police" gives a detailed account of the hierarchy and divisions within the French legal system. He describes the complex, unstable, and heterogeneous nature of the system. On the advent of a lawyer class and the relationship between a bourgeois identity and ancien régime judicial practice, see Bell, *Lawyers and Citizens*.

37 In his address "Au lecteur," Racine emphasizes that he put little thought into the play and says he was helped by friends. See his *Œuvres complètes – Théâtre-poésie*, 301–2.

38 All quotes taken from Racine, *Les Plaideurs*, in *Œuvres complètes – Théâtre-poésie*.

39 Racine's decision to locate *Les Plaideurs* in Normandy can be explained by a variety of motives, beyond the region's perceived provincialism. It was, of course, the birthplace of Corneille, and a region with a history of legal opposition to the Crown through the assertion of its unique rights under the *Chartre Normande*. For a reading of Normandy as an independently minded region rebellious to the centralizing goals of the monarchy, all of which may have influenced Corneille, and therefore Racine's, dramatic production, see Blocker, "Une 'muse de province' négocie sa centralité."

40 Furetière, *Dictionnaire universel*, "Peinture." It should be noted that rather than cite Corneille's negative appraisal of the king that appears

in Corneille's play, Furetière chooses instead to quote from Molière's *Les Fâcheux* (1661) where it is asserted that the king is most definitely not a "*roi en peinture*."

41 See Soll, *The Information Master*, and Blanchard, *Eminence*.

42 See ch. 1 for a discussion of Saint Louis's place in the French iconography of royal judgment.

4 Learning from Experience: On Corneille and Coherence

1 Benjamin, *The Origin of German Tragic Drama*, 137.

2 Chris Braider, David Clarke, Thomas Pavel, and Mitchell Greenberg at times fall prey to lumping Cornelian sovereigns together and placing them under the same banner of absolutism. Astoundingly, for example, Clarke in *Pierre Corneille* sees Corneille as putting into practice Jean Bodin's theories on sovereignty, such as in the following case: "Si la justice est la fin de la loi, la loi œuvre du Prince, le Prince est image de Dieu, il faut par même suite de raison que la loi du Prince soit faite modèle de la loi de Dieu" (161) [If justice is the aim of law, the law the work of the Prince, the Prince the image of God, then it follows that the law of the Prince be made a model of God's law]. This is a passage Clarke cites in reference to *Clitandre*. For him, Corneille's tragicomedy illustrates, "a Christian ideal of glory in conformity with Bodin's celebrated definition of a *grand capitaine* fully reconciled with the justice and authority of the Crown," 124.

3 This type of reading no doubt stems from the earlier plays' imperfect fit in the teleology of Cornelian heroism. George Couton, the editor of the *Œuvres complètes*, speaks of Corneille's early plays as "pre-Cornelian," as though in writing them he were not yet the author he was destined to become. Couton, however, does see their revelatory value: "Cette tragédie, encore qu'à certains points de vue elle soit *précornélienne*, a beaucoup à révéler sur ce que seront la dramaturgie et l'éthique cornélienne" (*Œuvres complètes*, 1:1381) [This tragedy, although from a certain perspective is pre-Cornelian, has a great deal to reveal about what the Cornelian dramaturgy and ethos will be].

4 Increasingly, historiographical studies on the changing portrait of the *héros cornélien* have become fertile ground for research. For an account of how the term was forged in the nineteenth century, especially in the patriotic fervour of the Third Republic, see Albanese, *Corneille à l'école républicaine*. John Lyons remarkably synthesizes the mostly French critics of Corneille's *héroisme cornélien* in "Le Mythe du héros cornélien." See also *Postérités du Grand Siècle* ed. Guillouz, and *Corneille des Romantiques* ed. Dufour-Maître

and Naugrette. For twentieth-century scholarship, Brasillach, *Pierre Corneille*; Nadal, *Le Sentiment de l'amour*; Bénichou, *Morales du Grand Siècle*; Starobinski, *L'Œil vivant*; Doubrovsky, *Corneille et la dialectique du héros*; and Prigent, *Le héros et l'etat dans la tragédie de Pierre Corneille*, most notably contributed to shaping the notion of Cornelian heroism.

5 For a reading of *Clitandre* as an effort by Corneille to rebuke the theatrical unities, and the unity of time in particular, see Hawcroft, "Corneille's *Clitandre* and the Theatrical Illusion."

6 Corneille, "Préface de *Clitandre*," *Œuvres complètes*, 1:57. *Clitandre*'s plot is so famously convoluted that Corneille himself declared that one would need to watch the play more than once to understand it. In the 1660 edition, he goes so far as to include a plot summary to guide his readers. In the interest of brevity and clarity, I provide a broad summary of the dramatic action based on Corneille's own description: Two young noblewomen, Dorise and Caliste, are in love with Rosidor, the king's favourite. Rosidor loves Caliste. Yet Clitandre – the royal *dauphin*'s favourite – also loves Caliste. Meanwhile, another gentleman of the court, Pymante, loves Dorise, though she spurns him. Dorise, wanting Rosidor for herself, decides to kill her rival, so she lures Caliste into the nearby woods, close to a place where she had, by chance, found a sword the previous day. Rosidor intervenes just as Dorise is about to kill Caliste, and stops her. She flees. Rosidor's presence in the woods is explained by Pymante's own scheme to rid himself of a rival. Pymante had bribed Clitandre's servants and falsified a letter in Clitandre's handwriting, telling Rosidor to meet him in the forest. The disguised Pymante and Clitandre's servants then ambushed Rosidor who managed *in extremis* to kill the servants and get away. When Dorise flees, she finds these servants' clothes and dresses in them to hide her identity. She then encounters Pymante, who at first takes her for one of Clitandre's servants, but then recognizes her and tries to rape her. She defends herself by stabbing him in the eye with her hairpin. Meanwhile, Clitandre, who had been out hunting with the prince, is accused of attempting to kill Rosidor and is put in jail and sentenced to die, despite the nobleman's protestations of innocence. The prince, still in the woods, sees Pymante trying to kill a young man (Dorise), he defends him/her in a sword fight, and Dorise helps the prince by hanging on to Pymante's legs and making him trip. The prince then overpowers Pymante. Dorise divulges to the Prince everything that occurred in the woods. Back at the court, the king, who has already decided to give Caliste to Rosidor in marriage, frees the imprisoned Clitandre, gives him Dorise in marriage, and calls for the members of his *Conseil* to give Pymante a sentence that they deem appropriately severe to meet the king's approval.

7 Exceptions to reading the play as cut off from the theatre that follows are the following: Baker, *Dissonant Harmonies*, and Zuerner, "Disguise and the Gendering of Royal Authority in Corneille's *Clitandre*," who both ground the gender dynamics in *Clitantre* in the historical context of the play and show how it sets the stage for later paradigmatic encounters of the Cornelian hero and heroine.

8 See Benjamin, *The Origin of German Tragic Drama*. Benjamin explains: "Whereas [incarnating a form] is the business of the poetic elect, [giving it its characteristic expression] is often done incomparably more distinctly in the laborious efforts of minor writers. The life of the form is not identical with that of the works which are determined by it, indeed the clarity with which it is expressed can sometimes be in inverse proportion to the perfection of a literary work; and the form itself becomes evident precisely in the lean body of the inferior work, as its skeleton so to speak" (58).

9 It was not until Corneille's in-depth edits of the play in 1660 that the playwright decided to name the nameless king and prince; up until then the royal characters were known, simply, as, "le roi" and "le prince"; see Couton, "Notice," *Œuvres complètes*, 1:1196–1233.

10 For a reading of *Clitandre* at the antipodes of my own, see Clarke, *Pierre Corneille*, 119–34, who sees it as a subtle portrayal of Richelieu's execution of the nobleman Marillac.

11 The play's original title was *Clitandre ou l'innocence délivrée*, which emphasized the passive mode of the "deliverance," as well as the centrality of the wronged captive, especially in comparison to the king. In the 1660 edition, written as Corneille edits his works and embraces tragic poetics, he revises the title to *Clitandre* and re-labels the play a tragedy. Beyond a testament to the popularity of the more "noble" genre, the change in title attests to an idea that has gained currency: titles should not give away the play's ending and tragedies can end happily.

12 See chapter 1 for a discussion of Corneille's "Examen de *Clitandre*," in which he articulates a rule against kings such as Alcandre.

13 The king goes so far as to forbid the indifferent Clitandre and Doriste from expressing their indifference to each other: "Clitandre en attendant cette heureuse journée [celle de l'hyménée] / Tâchera d'allumer en son âme des feux / Pour celle que mon fils désire, et que je veux / A qui pour réparer sa faute criminelle / Je défends désormais de se montrer cruelle: / Ainsi nous verrons lors cueillir en même jour / A deux couples d'amants les fruits de leur amour" (vv. 1866–72) [While awaiting this joyous day, / Clitandre will attempt to ignite within his soul the flames of love / For the woman whom my son desires and that I order / To repair her criminal mistake / (the

woman) Whom I hereby forbid from showing herself cruel; / Thus we will see grow in one day/ In two couples the fruits of their love].

14 Merlin-Kajman, *L'Absolutisme dans les lettres*, 69.
15 See Mousnier, *Des offices*, 132.
16 Corneille, "Examen de *Clitandre*," *Œuvres complètes*, 1:102.
17 See Bilis, "Voir la Sorcière de Colchis."
18 See Longino, *Orientalism in French Classical Drama*; and Greenberg, *Subjectivity and Subjugation*, and *Canonical States, Canonical Stages*. Braider, *Matter of Mind*, ch. 3, "The Witch from Colchis: Corneille's *Médée*, Chimène's *Le Cid*, and the Invention of Classical Genius," 122–49.
19 Corneille, "Dédicace à Monsieur P.T.N.G.," *Œuvres complètes*, 1:535.
20 Jason plainly admits: "Aussi je ne suis pas de ces amants vulgaires, / J'accommode ma flamme au bien de mes affaires" (vv. 25–6) [I am not one of those vulgar lovers / I accommodate my flame to the betterment of my affairs].
21 Corneille, "Examen de *Médée*," *Œuvres complètes*, 1:537.
22 Ibid., 1:536.
23 Ibid., 1:539.
24 Ibid.
25 Ibid., 1:540.
26 Ibid.
27 Corneille, "Discours sur le poème dramatique," *Œuvres complètes*, 3:124.
28 Doubrovsky, *Corneille et la dialectique du héros*, and Prigent, *Le héros et l'état dans la tragédie de Pierre Corneille*, have famously read *Suréna* as the culmination of the Cornelian hero's "demolition."
29 Among the playwright's most influential and enduring "demolition critics" are Bénichou, *Morales du Grand Siècle*; Doubrovsky, *Corneille et la dialectique du héros*; Prigent, *Le héros et l'état dans la tragédie de Pierre Corneille*; Starobinski, *L'Œil vivant*; Pavel, *L'Art de l'éloignement*; and also Greenberg, *Subjectivity and Subjugation* who all propose varied distillations of the demolition thesis.
30 See Pavel, *L'art de l'éloignement*, 201–5.
31 For details on the *variantes* and on the 1648 edition versus the 1637 one, see Corneille, "Notice du Cid," 1:1449–1510. Clarke, *Pierre Corneille*, for example, interprets *Le Cid*'s change in genre as inevitable: "The new subtitle recognizes the degree in which his tragicomedy had exceeded the limits of its classification by the prominence it gave to the political significance of the lovers' entanglement in public affairs" (138); Margitiç, "Les Deux *Cid*" provides an insightful analysis of the reasons behind this change in the label.
32 The new edition of Corneille's comedies grouped together in one volume represents an important effort to present the playwright in the full range of his theatrical dimensions. See Pierre Corneille, *Théâtre*.

33 For a reading that sets *L'Illusion comique* in the context of the newly formed authority of the Académie Française and the emphasis on dramatic rules, see Blocker, *Instituter un "art,"* ch. 5, "Magie, doctrine, usages: Corneille et son "art," 365–97.

34 Whether by "first scene" we mean the original first scene where Don Gomès and Elvire discuss his choice, or the amended, post-1648, first scene where Elvire announces to Chimène her father's decision, both replicate the celebratory matrimonial endings of the comedic genre. For a reading of *Le Cid* in light of Corneille's comedies that preceded it, see Fumaroli, *Héros et orateurs*, ch. 4, "*Du Cid* à *Polyeucte*: une dramaturgie du couple."

35 Don Diègue tells Don Gomès: "Vous voyez toutefois qu'en cette concurrence / Un monarque entre nous met quelque différence" (vv. 213–14) [You see however that in this rivalry / The king notes some differences between the two of us].

36 Merlin-Kajman, *L'Absolutisme dans les lettres*, 210.

37 Don Diègue who is concerned by the public's opinion of his family's honour protests Don Fernand's justice: "[…] vous renversez des lois / Qu'a vu toute la Cour observer tant de fois / Que croira votre peuple et que dira l'envie / Si sous votre défense il ménage sa vie" (vv.1425–8) [… You reverse laws / That all of the court has seen observed many times / What will the people think and what will envy say, / If under your defense his life is spared].

38 Corneille, *Œuvres complètes*, 1:702.

39 She decisively states: "Je la [ta tête] dois attaquer, mais tu dois la défendre; / C'est d'un autre que toi qu'il me faut l'obtenir, / Et je dois te poursuivre, et non pas te punir" (vv. 952–4) [I must attack it [your head], but you must defend it; / It is from someone other than you that I must obtain it, / And I must pursue you, but not punish you].

40 For a reading of the sexist undertones of this encounter see Carlin, *Women Reading Corneille*.

41 Scudéry's comments on the play focus on the distressing speed of events: "De faire entrer dans un même esprit, et dans moins de vingt-quatre heures, deux pensées si opposées l'une à l'autre comme sont la poursuite de la mort d'un père, et le consentement d'épouser son meurtrier; et d'accorder en un même jour deux choses qui ne se pouvaient souffrir dans toute une vie" (*Observations sur* Le Cid, 369–70) [To make occur, to the same mind, and in less than twenty-four hours, two thoughts so opposed to one another as are the persecution for the murder of a father, and the consent to marry his murderer; and to grant in the same day two things that would not have been acceptable in a whole lifetime].

42 Frye, *Shakespeare*, "The Argument of Comedy," 81.

43 Addressing the parallels between the criminal heroes in *Le Cid* and *Horace*, Merlin-Kajman describes Corneille as a "récidiviste," a second-time offender; see "Réécriture cornélienne du crime."

44 This performance was preceded by a private reading held for Richelieu in the Palais Cardinal two months earlier in the presence of Chapelain and d'Aubignac. See Corneille, "Notice de *Horace*," *Œuvres complètes*, 1:1533–9.

45 See Forestier, *Essai de génétique théâtrale* "Esthétique," 74, 81, 111, 281–2.

46 Lyons, *The Tragedy of Origins*, aptly summarizes the anyway-you-look-at-it guilt of Horace: "Horace condemns himself, for in the first case he is enacting the obsolete gesture of a family claiming superiority over a newly strengthened state, and in the second case he violates the hierarchy of the state by presuming to incarnate its authority when he is only an executor of royal authority" (57).

47 See Corneille, *Horace*, "Le héros et son double," 181–91.

48 "J'excuse ta chaleur à venger ton offense / Et l'Etat défendu me parle en ta défense: / Crois que dorénavant Chimène a beau parler, / Je ne l'écoute plus que pour la consoler" (vv. 1263–6) [I excuse your lust in avenging your offence / And the State defended speaks to me in your defence: / Believe that from now on Chimène can keep talking, / I will only listen to her to console her].

49 Both the Latin version given by Corneille and a sixteenth-century French version are cited in Corneille *Œuvres complètes*, 1:835–8 and 1555–60. It is from this excerpt that I draw.

50 As Corneille sycophantically states in the play's dedication to Richelieu: "C'est là que lisant sur son visage [Richelieu's] ce qui lui plaît, et ce qui ne lui plaît pas, que nous nous instruisons avec certitude de ce qui est bon, et de ce qui est mauvais, et tirons des règles infaillibles de ce qu'il faut suivre et de ce qu'il faut éviter" (Corneille, "A Monseigneur le Cardinal Duc de Richelieu," *Œuvres complètes*, 1:834) [It is there that reading from his face what pleases him, and what displeases him, that we learn with certainty what is right, what is wrong, and we draw infallible rules of what must be followed or avoided]. On the different readings of this dedication, especially in light of Corneille's difficult relations with Richelieu, see Jouhaud, *Les Pouvoirs de la littérature*, and Merlin-Kajman, *L'Absolutisme dans les lettres*.

51 Cardin Le Bret was prominent among such theorists advocating the prince's right to transgress positive law: "La souveraineté est la puissance absolue et perpétuelle d'une république [...] Il faut que ceux-là qui sont souverains ne soient aucunement sujets aux commandements d'autruy et qu'ils puissent donner loy aux sujets et de casser ou anéantir les lois inutiles pour en faire d'autres" (*Traité de la souveraineté du roi*, 511) [Sovereignty is the absolute

and perpetual power over a republic ... Those who are sovereigns must not be subjects in any way to the commands of others and they must be able to give laws to their subjects and break or abolish useless laws in order to make others].

52 "[Ce crime] Vient de la même épée, et part du même bras / Qui *me* fait aujourd'hui maître de deux Etats. / Deux scèptres en *ma* main, Albe et Rome asservie, / Parlent bien hautement en faveur de sa vie. / Sans lui *j*'obéirais où *je* donne la loi, / Et *je* serais Sujet où *je* suis deux fois Roi" (vv. 1741–6, my emphasis) [(This crime) Stems from the same sword, and from the same arm / That makes me today master of two states. / Two sceptres in my hand, Alba and Rome subjugated, / Speak loudly in favour of his life: / Without him I would obey where I give the law, / And I would be a subject where I am twice King].

53 Couton, *Corneille et la tragédie politique*, 27.

54 Greenberg, *Corneille, Classicism, and the Ruses of Symmetry*, 87.

55 Valère is described as a "Chevalier romain" in the cast of characters; see Corneille, *Œuvres complètes*, 1:844. Cutting off Valère, Tulle states: "Valère, c'est assez/ Vos discours par les leurs ne sont pas effacés" (vv. 1729–30) [Valère, that's enough / Your speeches are not erased by theirs].

56 Aubignac, cited in "Notice de *Horace*," in Corneille, *Œuvres complètes*, 1:1537. Chapelain, in a letter to Guez de Balzac, also criticizes Camille's murder: "Dès l'année passée [1639] je lui [à Corneille] dis qu'il fallait changer son cinquième acte des *Horaces*, et lui dis par le menu comment; à quoi il·avait résisté toujours depuis, quoique tout le monde lui criât que sa fin était brutale et froide et qu'elle en devait passer par mon avis" ("Notice de Horace," 1:1537) [As early as last year, I told him he needed to change his fifth Act of *Horace*, and even described to him how to do so; but he resisted this, although everyone told him his ending was cold and brutal and that it would benefit from my advice].

57 Stone, *The Classical Model*, 57.

58 See Foucault, *Discipline and Punish*, 3–31.

59 Stone, *Royal Disclosure*, 31. Stone adds: "The play's final scene is less a sacrifice of her difference than a tribute to it. Entombed with her lover, Camille represents the violation of all synthesis, the triumph of diversity and dissention within a traditional oneness."

60 Corneille, "Examen d'*Horace*," *Œuvres complètes*, 1:842.

61 Ibid.

62 In his arrest of Tartuffe, the *Exempt* describes the intervention as the result of the king's all-seeing nature: "Un Prince dont les yeux se font jour dans les cœurs / Et que ne peut tromper tout l'art des imposteurs. / D'un fin

discernement sa grand âme pourvue / Sur les choses jette une droite
vue; / Chez elle [sa majesté] jamais rien ne surprend trop d'accès, / Et sa
ferme raison ne tombe en nul excès" (Molière, *Tartuffe*, vv. 1907–12)
[A Prince whose eyes see the light of day in hearts / And whom the art of
imposters cannot fool. / Of judgment his soul is blessed / Upon all things
sees clearly; / In his majesty nothing ever surprises access, / And his firm
reason never falls into any excess].

63 Corneille, "Examen d'*Horace*," *Œuvres complètes*, 1:843.

64 He reflects further on the play's overall deficiencies in terms of timing,
including the momentum of the tragedy and the dual action that Camille's
death constitutes. After Horace vanquishes the Curiace brothers, the tragic
action on which the play had centred reaches an end. Camille's death
therefore appears tangential: "Cette action qui devient la principale de
la pièce n'est que momentanée, et n'a point cette juste grandeur que lui
demande Aristote, et qui consiste en un commencement, un milieu et une
fin" (Corneille, "Examen d'*Horace*," in *Œuvres complètes*, 1:840) [This action
that becomes the main one of the play is only momentary, and does not
possess that perfect grandeur which Aristotle asks of it, and which consists
of a beginning, a middle, and an end].

5 Corneille's *Cinna* and Rotrou's *Crisante*: A Search
for the Emperor's Judgment

1 Corneille, *Œuvres complètes*, 1:1574. Pierre Bourdelot, the Prince de Condé's
personal doctor, is the author of a letter that contains this passage. For
commentary on the contested date of *Cinna*'s first staging – 1641 or 1642 –
see Couton's, "Notice," as well as details on the conditions and (favourable)
reception of the play, ibid., 1573–97.

2 In *Cinna*'s "Examen" Corneille, perhaps self-servingly, underscores the
unanimous success of his play: "Ce poème a tant de suffrages qui lui
donnent le premier rang parmi les miens, que je me ferais trop d'importants
ennemis si j'en disais du mal: je ne le suis pas assez de moi-même pour
chercher des défauts où ils n'en ont point voulu voir, et accuser le jugement
qu'ils en ont fait, pour obscurcir la gloire qu'il m'en ont donnée" (*Œuvres
complètes*, 1:910) [This poem has received so much support that it is in the
first rank among my works, that I would make too many important enemies
for myself if I found any fault with it: I am not enough of my own enemy to
seek flaws where others have not found them, and to accuse the judgment
they have made and darken the glory they have given me].

3 Corneille, "Examen de *Cinna*," in *Œuvres complètes*, 1:910.

4 Merlin-Kajman *L'Absolutisme dans les lettres*, 52.

5 Greenberg, *Subjectivity and Subjugation*, 61.

6 Among many contributions in this vein, I note the following for their emphasis on *Cinna* as a contemporary political mirror: Georges Couton remarks that "la noblesse française était en état permanent de vendetta contre le Cardinal" [the French nobility was in a state of constant vendetta against the Cardinal], and offers a *lecture à clef* of Auguste's clemency as a reflection of Richelieu's strategy: "[le ministre] assume maintenant un rôle analogue à celui d'Auguste, de restaurateur de l'Etat [...] il lui appartient de modifier la conjoncture politique en y introduisant un facteur nouveau, la clémence" (*Œuvres complètes*, 1:1588) [the minister now plays an analogous role to Auguste, as restorer of the State ... It is up to him to modify the political situation by introducing a new factor, clemency]. Meanwhile, Georges Forestier sees an unambiguous legitimization of the sovereign's victory over "les factions féodales qui résistent à l'absolutisme" [the feudal factions that resisted absolutism]: "On conçoit l'intelligence politique d'un Corneille montrant à tous comment un grand règne et un grand empire sont sortis d'une ultime conjuration qui se légitimait en croyant à tort s'attaquer à un pouvoir tyrannique" (*Cinna*, "Préface," ed. Forestier, 15) [We can conceive of the political intelligence of Corneille demonstrating how a great reign and a great empire came out of a last plot that legitimized itself by wrongly believing it was attacking a tyrannical power]. In contrast, François Lasserre underlines the playwright's conflicted blend of admiration and condemnation for the cardinal. Auguste becomes what Richelieu could be if only he used his political savoir-faire for the public good: "Corneille nourrissait une bonne dose de méfiance, bientôt doublée de haine personnelle, désapprouvait et craignait terriblement son machiavélisme [celui de Richelieu], ne demandait qu'à s'enthousiasmer pour son action politique" (*Corneille de 1638 à 1642*, 182) [Corneille harboured a strong degree of distrust, soon amplified by personal hatred, and terribly disapproved of and feared his Machiavellianism, seeking only to approve of his political action]. In John Lyons's view, which I discuss below, Corneille depicts the victory of Richelieu's "policy of the non-sequitur" as a Machiavellian means of ending violence tied to the past, but, declining to turn the playwright into a "spokesman for Richelieu" (76), he leaves open to debate the playwright's approval of this transformation; see *The Tragedy of Origins*, 71–108.

7 Fumaroli, *Héros et Orateurs*, 48.

8 Lyons, *French Literature*, 38.

9 Corneille, "De la tragédie," in *Œuvres complètes*, 3:68.

10 See discussion of "Tragedies of the Scaffolds," chapter 2.

11 See Langer, *Vertu du discours*, and Poirier, *Corneille et la vertu de prudence* for the reception and application of these traditions in the portrayal of the virtuous prince. For insightful summaries of justice as the indispensable virtue of a prince, see Skinner, "Political Philosophy," and Nelson, "The Problem of the Prince."

12 Barden Dowling, *Clemency and Cruelty in the Roman World*, gives a detailed history of the private and political uses of clemency in ancient Rome. Regarding the dialectic of power inherent in clemency, she writes: "One cannot claim to have won if no one acknowledges defeat: if the person is being spared (or the witnesses who observe) does not acknowledge the suspension of punishment, the act is meaningless" (9). My summary of the historicization of Augustan clemency is largely based on Barden Dowling's thorough account. See also Galinsky, *Augustan Culture* on the four imperial virtues, and Noreña, "The Communication of the Emperor's Virtues" where he discusses the reasons behind clemency's rare appearance on Roman coinage designed to celebrate imperial qualities.

13 Seneca, "On Clemency, 166.

14 Corneille, "Examen de *La Mort de Pompée*," in *Œuvres complètes*, 1:1076.

15 See Dyer "Rhetoric and Intention in Cicero," for a discussion of how charges of Julius Caesar's despotism were linked to his policy of clemency, especially as portrayed by Cicero. On clemency motivating Caesar's assassination, see Wallace-Hadrill, "The Emperor and his Virtues."

16 This is Barden Dowling's argument in linking *clementia* to its mirror image, *crudelitas* – also irrational and potentially limitless (*Clemency and Cruelty*, 27). The two concepts evolve together, their definitions serving as indissoluble foils. See also Konstan, "Clemency as a Virtue," who offers a broad historical account of clemency's place within Roman culture. He argues that although clemency was most often tied to political calculation in the Roman classical age, it was not always associated with strategy.

17 The nobility leading up to the *Fronde* saw itself as the source of legal power within the state, giving the aristocracy a collective identity regarding its rights and privileges as well as its political importance; see Jouanna, *Le Devoir de* révolte.

18 "Ma haine va mourir, que j'ai cru immortelle, / Elle est morte, et ce cœur devient Sujet fidèle / Et prenant désormais cette haine en horreur, / L'ardeur de vous servir succède à sa fureur" (vv. 1725–8) [My hatred will die, that which I thought immortal / It is dead, and this heart has become a faithful subject / And seeing from now on this hatred with horror, / The ardour to serve you replaces its furore].

19   Soyons amis, Cinna, c'est moi qui t'en convie:
     Comme à mon ennemi je t'ai donné la vie,
     Et malgré la fureur de ton lâche destin,
     Je te la donne encore comme à mon assassin.
     Commençons un combat qui montre par l'issue
     Qui l'aura mieux de nous, ou donnée ou reçue.
     Tu trahis mes bienfaits, je les veux redoubler
     Avec cette beauté que je t'avais donnée
     Reçois le Consulat pour la prochaine année.   (vv. 1701–9)

     [Let us be friends, Cinna, I urge you:
     Just as with my enemy, I have given you life,
     And despite the furore of your cowardly destiny,
     I give it to you again as to my assassin.
     Let us begin a struggle that will show by its outcome
     Who between us will have best, either given or received.
     You betray my gifts, and I want to double them
     With this beauty that I had given to you
     Receive the Consulate for next year.]

20   See Fernandez-Lacôte, *Les Procès du Cardinal de Richelieu*, ch. 3,
     "Institutions," 179:

     "La distinction entre intrigue de cabinet et conspiration de grande
     envergure ne doit donc pas être regardée comme un anachronisme; c'est
     au contraire l'attitude du pouvoir politique qui provoque l'étonnement
     des acteurs et des observateurs de la cour. Le procès d'Etat est bien
     devenu, au cours des années du ministère de Richelieu, une des armes
     du pouvoir – il s'est trouvé amplifié, consolidé et s'est révélé d'une
     efficacité redoutable comme instrument de mise en ordre de l'histoire
     en train de se faire" [The distinction between cabinet intrigue and
     large-scale conspiracy must not be seen as an anachronism; it is on the
     contrary, the attitude of the political powers that provokes the surprise
     of the actors and observers of the court. The political trial becomes,
     during the Richelieu years, one of the weapons of power – it is amplified,
     consolidated, and is revealed to be of surprising efficiency as an ordering
     instrument of history in the making]. See also Delatour, "'Les armes en
     main et les larmes aux yeux': Le procès de Cinq-Mars et de Thou."

21   For a summary of the growing opposition between the *officiers,* who held
     their positions on a hereditary basis, and the *commissaires,* who were
     appointed for specific and contingent legal commissions, as a result of the

increasing efforts by the absolutist-inclined monarchy to shift legal authority away from more independent-minded entities like the *Parlements*, see Gordon, *Citizens without Sovereignty*, esp., 9–42 ("Absolutism and the Ideal Type of Sociability"). For local examples that speak to the larger issue of the battle for authority and a notion of legality separate from the monarch see, Biek, *Absolutism and Society*, and Kettering, *Judicial Politics and Urban Revolt in Seventeenth-Century France*. See also McClure, *Sunspots and the Sun King*, esp. 1–67.

22 See Alain Couprie for a study of prisons in Corneille's theatre, "Prison et prisonniers dans le théâtre de Corneille." He lists further examples of euphemisms for prisons, such as the increased use of "chambre" or "appartement" to refer to prison cells.

23 Corneille, "Examen de *Médée*," in *Œuvres complètes*, 1:539.

24 We should be inclined to read this easy purging of guilt with suspicion given Corneille's reliance on Seneca who minimizes Augustus's ability to erase his past crimes. Despite the glory of Augustus's decision, Seneca emphasizes the brutal path that led to it: "I do not call exhausted cruelty 'clemency.'" See "On Clemency," 157.

25 Lyons, *The Phantom of Chance*, 255.

26 D'Aubignac, "Des délibérations," in *La Pratique du théâtre*, 431: "Les Stances de Rodrigue, où son esprit délibère entre son amour et son devoir, ont ravi toute la cour et tout Paris" [Rodrigue's *stances*, where his spirit deliberates between his love and his duty, pleased all of the court and all of Paris].

27 Ibid., 431 (my emphasis).

28 In *Horace*'s "Examen," Corneille had commented on the ill-timed speeches of his characters: "Tout ce cinquième est encore une des causes du peu de satisfaction que laisse cette Tragédie: il est tout en plaidoyers, et ce n'est pas là la place des harangues, ni des longs discours. Ils peuvent être supportés en un commencement de Pièce où l'action n'est pas encore échauffée: mais le cinquième Acte doit plus agir, que discourir. L'attention de l'Auditeur déjà lassée se rebute de ces conclusions qui traînent, et tirent la fin en longueur" (Corneille, "Examen," *Horace*, in *Œuvres complètes*, 1:843) [This entire fifth Act is one of the reasons for the lack of satisfaction that this Tragedy provokes: it is made up entirely of speeches, and that is not the space for harangues, nor for long discourses. They can be withstood at the start of a play where the action has not yet warmed up: but the fifth Act must more act than discuss. The Auditor's attention has already been worn and objects to these conclusions that drag on, and lengthen the end].

29 Marin, "Pour une théorie baroque de l'action politique," 23.

30 In between *Cinna* and *Venceslas*, Tristan l'Hermite also ponders the relationship between tyranny, clemency, and tragedy in *La Mort de Sénèque* (1645). On the dialogue between that play and *Cinna*, I refer you to Bilis, "The Silence of Subjects."

31 Le Bret refers to the king using this term. See *Traité De la Souveraineté du Roi*.

32 Cornette, "Fiction et réalité de l'état baroque," 27.

33 McClure, *Sunspots and the Sun King*, 224.

34 See Tollet, "La Pologne vue par les Français."

35 Treilhou-Balaudé, "Rotrou poète de la scène," 226.

36 Vuillemin, *Baroquisme et theatralité*, 137.

37 According to Benjamin, the baroque royal figure is less important as an individual human being than as a representation of collective forces, and the *Trauerspiel* culminates in a grotesque disintegration of the main character. See Benjamin, *The Origins of German Tragic Drama*.

38 Forestier, *La Tragédie française*, "Psychologie tragique: la dialectique des passions et des caractères," 264.

39 Voltaire, *Le Siècle de Louis XIV*, 1200.

40 Vuillemin, *Baroquisme et théâlité*, 108.

41 See Forestier, *Le Théâtre dans le théâtre*, and Baby, *La tragi-comédie de Corneille à Quinault*. Its very presence on the "programme de l'agrégation de lettres modernes" in 2008 attests to Rotrou's rise in literary status and to the more general appeal of his works. *Saint Genest* remains, as it was throughout the twentieth century, the major play of Rotrou's thirty-five-play corpus. Its appearance on the Agrégation reading list generated great efforts to rescue Rotrou from the critical margins with a special issue of *Littératures Classiques* 63 (2007), edited by Pierre Pasquier, devoted to "Le théâtre de Rotrou." The emphasis there, however, was still mostly placed on Rotrou's blending of dramatic genres and the influence of Spanish drama, or on the staging of his plays (Rotrou is known for his unusual affinity for *didascalies*). Only two of the twenty-one articles assembled in that issue consider power relations in Rotrou within a political context: Treilhou-Balaudé's "Poète de la scène" considers the monarchical figures in *Venceslas* and *Saint Genest*, and Jean-Claude Vuillemin's "Jeux de théâtre et enjeux du regard dans le théâtre de Rotrou." Another recent overview of Rotrou and his œuvre, including an up-to-date bibliography, is provided in Vialleton, *Rotrou, dramaturgie de l'ingénuosité*.

42 Rotrou, *Théâtre complet*. 10 vols.

43 Notable exceptions include Biet, "Droit divin, droit naturel et droit humain dans *Antigone* de Jean Rotrou"; Jondorf, "What Is a King? The Figure of

the King in Rotrou"; Matthews, "The Tyrannical Sovereign in the Pre-1640 French Tragicomedy"; Wolfe, "Royal Discourse in Rotrou's *Venceslas.*"

44 I give here the date of its royal *privilège* (7 February 1637). The dating of *Crisante* has been the subject of much speculation since no document attests with certainty to its first staging. See Gethner, "La chronologie du théâtre de Rotrou." Various hypotheses on its date, spanning the period from 1630 to 1635 have been advanced regarding its first representation at the Hôtel de Bourgogne, but, following Gethner and the editors of Jean de Rotrou *Théâtre complet, Crisante,* ed. Anne Duroux, vol. 4 (Paris: Société des Textes Français Modernes, 2001) I understand it to have first appeared in 1635 with a publication in 1637.

45 On the five authors and their relationship to Richelieu and his theatrical projects, see Blocker, *Instituer un "art,"* 185–275.

46 Benjamin defines the sovereign of seventeenth-century German drama according to the following principle: "Whereas the modern concept of sovereignty amounts to a supreme executive power on the part of the prince, the baroque concept emerges from a discussion of the state of emergency, and makes it the most important function of the prince to avert this" (*The Origin of German Tragic Drama*, 65). Antioche possesses the "extravagant tone of plaintive lamentation" and an "incessant hand-wringing mode of expression" that Benjamin links to the sovereigns of *Trauerspiel* (64).

47 Hampton, "Baroque Topographies," where he links the baroque aesthetic to a problem of location and to a question of territoriality.

48 Jacobson, "Is There a Woman in This Text?"

49 Cited in Descimon, "Les fonctions de la métaphore, 1127–47.

50 Edouard Regnard cited in Descimon, "Les fonctions de la métaphore du marriage, 1139.

51 Le Bret, *De la souveraineté du Roy,* 48.

52 For an analysis of Lucrèce's character, rape, and suicide as portrayed in seventeenth-century France, see Bousquet, "Le suicide féminin au XVIIe siècle: un acte héroïque?" See also Miola, *Shakespeare's Rome.* Miola's comment on Lucretia could very well apply to Crisante: "The Rape of Lucretia balances itself between tragedy and history as it progresses through disorder, loss, and sorrow to the costly expiation of evil and the chastened emergence of a new order (19).

53 This is a paraphrase of the plot summary given in the introduction to Rotrou, *Crisante,* in *Théâtre complet,* vol. 4, ed. Anne Duroux, 14–21.

54 Ibid., 4:15.

55 Gilhuly, "Corinth, Courteseans, and the Politics of Place, 171–99.

56 See Plutarque, *Vie parallèles*: "Timoléon," "Agésilas," "César," and "Aratos."

57 "Un jour nous est honteux s'il passe sans combats, / Et déjà le repos afflige nos soldats, / Ne pouvant autre part exercer leur courages, / Eux-mêmes il se font les objets de leurs rages; / L'un l'autre en ce repos ne peut supporter, / Ils trouvent des ébats chacun à s'affronter; / De leur sang à toute heure on voit rougir la terre, / L'aise les incommode, et leur paix fait la guerre" (vv. 1085–92) [A day is shameful to us if it goes without battle, / And already rest afflicts our soldiers, / Unable to exert their courage, / They become the objects of their own rage; / None can stand this rest, / They each find fights to defy each other for; / Of their blood at all hours we see the ground redden, / Rest bothers them, and peace makes war].

58 "Mais de plus près que tous cet affront me regarde, / Qui ne vous choisis pas une plus sûre garde, / Et qui ne pus juger du lubrique dessein, / Dont ce jeune insolent sentait brûler son sein" (vv. 1147–50) [But this affront affects me most dearly, / Because I did not choose a more certain guard, / And did not judge the lascivious designs, / That this young insolent felt burning in his chest].

59 Biet, *Droit et littérature sous l'Ancien Régime*.

60 "Que coupée, au plus tôt, en ses mains on la [la tête de Manilie] lui rende / Et qui sera tenté d'un acte si brutal, / Craigne par son exemple un châtiment égal" (vv. 1256–8) [That cut, swiftly, it be placed in her hands / And that whoever would attempt such a brutal act, / Fear that he shall receive such an exemplary punishment].

61 The stage directions indicate, "Antioche ouvrant le rideau sort du lit, tirant de son corps une épée teinte de sang, et va tomber sur le corps de Crisante" (vv. 1470–1) [Antioche opens the curtain and leaves the bed, pulling from his body a sword covered in blood, and falls on Crisante's body].

6 Racine and Royal Fathers of Injustice – *Mithridate* and *Phèdre*

1 "Who has betrayed me? Why have I not been avenged?"

2 "Let us see, let us examine. But where to begin? / Who will enlighten me? What witnesses? Which clue?"

3 Barthes, *Sur Racine*, 38.

4 Ibid. See also Scherer: "Le passage des générations est un puissant créateur de haine. La deuxième génération contient en germe la mort du Père et permet ainsi à la cérémonie poétique de se renouveler, en paraissant contredire, la cérémonie dramatique" [The passage of generations is a

powerful creator of hate. The second generation contains within itself the death of the Father and enables the poetic ceremony to renew itself, by seemingly contradicting, the theatrical ceremony" (Scherer, *Racine et/ou la cérémonie*, 190). More recently, Mitchell Greenberg has spoken of Racinian tragedy as the space of "The law of the Father [...] the law of no, of renunciation, of difference, and of exclusion that structures the possibilities of social life and that permits its perpetuation within order, within history, within the state" (*Canonical States, Canonical Stages*, 163). See also Greenberg, *Baroque Bodies*.

5 Racine, *Andromache*, trans., John Edmunds.

6 For the psychoanalytical vein, see Mauron, *L'Inconscient dans l'oeuvre et la vie de Racine*, 29. Other notable psychoanalytical readings of Racine include, Apostolidès, "Image du père et peur du tyran au XVIIe siècle."

7 Aristotle, *Theory of Poetry and Fine Art*, ch. XIV, 49.

8 In *Britannicus*, Junie describes herself as, "Seule reste du débris d'une illustre famille" (v. 556) [The only remains of the debris of an illustrious family], alluding to her status as a descendant of Auguste, whose shadow weighs over the plot as the foil to Néron's corrupt reign. It is Auguste's statue that protects her at the tragedy's end when she escapes into the temple of the Vestals. In parallel, the memory of the emperor Claudius, Britannicus's father, inspires Néron's fears since Agrippine can threaten to restore the legitimate Britannicus to the throne if he does not obey her. In *Bérénice*, the death and burial of Titus's father, Vespasien, means that Titus is now "master of the universe." The queen of Palestine believes that as the new Roman emperor, her lover will marry her as he has promised, but it is precisely because of the father's death and the weight that has come with that succession that Titus can no longer keep his promise to Bérénice and must choose faithfulness to the laws of Rome instead. Finally, in *Bajazet*, we do not find a father per se, but a brother-father figure in the person of Sultan Amurat who never appears onstage but whose imminent return threatens to fatally punish those who have betrayed him.

9 Racine, *Œuvres complètes*, vol. 1, "Préface (1660–1672)," 126.

10 Ibid., "Dissertation sur le Grand Alexandre," 183.

11 Ibid., 184.

12 Ibid.

13 In the "Préface d'*Alexandre le Grand*," 191–2, he adamantly defends both Alexandre and Porus's prestige and honour based on his adherence to historical descriptions.

14 Racine, *Œuvres complètes*, vol. 1, "Préface, *Britannicus*," 372: "C'est ici un monstre naissant. Il n'a pas encore mis le feu à Rome. Il n'a pas encore tué

sa Mère, sa Femme, ses Gouverneurs" [He is here a nascent monster. He has not yet set Rome on fire. He has not yet killed his Mother, his Wife, and his Governors].

15 "Je fuis, je l'avouerai, cette jeune Aricie, / Reste d'un sang fatal conjuré contre nous" (vv. 50–1) [I will confess: I'm fleeing from young Aricia, / Last of that fatal blood which would destroy us] (*Phaedra*, trans. John Edmunds). All English translations of *Phèdre* are taken from this edition.

16 Barthes, *Sur Racine*, 39.

17 Zanger, *Scenes from the Marriage of Louis XIV*, 8.

18 Goodkin, *Birth Marks*, 188. Italics in the original.

19 She tells him: "épargnez votre race, respectez votre sang" (v. 1117) [Spare your race, respect your blood].

20 Scherer, *Racine et/ou la cérémonie*, 87.

21 "Le roi et le prince son fils paraissent [dans *Clitandre*] dans un emploi fort en-dessous de leur Dignité: l'un n'y est *que comme juge*, et l'autre comme confident de son favori. Ce défaut n'a pas accoutumé de passer pour défaut: aussi n'est-ce qu'un sentiment particulier dont je me fais une Règle, qui peut-être ne semblera pas déraisonnable, bien que nouvelle" [The king and the prince his son appear [in *Clitandre*] in a function far beneath their Dignity: one is there *only as a judge*, and the other as the confidant of his favourite. This defect has not usually been recognized as a defect: therefore it is only a personal feeling from which I make a Rule for myself, that perhaps will not seem unreasonable despite its newness] (Corneille, "Examen de *Clitandre*," in *Œuvres complètes*, 1:102, my emphasis).

22 I echo here Jean Rohou's characterization of Mithridate's transformation at the play's close as a "conversion du monstre." See Rohou, "Structure et signification dans *Britannicus, Bérénice* et *Mithridate*," 51–72.

23 See Giesey, *Rulership in France, 15th–17th Centuries*.

24 Guyot, *Racine et le corps tragique*, 102.

25 "Mais vous me tenez lieu d'Empire et de Couronne. / Vous seule me restez. Souffez que je vous donne, / Madame, et tous ces vœux que j'exigeais de vous, / Mon Cœur pour Xipharès vous les demande tous" (vv. 1765–8) [But you replace my Empire and Crown, / You alone remain mine. Suffer that I give you to him, / Madam, and all those wishes that I demanded of you, / My heart for Xipharès asks them all of you now].

26 "Et si quelque vengeance à ma mort est promise / Que c'est à leur [celle des Romains] valeur que le Ciel l'a remise" (v. 1704–5) [And if some vengeance to my death is promised / That it is to their [the Romans'] bravery that the Heavens have left it].

27 Donneau de Visé, *Mercure galant*, T.IV, cited in Vincent, *Présentation de la première revue féminine*, 178.

28 "Allons de mon erreur, hélas! Trop éclaircis / Mêler nos pleurs au sang
    de mon malheureux fils. / Allons de ce cher fils embrasser ce qui reste. /
    Expier la fureur d'un vœu que je déteste" (vv. 1647–50) [Let us, now that
    my error's all too clear / Blend our tears with the blood of my unfortunate
    son. / Let us embrace what remains of that dear son. / Expiate my mad
    atrocious wish].

29 Biet, *Droit et littérature sous l'Ancien Régime.*

Bibliography

Agamben, Giorgio. *State of Exception*. Translated by Kevin Attell. Chicago: University of Chicago Press, 2004.

Apostolidès, Jean-Marie. "Image du père et peur du tyran au XVIIe siècle." *Revue française de psychanlyse* 44 (January 1980): 7–14.

– *Le Roi-Machine: spectacle et politique au temps de Louis XIV*. Paris: Minuit, 1981.

Aristotle. *Theory of Poetry and Fine Art*. Translated and edited by S.H. Butcher. New York: Dover, 1951.

Assaf, Francis. *La Mort du roi: Une thanatographie de Louis XIV*. Tübingen: Gunter Narr Verlag, 1999.

Aubignac, François Hédelin, abbé d.' "Commentaires sur Corneille," "Lettre sur Œdipe," and "Troisième dissertation concernant le poème dramatique, en forme de remarques sur la tragédie de M. Corneille, intitulée l'Œdipe Envoyée à Madame la Duchesse de R." In *Œdipe (Corneille et Voltaire)*. Edited by Laurent Thirouin and Denis Raynaud. Saint-Etienne: Publications de l'Université de Saint-Etienne, 2004.

– *La Pratique du théâtre*. Edited by Hélène Baby. Paris: Champions Classiques, 2011.

Baby, Hélène. *La Tragi-comédie de Corneille à Quinault*. Paris: Klincksieck, 2001.

Baker, Susan Read. *Dissonant Harmonies: Drama and Ideology in Five Neglected Plays by Pierre Corneille*. Tübingen: Gunther Narr Verlag, 1990.

Bakhtin, Mikail M. *The Dialogic Imagination: Four Essays by M.M. Bakhtin*. Edited by Michael Holquist. Translated by Caryl Emerson and Michael Holquist. Austin: University of Texas Press, 1981.

Barden Dowling, Marissa. *Clemency and Cruelty in the Roman World*. Ann Arbor: University of Michigan Press, 2006.

Barthes, Roland. *Sur Racine*. Paris: Editions du Seuil, 1963.

Bell, David A. *Lawyers and Citizens: The Making of a Political Elite in Old Regime France*. New York: Oxford University Press, 1994.

Bénichou, Paul. *Morales du Grand Siècle*. Paris: Gallimard, 1948.

Benjamin, Walter. *On the Origin of German Tragic Drama*. Translated by John Osborne. London: NLB, 1977.

Bercé, Yves-Marie, and Elena Fasano Guarini, eds. *Complots et conjurations dans l'Europe moderne: actes du colloque international de Rome*. Rome: Collection de l'École de Rome, 1993.

Biek, William. *Absolutism and Society in Seventeenth-Century France: State Power and Provincial Aristocracy in Languedoc*. Cambridge: Cambridge University Press, 1985.

Biet, Christian. "Droit divin, droit naturel et droit humain dans *Antigone* de Jean Rotrou." *Littératures Classiques* 17 (1992): 65–83.

– *Droit et littérature sous l'Ancien Régime: le jeu de la valeur et de la loi*. Paris: Honoré Champion, 2002.

– "La plume et la loi." In *L'Ecriture des juristes, XVIe–XVIIIe siècle*, edited by Laurence Giavarini, 183–203. Paris: Classiques Garnier, 2010.

– *Racine ou la passion des larmes*. Paris: Hachette, 1996.

– "Le Spectacle du sang, l'incapacité des rois et l'impuissance du public: représentation de la souveraineté et spectacle violent dans les tragédies du tout premier XVIIe siècle: *Scédase* d'Alexandre Hardy." In *L'invraisemblance du pouvoir: Mises en scène de la souveraineté au XVIIe siècle*, edited by Jean-Vincent Blanchard and Hélène Visentin, 31–51. Paris: Presses Universitaires de Paris-Sorbonne, 2002.

– *Théâtre de la cruauté et récits sanglants en France (XVIe–XVIIe siècles)*. Paris: Editions Robert Laffont, 2006.

Biet, Christian, Charlotte Bouteille, Sybile Chevallier, and Romain Jobez. "L'écriture du crime dans le théâtre de la cruauté et les récits sanglants français de la fin du XVIe au début du XVIIe siècle." In *Littératures Classiques. Réécritures du crime: l'acte sanglant sur la scène, XVIe–XVIIIe siècle*, edited by Laurence Marie and Zoé Schweitzer, 67 (spring, 2008): 231–47.

Bilis, Hélène. "The Silence of Subjects: Tragedy and the Refusal to Speak in Tristan's *La Mort de Sénèque*." In *L'Eloquence du Silence: dramaturgie du non-dit sur la scène théâtrale des 17e et 18e siècles*, edited by Hélène Bilis and Jennifer Tamas, 114–35. Paris: Classiques Garnier, 2014.

– "Voir la Sorcière de Colchis d'un nouvel œil ou comment rendre visible la dignité." *Littératures Classiques*, edited by Sylvaine Guyot and Tom Conley, 83 (winter 2013): 233–45.

Blanchard, Jean-Vincent. *Eminence: Cardinal Richelieu and the Rise of France*. New York: Walker and Company, 2011.

Blocker, Déborah. *Instituer un "art": politiques du théâtre dans la France du premier XVIIe siècle*. Paris: Honoré Champion, 2009.

– "Une 'muse de province' négocie sa centralité: Corneille et ses lieux." *Les Dossiers du Grihl,* 2008–1, *Localités: localisation des écrits et production locale d'actions,* July 2008, http://dossiersgrihl.revues.org/2133.

Bodin, Jean. *Les Six livres de la République* [1576]. 6 vols. Paris: Fayard, 1986.

Boureau, Alain. *Le Simple corps du roi: l'impossible sacralité des souverains français, XVe–XVIIIe siècle.* Paris: Les Editions de Paris, 2000.

Bousquet, Philippe. "Le suicide féminin au XVIIe siècle: un acte héroïque?" In *La Femme au XVIIe siècle. Actes du colloque de Vancouver,* edited by Richard Hodgson, 183–200. Tübingen: Gunter Narr Verlag: 2000.

Braider, Christopher. *Indiscernible Counterparts: The Invention of Text in French Classical Drama.* North Carolina Studies in the Romance Languages and Literatures. Chapel Hill: University of North Carolina Press, 2002.

– *Matter of the Mind: Reason and Experience in the Age of Descartes.* Toronto: University of Toronto Press, 2012.

Bray, René. *La formation de la doctrine classique en France.* Paris: Hachette, 1927.

Burke, Peter. *The Fabrication of Louis XIV.* New Haven: Yale University Press, 1992.

Canova-Green, Marie-Claude. *La Politique-Spectacle au grand siècle: les rapports franco-anglais.* Tübingen: Gunter Narr Verlag, 1993.

Carlin, Claire. *Women Reading Corneille: Feminist Psychocriticisms of* Le Cid. New York: Peter Lang, 2000.

Cave, Terrence. *Recognitions: A Study in Poetics.* Oxford: Clarendon Press, 1988.

Chapelain, Jean. "Discours de la poésie representative." In *Chapelain: Opuscules critiques,* edited by Alfred C. Hunter and Anne Duprat, 272–5. Geneva: Droz, 2007.

– *Les Sentiments de l'Académie Francaise sur la tragi-comédie du* Cid. In *La Querelle du Cid (1637–1638),* edited by Jean-Marc Civardi, 50–74. Paris: Honoré Champion, 2004.

– *Les Sentiments de l'Académie Française touchant les observations faites sur la tragi-comédie du* Cid. In *Chapelain: Opuscules critiques,* edited by Alfred C. Hunter and Anne Duprat, 280–316. Geneva: Droz, 2007.

Chaouche, Sabine. *L'art du comédien: déclamation et jeu scénique en France à l'âge classique 1629–1680.* Paris: Honoré Champion, 2001.

Chatelain, Jean-Marc. "Héros Togatus: culture cicéronienne et gloire de la robe dans la France d'Henri IV." *Journal des Savants* (July–September, 1991): 263–87.

Chiffoleau, Jacques. "Le Crime de majesté, la politique et l'extraordinaire: note sur les collections érudites du procès de lèse-majesté du XVIIe siècle français et sur leurs exemples médiévaux." In *Genèse de l'Etat moderne en Méditerranée,* 183–213. Rome: Ecole Française de Rome, 1993.

Civardi, Jean-Marc. *La Querelle du Cid (1637–1638).* Paris: Honoré Champion, 2004.

Clarke, David. *Pierre Corneille: Poetics and Political Drama under Louis XIII.* Cambridge: Cambridge University Press, 1992.

Constant, Jean-Marie. *La Noblesse en liberté. XVI–XVIIe siècles.* Rennes: Presses Universitaires de Rennes, 2004.

Corneille, Pierre. *Œuvres complètes.* 3 vols. Edited by Georges Couton. Paris: Gallimard, Bibliothèque de la Pléiade, 1980–7.

– *The Cid/Cinna/The Theatrical Illusion.* Translated by John Carincross. London: Penguin Classics, 1973.

– *Cinna.* Edited by Georges Forestier. Paris: Gallimard Folio Classique, 2005.

– *Horace.* Edited by Marc Escola. Paris: GF Flammarion, 2007.

– *Théâtre.* Edited by Claire Carlin, Jean de Guardia, Liliane Picciola, and Marc Vuillermoz. Paris: Garnier, 2014.

– *Trois discours sur le poème dramatique.* Edited by Marc Escola and Bénédicte Louvat. Paris: GF Flammarion, 1999.

Cornette, Joël. "Fiction et réalité de l'état baroque (1610–1652)." In *L'Etat Baroque 1610–1652,* edited by Henry Méchoulan, 8–25. Paris: J. Vrin, 1985.

Cosandey, Fanny. *La Reine de France: symbole et pouvoir.* Paris: Gallimard, Bibliothèque des histoires, 2000.

Couprie, Alain. "Prison et prisonniers dans le théâtre de Corneille." *Cahiers de l'Association internationale des études françaises* 37 (1985): 137–50.

Couton, Georges. *Corneille et la tragédie politique.* Paris: Broché, 1990.

Declercq, Gilles. "L'identification des genres oratoires en tragédie française du 17e siècle (*Iphigénie, Cinna*)." In *Theatrum mundi: Studies in Honor of R. Tobin,* edited by Claire Carlin and Kathleen Wine, 230–7. Charlottesville, VA: Rookwood Press, 2003.

Deierkauf-Holsboer, Wilma S. *Vie d'Alexandre Hardy, poète du roi, 1572–1632: 47 documents inédits.* Paris: Nizet, 1972.

Delatour, Jérome. "'Les armes en main et les larmes aux yeux': le procès de Cinq-Mars et de Thou." In *Les Procès politiques (XIVe–XVIIe siècles),* edited by Yves-Marie Bercé, 351–93. Rome: Collection de l'Ecole de Rome, 2007.

Delmas, Christian. *La Tragédie de l'Age Classique 1553–1770.* Seuil: Paris, 1994.

Descimon, Robert. "Les fonctions de la métaphore du mariage politique du roi et de la république: France, XVe–XVIII siècles." *Annales ESC* 43 (November–December 1992): 1127–47.

– "Les Paradoxes d'un juge seigneurial: Charles Loyseau (1564–1627)" *Cahiers du CRH* 27, "Officiers moyens (II)," 2001, http://ccrh.revues.org/1333.

De Smet, Ingrid. *Thuanus: The Making of Jacques-Auguste de Thou.* Geneva: Droz, 2006.

De Thou, Jacques-Auguste. *Histoire universelle traduite sur l'édition latine de Londres.* 16 vols. London, 1734.

Dewald, Jonathan. *Aristocratic Experience and the Origins of Modern Culture: France, 1570–1715.* Berkeley: University of California Press, 1993.

Dotoli, Giovanni. *Temps des Préfaces: le débat théâtral en France de Hardy à la querelle du Cid.* Paris: Klincksieck, 1996.

Doubrovsky, Serge. *Corneille et la dialectique du héros.* Paris: Gallimard, 1963.

Dowling, Melissa Barden. *Clemency and Cruelty in the Roman World.* Ann Arbor: University of Michigan Press, 2006.

Dufour-Maître, Myriam, and Florence Naugrette, eds. *Corneille des Romantiques.* Mont-Saint-Aignan: Universités de Rouen et du Havre, 2006.

Dyer, R.R. "Rhetoric and Intention in Cicero's *Pro Marcello*." *Journal of Roman Studies* 80 (1990): 17–30.

Ekstein, Nina. "The Conversion of *Polyeucte*'s Félix: The Problem of Religion and Theater." *French Forum* 34.1 (2009): 1–17.

Escola, Marc. "Introduction à Horace." In *Horace*, edited by Marc Escola. 19–46. Paris: GF Flammarion, 2007.

Escola, Marc, and Bénédicte Louvat. "Le statut de l'épisode dans la tragédie classique: *Œdipe* de Corneille ou le complexe de Dircé." *XVIIe siècle* 200 (July–September 1998): 453–70.

Fernandez, Hélène. "Représenter un procès politique au XVIIe siècle: Michel de Marillac à Rueil." In *Représentations du procès; droit, théâtre, littérature, cinéma*, edited by Christian Biet and Laurence Schifano, 203–27. Nanterre: Université Paris X: Collection Représentation, 2003.

Fernandez-Lacôte, Hélène. *Les Procès du Cardinal de Richelieu: droit, grâce et politique sous Louis le Juste.* Paris: Champ Vallon, 2010.

Ferrier-Caverivière, Nicole. *L'Image de Louis XIV dans la littérature de 1660 à 1715.* Paris: Presses Universitaires de France, 1981.

Forestier, Georges. *Corneille: le sens d'une dramaturgie.* Paris: Sedes, 1998.

– *Essai de génétique théâtrale: Corneille à l'œuvre.* Paris: Klincksieck, 1996.

– "Imitation parfaite et vraisemblance absolue: réflexions sur un paradoxe classique." *Poétique* 82 (1990): 187–202.

– *Le Théâtre dans le théâtre sur la scène française du XVIIe siècle.* Geneva: Droz, 1996.

– *La Tragédie française: passions tragiques et règles classiques.* Paris: Armand Colin, 2003.

Foucault, Michel. *Discipline and Punish: The Birth of the Prison.* Translated by Alan Sheridan. New York: Vintage Books, 1977.

– *"Il faut défendre la société": Cours au Collège de France (1975–1976)*. Edited by François Ewald and Alessandro Fontana. Paris: Seuil/Gallimard, 1997.

Frisch, Andrea. "French Tragedy and the Civil Wars." *Modern Language Quarterly* 67.3 (2006): 287–312.

– *The Invention of the Eyewitness: Witnessing and Testimony in Early Modern France*. North Carolina Studies in the Romance Languages and Literatures. Chapel Hill: University of North Carolina Press, 2004.

Frye, Northrop. *Shakespeare: Modern Essays in Criticism*. Edited by Leonard F. Deran. Oxford: Oxford University Press, 1957.

Fumaroli, Marc. *L'Age de l'éloquence: rhétorique et res literaria de la Renaissance au seuil de l'époque classique*. Paris: Albin Michel, 1994.

– *Héros et Orateurs: rhétorique et dramaturgie cornéliennes*. Geneva: Droz, 1990.

Furetière, Antoine. *Le Dictionnaire universel d'Antoine Furetière*, préfacé par Pierre Bayle, précédé d'une biographie de son auteur et d'une analyse de l'ouvrage par Alain Rey. 3 vols. The Hague and Rotterdam: Leers, 1690; Paris: Le Robert, 1973.

Galinsky, Karl. *Augustan Culture: An Interpretive Introduction*. Princeton: Princeton University Press, 1996.

Genette, Gérard. "Vraisemblance et motivation." In *Figures II*, 71–99. Paris: Le Seuil, 1969.

Gethner, Perry. "La chronologie du théâtre de Rotrou." *R.H.T.* 3 (1991.3): 242–57.

Giesey, Ralph. *The Royal Funeral Ceremony in Renaissance France*. Geneva: Droz, 1960.

– *Rulership in France, 15th–17th Centuries*. Hampshire, UK: Ashgate, 1996.

Gilhuly, Kate. "Corinth, Courtesans, and the Politics of Place." In *Space, Place, and Landscape in Ancient Greek Literature and Culture*, edited by Kate Gilhuly and Nancy Worman, 171–99. Cambridge: Cambridge University Press, 2014.

Goodkin, Richard, E. *Birth Marks: The Tragedy of Primogeniture in Pierre Corneille, Thomas Corneille, and Jean Racine*. Philadelphia: University of Pennsylvania Press, 2000.

Gordon, Daniel. Citizens without Sovereignty: Equality and Sociability in French Thought, 1670–1789. Princeton: Princeton University Press, 1994.

Greenberg, Mitchell. *Baroque Bodies: Psychoanalysis and the Culture of French Absolutism*. Ithaca, NY: Cornell University Press, 2001.

– *Canonical States, Canonical Stages: Œdipus, Othering, and Seventeenth-Century Drama*. Minneapolis: University of Minnesota Press, 1994.

– *Corneille, Classicism, and the Ruses of Symmetry*. Cambridge: Cambridge University Press, 1987.

– *Subjectivity and Subjugation in Seventeenth-Century Drama and Prose.* Cambridge: Cambridge University Press, 1992.

Guichemerre, Roger. *La Tragi-comédie.* Paris: Presses Universitaires de France, 1981.

Guyot, Sylvaine. "En contrechamp: le héros sous le regard des personnages – éléments pour une réflexion sur les scénographies de l'éblouissement chez Corneille." In *Héros ou personnages? Le personnel du théâtre de Pierre Corneille,* edited by Myriam Dufour-Maitre, 95–109. Rouen: Presses Universitaires de Rouen et du Havre, 2013.

– *Racine et le corps tragique.* Paris: Presses Universitaires de France, 2014.

– "'Un silence d'étonnement et d'admiration': Racine, ou la discrète réticence du théâtre encomiastique." In *L'Eloquence du Silence: Dramaturgie du non-dit sur la scène théâtrale des 17e et 18e siècles,* edited by Hélène Bilis and Jennifer Tamas, 241–60. Paris: Classiques Garnier, 2014.

Hampton, Timothy. "Introduction: Baroques." In *Baroque Topographies: Literature/ History/ Philosophy,* 2–10. Yale French Studies 80. New Haven: Yale University Press, 1991.

Hanley, Sarah. *The* Lit de Justice *of the Kings of France.* Princeton: Princeton University Press, 1983.

Hardy, Alexandre. *Scédase ou l'hospitalité violée.* In *Théâtre du XVIIe siècle,* edited by Jacques Scherer. Vol. 1. Paris: Bibliothèque de la Pléiade Gallimard, 1975.

Hawcroft, Micheal. "Corneille's *Clitandre* and the Theatrical Illusion." *French Studies* 47:2 (1993): 142–55.

Howe, Alan, and Richard Waller. "Alexandre Hardy and the French Theater in 1615." *Seventeenth-Century French Studies* 9 (1987): 26–34.

– *En Marge du Classicisme: Essays on the French Theater from the Renaissance to the Enlightenment.* Liverpool: Liverpool University Press, 1987.

Hutson, Lorna. *The Invention of Suspicion.* Oxford: Oxford University Press, 2008.

– *Rhetoric and Law in Early Modern Europe.* Edited by Lorna Hutson and Victoria Kahn. New Haven: Yale University Press, 2001.

Ibbett, Katherine. "Mon ami, ce héros." In *Héros ou personnages? Le personnel du théâtre de Pierre Corneille,* edited by Myriam Dufour-Maître, 275–93. Rouen: Presses Universitaires de Rouen et du Havre, 2013.

– *The Style of the State in French Theater, 1630–1660: Neoclassicism and Government.* Aldershot, UK: Ashgate, 2009.

Jackson, Richard. *Vive le Roi! A History of the French Coronation from Charles V to Charles X.* Chapel Hill: University of North Carolina Press, 1984.

Jacobson, Mary. "Is There a Woman in This Text?" *New Literary History* 14.1 (autumn, 1982): 117–41.

Jondorf, Gillian. "What Is a King? The Figure of the King in Rotrou." *Seventeenth-century French Studies* 10 (1988): 40–52.

Jouanna, Arlette. "Conclusions." In *Les Procès politiques, XIVe–XVIIe siècles*, edited by Yves-Marie Bercé, 661–7. Rome: Collection de l'Ecole de Rome, 2007.

– *Le Devoir de révolte: la noblesse française et la gestation de l'Etat moderne, 1559–1661*. Paris: Fayard, 1989.

– *Le Pouvoir Absolu: naissance de l'imaginaire politique de la royauté*. Paris: Gallimard, 2013.

Jouhaud, Christian. *Les Pouvoirs de la littérature: histoire d'un paradoxe*. Paris: Gallimard NRF, 2000.

– *Sauver le Grand-Siècle? Présence et transmission du passé*. Paris: Le Seuil, 2007.

Kahn, Victoria. *The Future of Illusion: Political Theology and Early Modern Texts*. Chicago: University of Chicago Press, 2013.

Kantorowicz, Ernst. *The King's Two Bodies: A Study in Medieval Political Theology*. Princeton: Princeton University Press, 1957.

Kettering, Sharon. *Judicial Politics and Urban Revolt in Seventeenth-Century France. The Parlement of Aix, 1629–1659*. Princeton, NJ: Princeton University Press, 1978.

Kitchens III, James. "Judicial Commissaires and the Parlement of Paris: The Case of the Chambre de l'Arsenal." *French Historical Studies* 12.3 (spring, 1982): 323–50.

Konstan, David. "Clemency as a Virtue." *Classical Philology* 100.4 (October, 2005): 337–46.

Lahouati, Gérard, and Paul Mirronneau, eds. *Figures de l'histoire de France dans le théâtre au tournant des Lumières 1760–1830*. Oxford: Voltaire Foundation, 2007.

La Mesnardière, Hippolyte-Jules Pilet de. *La Poétique*. Paris, 1640. Reprint, Geneva: Slatkine, 1972.

Langer, Ullrich. *Vertu du discours, discours de la vertu: littérature et philosophie morale au XVIe siècle en France*. Geneva: Droz, 1999.

Lanson, Gustave. *Esquisse d'une histoire de la tragédie française*. New York: Columbia University Press, 1920.

Lasserre, François. *Corneille de 1638 à 1642: la crise technique d'*Horace, Cinna et Polyeucte. Paris and Tubingen: Biblio 17 Gunter Narr, 1990.

Le Bret, Cardin. Traité *de la souveraineté du Roy, de son domaine et de sa couronne*. In *Les Œuvres de Messire C. Le Bret* [1632]. Rouen: Charles Osmont, 1689.

Le Goff, Jacques. *Saint Louis*. Paris: Gallimard, 1996.

Le Roux, Nicolas. *Le Roi, la cour, l'état de la Renaissance à l'absolutisme*. Paris: Champ Vallon, 2013.

Longino, Michèle. *Orientalism in French Classical Drama*. Cambridge: Cambridge University Press, 2000.

Loyseau, Charles. "Traité des Seigneuries." In *Les Œuvres de Maistre Charles Loyseau, avocat en Parlement … derniere edition, plus exacte que les precedentes.* Lyon: la Compagnie des Libraires, 1701.

Lyons, John D. *French Literature: A Very Short Introduction.* Oxford: Oxford University Press, 2010.

– *Kingdom of Disorder: The Theory of Tragedy in Classical France.* West Lafayette, IN: Purdue University Press, 1999.

– "Material Fatality: Props and the Baroque Drama of Chance." In *Walter Benjamin's Hypothetical French Trauerspiel,* edited by Katherine Ibbett and Hall Bjornstad, 36–49. Yale French Studies 124. New Haven: Yale University Press, 2013.

– "Le Mythe du héros cornélien." *Revue d'histoire littéraire de la France* (April–June, 2007): 433–48.

– *The Phantom of Chance: From Fortune to Randomness in Seventeenth-Century French Literature.* Edinburgh: Edinburgh University Press, 2012.

– *The Tragedy of Origins: Pierre Corneille and Historical Perspective.* Stanford: Stanford University Press, 1996.

Mairet, Jean. "Préface, en forme de discours poétique." In *Théâtre du XVIIe siècle,* edited by Jacques Scherer, 1:479–88. Paris: Gallimard, Bibliothèque de la Pléiade, 1975.

Margitiç, M.R. "Les Deux *Cid*: de la tragi-comédie à la pseudo-tragédie classique." *Papers on French Seventeenth-Century Literature* 11 (1984): 409–25.

Marin, Louis. *Le Portrait du roi.* Paris: Editions de Minuit, 1981.

– "Pour une théorie baroque de l'action politique." In *Considérations politiques sur les coups d'Etat.* Paris: Les Editions de Paris, 1988.

– *Les Pouvoirs de l'image.* Paris: Seuil, 1993.

Marvick, Elizabeth Wirth. *Louis XIII: The Making of a King.* New Haven: Yale University Press, 1986.

Matthews, James D. "The Tyrannical Sovereign in the Pre-1640 French Tragicomedy: Political Statement or Dramatic Necessity?" In *L'Image du soverain dans le théâtre de 1600 à 1650,* edited by M.R. Margitic and B.R. Wells, 147–58. Paris-Tubingen: Gunter Narr, 1987.

Maulnier, Thierry. *Racine.* Paris: Librairie Revue Française, 1935.

Mauron, Charles. *L'Inconscient dans l'œuvre et la vie de Racine.* Geneva: Slatkine, 1986.

McClure, Ellen. *Sunspots and the Sun King: Sovereignty and Mediation in Seventeenth-Century France.* Chicago: University of Illinois Press, 2006.

Merlin-Kajman, Hélène. *L'Absolutisme dans les lettres et la théorie des deux corps: passions et politique.* Paris: Honoré Champion, 2000.

– *Public et littérature en France au XVIIe siècle.* Paris: Belles Lettres, 1994.

- "Réécriture cornélienne du crime: le cas d'*Horace.*" *Littératures Classiques* 67 (2008:3): 101–14.

Miola, Robert. *Shakespeare's Rome.* Cambridge: Cambridge University Press, 1983.

Molière. *Œuvres complètes.* 2 vols. Edited by Georges Couton. Paris: Bibliothèque de la Pléiade, 1971.

- *Tartuffe.* In *Œuvres complètes.* 2 vols. Edited by Georges Forestier. Paris: Bibliothèque de la Pléiade, 2010.

Moote, A. Lloyd. *Louis XIII, The Just.* Berkeley: University of California Press, 1989.

- *The Revolt of the Judges: The Parlement of Paris and the Fronde, 1643–1652.* Princeton: Princeton University Press, 1971.

Morel, Jacques. *Agréables mensonges: essais sur le théâtre français du XVIIe.* Paris: Klincksieck, 1991.

- *Jean Rotrou: dramaturge de l'ambiguïté.* Paris: Armand Colin, 1968.

Mousnier, Roland. *Les Institutions de la France sous la monarchie absolue (1598–1789).* Paris: Presses Universitaires de France, 1992.

- *La Vénalité des offices sous Henri IV et Louis XIII.* Vol. I. Paris: Presses Universitaires de France, 1971.

Murray, Timothy. "Richelieu's Theater: The Mirror of a Prince." *Renaissance Drama* 8 (1977): 275–97.

Nelson, Eric. "The Problem of the Prince." In *The Cambridge Companion to Renaissance History,* edited by James Hankins, 319–39. Cambridge: Cambridge University Press, 2007.

Noreña, Carlos. "The Communication of the Emperor's Virtues." *Journal of Roman Studies* 91 (2001): 146–68.

Pavel, Thomas. *L'Art de l'éloignement: essai sur l'éloignement classique.* Paris: Gallimard, Folio Essais, 1996.

Plutarque. *Vies parallèles.* Paris: Gallimard, 2001.

Poirier, Germain. *Corneille et la vertu de Prudence.* Geneva: Droz, 1984.

Prigent, Michel. *Le héros et l'état dans la tragédie de Pierre Corneille.* Paris: Presses Universitaires de France, 1986.

Racine, Jean. *Œuves completes – Théâtre-poésie.* Vol. 1. Edited by Georges Forestier. Paris: Gallimard, 1999.

- *Œuvres complètes – Prose.* Vol. 2. Edited by Raymond Picard. Paris: Gallimard, 1966.

- *Andromache.* Translated by John Edmunds. In *Corneille, Molière, Racine: Four French Plays, Cinna, The Misanthrope, Andromache, Phaedra.* London: Penguin Classics, 2013.

- *Phaedra.* Translated by John Edmunds. In *Corneille, Molière, Racine: Four French Plays, Cinna, The Misanthrope, Andromache, Phaedra.* London: Penguin Classics, 2013.

Ranum, Orest. *Richelieu and the Councillors of Louis XIII*. Oxford: Oxford University Press, 1963.

Reiss, Timothy. *Toward Dramatic Illusion: Theatrical Technique and Meaning from Hardy to Horace*. New Haven: Yale University Press, 1971.

Ribard, Dinah, and Alain Viala. *Le Tragique*. Paris: Bibliothèque Gallimard, 2002.

Richard, Jean. *Saint Louis, roi d'une France féodale*. Paris, Fayard, 1983.

Rigal, Eugène. *Alexandre Hardy et le théâtre français à la fin du XVIe siècle et au commencement du XVIIe*. Paris: Hachette, 1891.

Rohou, Jean. "Structure et signification dans *Britannicus, Bérénice* et *Mithridate*." *Littératures Classiques* 26 (January, 1996): 51–72.

Rotrou, Jean. *Théâtre complet*. 10 vols. Edited by Georges Forestier et al. Paris: Société des textes français modernes, 1998–2014.

Rousset, Jean. *Circé et le paon: la littérature de l'âge baroque en France*. Paris: José Corti, 1954.

Scherer, Jacques. *Racine et/ou la cérémonie*. Paris: Presses Universitaires de France, 1982.

Schmitt, Carl. *Political Theology: Four Chapters on the Theory of Sovereignty*. Translated by George Schwab. Chicago: University of Chicago Press, 1985.

Scott, Paul. "'Ma force est trop petite': Authority and Kingship in *Le Cid*." *Forum for Modern Language Studies* 45 (2009): 292–304.

Scudéry, Georges de. *Apologie du théâtre*. Paris: Presses Universitaires de France, 2012.

– *Observations sur* Le Cid*:* In *La Querelle* du Cid. Edited by Jean-Marc Civardi. Paris: Honoré Champion, 2004.

Seneca. "On Clemency." In *Anger, Mercy, Revenge*, translated and edited by Robert A. Kaster and Martha C. Nussbaum, 146–80. Chicago: University of Chicago Press, 2010.

Skinner, Quentin. "Political Philosophy." In *The Cambridge History of Renaissance Philosophy*, edited by Charles B. Schmitt, Quentin Skinner, Eckhard Kessler, 389–452. Cambridge: Cambridge University Press, 1988.

Soll, Jacob. *The Information Master: Jean-Baptiste Colbert's Secret State Intelligence System*. Ann Arbor, MI: University of Michigan Press, 2009.

Soman, Alfred. *Sorcellerie et justice criminelle: le Parlement de Paris 16e–18e siècles*. Hampshire-Brookfield: Variorum, 1992.

Starobinski, Jean. *L'Œil vivant: Corneille, Racine, La Bruyère, Rousseau, Stendhal*. Paris: Gallimard, 1961.

Stone, Harriet. *The Classical Model: Literature and Knowledge in Seventeenth-Century France*. Ithaca: Cornell University Press, 1996.

– *Royal Disclosure: Problematics of Representation in French Classical Tragedy*. Birmingham, AL: Summa Publications, 1987.

Tesissier-Ensminger, Anne. "Histoire de re-dire le droit: la mémoire en procès de l'historien de Thou." In *Dire le droit: normes, juges, jurisconsultes,* edited by Barbara Anagnostou-Canas, 285–327. Paris: Panthéon-Assas "Colloques," 2006.

Thirouin, Laurent. *L'Aveuglement salutaire: le réquisitoire contre le théâtre dans la France classique.* Paris: Honoré Champion, 1997.

Tollet, Daniel. "La Pologne vue par les Français (Fin du XVIe siècle, première moitié du XVIIe siècle)." In *L'Etat Baroque: regards sur la pensée politique de la France du premier XVIIe siècle (1610–1652),* edited by Henri Méchoulan, 447–56. Paris: Vrin, 1985.

Treilhou-Balaudé, Catherine. "Rotrou: poète de la scène." *Littératures Classiques* 63 (2007): 223–36.

Tristan l'Hermite, François. *Marianne.* Edited by Guillaume Peureux. Paris: GF Flammarion, 2003.

Vialleton, Jean-Yves. *Rotrou: dramaturgie de l'ingénuosité.* Paris: Presses Universitaires de France, 2007.

Vincent, Dominique. *Présentation de la première revue féminine d'information et de culture 1672–1710.* Paris: Honoré Champion, 2005.

Voltaire. "Avertissement de *Sémiramis.*" In *Œuvres complètes.* Vol. 52, edited by Louis Morland, 485–506. Paris: Garnier, 1877.

– "Lettre IV contenant la critique de l'*Œdipe* de Voltaire." In *Œdipe* (*Corneille et Voltaire*), edited by Laurent Thirouin and Denis Raynaud, 90–100. Saint-Etienne: Publications de l'Université de Saint-Etienne, 2004.

– *Le Siècle de Louis XIV: Œuvres historiques de Voltaire.* Edited by René Pomeau. Paris: Gallimard, 1957.

Vuillemin, Jean-Claude. *Baroquisme et théâtralité: le théâtre de Jean Rotrou.* Tubingen: Biblio 17 Gunter Narr, 1994.

Wallace-Hadrill, Andrew. "The Emperor and His Virtues." *Historia* 30 (1980): 293–323.

Wolfe, Kathryn. "Royal Discourse in Rotrou's *Venceslas.*" *Papers on French Seventeenth-Century Literature* 15 (1988): 677–84.

Zanger, Abby. *Scenes from the Marriage of Louis XIV: Nuptial Fictions and the Making of Absolute Power.* Palo Alto, CA: Stanford University Press, 1997.

Zuerner, Adrienne. "Disguise and the Gendering of Royal Authority in Corneille's *Clitandre.*" *The French Review* 71:5 (April, 1998): 757–74.

Index